KV-415-085

Berlin

Gisela Buddée

MERIAN TopTen

Highlights not to be missed

1 KaDeWe
The largest department store on the continent, with an amazing selection and gourmet food court (→ pp. 19, 31).

2 Hackesche Höfe
East Berlin's noble mile, with shops, studios, cinema and cafés, has been perfectly renovated (→ p. 55).

3 Pergamon Museum
Climb the steps to the Pergamon Altar under the watchful eyes of gods and giants (→ pp. 57, 76).

4 Potsdamer Platz
A new quarter emerged out of nowhere with hotels, a casino and a shopping mall (→ pp. 57, 80).

5 Kaiser-Wilhelm-Gedächtniskirche
A wonderful surprise awaits you inside this church (→ p. 62).

6 Waldbühne
An open-air concert or a classic film in the Murelle hills is an unforgettable experience (→ p. 64).

7 Reichstagsgebäude
Climb the spiral ramp to the glass dome of the Parliament Building where a wonderful view of the capital city awaits (→ p. 67).

8 Jewish Museum
An incredible architectural feat housing 2,000 years of Jewish history (→ p. 74).

9 Havel cruise
Take a leisurely cruise along the Havel into a Prussian arcadia (→ p. 88).

10 Sanssouci
One of Germany's most incredible rococo castles on more than 300 hectares of park with fountains, avenues and temples (→ p. 91).

MERIAN Tips ⋯⋯⟩
are on page 159

Contents

4 An introduction to Berlin
Interesting facts about your destination

10 **Where to...**
The best tips and addresses in the city

12 **Accommodation**
Luxurious or cosy, town or country?

17 **Food and Drink**
Berlin, just the kebab capital? Far from it!

29 **Shopping**
Kitsch, creativity and cuisine – it's all here

36 **Nightlife**
Where to dance, hear jazz, rock out or just have a beer

42 **Festivals and Events**
The best of the best. There is always something on in Berlin

46 **Tips for Families and Kids**
Science, stage, sea lions and more: exciting things for kids in Berlin

50 **Out and about in Berlin**
Brief descriptions of the most important sights and museums

53 **Mitte**
City of regents

62 **Charlottenburg**
The charming old West

64 **Köpenick**
Forests and lakes

65 **Steglitz**
Botanical treasures

66 **Spandau**
Where the Spree flows into the Havel

66 **Tiergarten**
Government yesterday and today

68 **Treptow**
Think monumental

68 **Weißensee**
The Jewish Cemetery

10 MERIAN TopTen
Highlights not to be missed
←⋯ p. 1

10 MERIAN Tips
Tips and recommendations for connoisseurs and individuals
p. 159 ⋯→

Legend

 Especially good for families and children

  These facilities are suitable for people with disabilities

 Dogs are allowed in these facilities

CREDIT *All credit cards are accepted here*

 *No credit cards accepted here*

Prices for one night in a double room without breakfast:
●●●● *above 200 €*   ●● *above 100 €*
●●● *above 150 €*   ● *up to 100 €*

Prices for a meal with appetizer and main course, without drinks:
●●●● *above 50 €*   ●● *above 20 €*
●●● *above 30 €*   ● *up to 13 €*

68 **Zehlendorf**
Love nest and garden art

70 **Museums and Galleries**
Old masters and new art from all
over the world

78 **Walking Tours and
Excursions**
*The best walks and excursions in
and around Berlin*

Walking Tours
80 Potsdamer Platz – High-tech
modernity in glass and steel
81 Prenzlauer Berg – visiting a legend
84 Parisian flair around Kurfürstendamm and Savignyplatz
86 Grunewald – the noble and idyllic
east bank of the Havel

Excursions
88 By steamer to Wannsee
91 Majestic residences
96 Rheinsberg Palace
97 Buckow – Pearl of
Märkische Schweiz

98 **EXTRA: Berlin Lexicon**
*Of locals and tourists, incidents
and inventions*

118 Interesting Facts about Berlin
*Practical tips and background
information*

120 **History**
A historical time line
122 **Phrase book**
Never again speechless
124 **Berlin from A–Z**
Useful addresses and travel
services

133 Maps
146 Street index
154 Locations and subject index
158 Credits

Maps

Overview map............*Front cover fold-out*
S- and U-Bahn map....... *Back cover fold-out*
Museumsinsel and Nikolaiviertel........... *75*
Prenzlauer Berg *82*
Kurfürstendamm *85*
Grunewald *87*
Berlin and Surroundings *89*
Park Sanssouci *93*
Maps *133–145*

*The letter-number combinations in the text
refer to the map quadrants, for example:*

⟶ S. 140, B 14   Maps
⟶ S. 75, c 2   Detailed map

With city map

An introduction to Berlin

The egg-shaped glass dome of the Reichstag (Parliament Building, → p. 67) symbolizes the transparency of modern democracy.

Berlin never quite seems finished: a wasteland becomes the New Mitte; a concrete jungle fills with colour; art conquers empty spaces; parks are never far away. And the Wall? Hardly a trace of it.

Sun shining on a comfortable lounge chair, bare feet resting in the warm sand, ice cubes clinking in a cloudy glass. Closing your eyes, you hear waves lapping against the banks, the horn of a steamer, and the wind scatters shreds of an explanation in your ear: "...visited daily by... a thousand people..." They must be talking about the Reichstag, the parliament building, which is visible from here. The summery Bundespressestrand (national press corps beach) really does exist, just like all the other beaches along the Spree river, and it certainly won't be the only surprise awaiting visitors to Berlin.

For curious Berliners–they are notoriously curious–and frequent visitors, it's a bit like a puzzle: What's changed at the Brandenburg Gate since last time? On Kurfürstendamm? Or on Potsdamer Platz? They put up with constant construction on Unter den Linden boulevard, take note with astonishment that the lift in a new hotel glides through an aquarium, and queue up patiently in front of a recently renovated museum. Or, for a different view of the city, they visit the Chancellor's offices or a new embassy. There is always something new here, and the seemingly unchanging rankings of tourist attractions are deceptive: Parliament and the other government buildings, Brandenburg Gate and Pariser Platz, Friedrichstrasse, Gendarmenmarkt and the neo-classical Unter den Linden boulevard are always up there. And Berliners are ever ready to show the city to guests and check for themselves on the city's progress. Foreigners look for the Wall but rarely find much more than an occasional trace in the pavement, odd derelict sites in Kreuzberg, or the painted East Side Gallery, which can hardly communicate that feeling of being enclosed or cut off in Berlin. The museum helps at Checkpoint Charlie, the former American border crossing for the Allies. At Brandenburg Gate, and on the banks of the river Spree, crosses commemorate those killed by Wall guards. But a sense of how it was to live in the divided city is hardly imparted to the visitor. And Berliners are not looking to relive it.

"We are one people..."

Berlin is different. It is the only place where East and West truly collided when the Wall came down in 1989. Almost half the original population has left the city since then, only to be replaced with roughly the same number of new citizens. Many West Berliners left the old "Island in the Sea of Red", as they once called their city, and moved to the old West or took the opportunity to start something new on the other side of the border in Brandenburg. This would have been impossible beforehand, of course. Many East Berliners lost their jobs in their now "liquidated" establishments and migrated in search of new ones, leaving the dilapidated buildings in places like Spandauer Vorstadt, Friedrichshain and Prenzlauer Berg. The Wall still exists in peoples' heads, as do the wage differences of East and West, but this residual feeling is slowly disappearing into the sandy soil of Brandenburg. Jokes, however, still linger: "We are ONE people," say East Germans. "So are WE!" counters the West.

Only the densely developed neighbourhood of Prenzlauer Berg, which has been part of Pankow since 2001 and seems more a legend than an actual district these days, is home to many former West Germans, West-Berlin Kreuzbergers and citizens from all parts of the former East. It is here that people live off the reputation of this formerly defiant pocket of resistance against the suffocating daily life of the former GDR. Nowhere else in Berlin will you find as many chic mothers pushing trendy strollers as in the cafés surrounding Kollwitzplatz. The number of expensive shops, hipster restaurants, swank clubs and bars is unparalleled here.

No celebrity benefits

Back in 1991, Berlin was expecting its status as the capital of Germany to spur robust population and economic growth. Free flights were offered to parliamentarians to ward off homesickness, an apartment complex was even built especially for them – the so-called parliamentarian snake –, and for particularly desperate cases a "permanent service" was set up to deliver Kölsch (the regional dark beer of Cologne) from the Rhine to the capital. Soon enough, however, there was no longer any need for the shuttle. Members of parliament moved to Steglitz, Pankow, Wedding and Friedrichshain, and the tavern near the parliamentary buildings on the Spree experienced a heyday. Berlin-

ers, for their part, barely noticed the new VIPs, which may have damaged the egos of some provincial politicians, who now shared anonymity with the likes of lesser-known journalists, and who had to accept that their usual celebrity status was not valid in Berlin. No, celebrities here are local heroes like the late actor Harald Juhnke, part of German entertainment for over 50 years, or the late singer without a voice, Hildegard Knef, who always had a suitcase in (West) Berlin, as the popular German song goes. In the West hardly anyone has heard of Helga Hahnemann and they are astonished to hear that the »Golden Hen« is presented in the East in her honour. But who is at once a celebrity in both East and West Berlin? Perhaps that will change in the future.

Lots of space for creativity

Young people from around the world are still coming to Berlin in droves. Perhaps the gaps between buildings and the crumbling balconies fill their creative minds with a desire to fill the empty spaces. Every

The interior of Köpenick City Hall (→ p. 64), where the self-appointed "Captain" made his appearance. Carl Zuckmayer created one of the best examples of popular theatre with his play The Captain of Köpenick.

cellar could be a new bar, every unused corner a snack stand, or an abandoned subway station a party venue. Much of this type of thing is still going on. People put the word out and then find their audience in front of the lector's stage, write jokes and appear on a comedy show, sing about their neighbourhood and land a summer hit. Swedes and Swiss, Russians and Poles, Americans, Iranians, Finns and Frenchmen have all come to stay for a year or longer, to start businesses, create art, fashion, or make music. Many move to the East where the future seems more open and flexible. But some vagabonds have managed to establish themselves, young authors have found publishers, the music industry actually followed the musicians here, and the Popcom music trade fair does not want to be left behind. The "art forum" fair has also stood the test. Berlin is hot, whether it's film, crime novels or just an anecdote that will most likely be forgotten by tomorrow.

Of hopefully more solid substance are the masterpieces to which internationally acclaimed architects have been inspired. If yesterday's subject of admiration was Berlin's star architect, Karl Friedrich Schinkel, whose work was the face of old Berlin, the attention, praise and acclaim of today belong to those who have discovered a new architectural language: disturbing as with Libeskind's Jewish Museum, cheery and colourful as with Rossi in Charlottenstrasse, reconciling old and new as with I.M. Pei in the German Historical Museum. Is Jahn's creation on Potsdamer Platz exemplary of the 21st century? Is this new glass ship on the Kranzlereck a betrayal of Ku'damm, as Berliners call their most famous boulevard. Outstanding constructions such as the Tempodrom's white tent add variety to urban uniformity. Foreign embassies along the Tiergarten, on Pariser Platz and along

Schinkel and his masterpieces

Among Berlin's most famous sights is the Reichstagsgebäude (Parliament Building, → p. 67), by far the most visited tourist attraction.

the Spree handsomely complement Berlin's cityscape with indigenous materials and chic designs. Strangers see more than the natives, for whom the provoking sights of yesterday are now already familiar. And what happened to the castle? Too late to ponder the subject. Its reconstruction has already been decided. The promenade Unter den Linden trails off into emptiness, the main point of reference for its buildings obviously missing. The GDR demolished the ruins of the Hohenzollern palace in 1950, declaring them "historical rubbish", but carefully rebuilt all the surrounding edifices. Of the 65 buildings along Unter den Linden, only 13 remained after the war.

The charm of the old West

Doesn't anyone care about the West any more? Sauntering down the Ku'damm can be very relaxing after the dust and noise of construction. This is the only proper place to go for a stroll, along Fasanenstrasse, Schlüterstrasse and Uhlandstrasse. It's also pleasant to sidle down Bleibtreustrasse and around Ludwigkirchplatz. At the weekend, tucked in among elegant restaurants you may find the door of a stately mansion open, affording you a peek at the mirrors, fine moulding and plaster cherubs. Your head abuzz with the activity of the East, you may be inclined to take a quiet dinner on Savignyplatz and still be surprised at the bustle there. It seems that people are once again beginning to enjoy the settled charm, shady trees, Parisian flair and familiar atmosphere of the West.

Bustling life in the East

The East consists of Mitte, Mitte West and Mitte East. Some complain that Berlin is a behemoth, but locals aren't bothered by it. They live in Kreuzberg and dance the night away in Golgatha. Or they reside in Pankow, in Köpenick, which feels like a village surrounded only by greenery and water. Black terns mate at Müggelsee lake and beavers are building dams again in Tegel. Residents of Spandau complain about the boars on there front lawns while the finest breeds of dog swim in Grunewald lake. All this is Berlin and if you take the underground or tram, you may just end up in a different town with its own markets, pretty squares, sights, parks, woods and waters. Not until 1920 was the metropolis of Berlin established through the unification of previously independent towns and rural communities. This is easily seen in the different districts when you begin to really explore the city and seek out the people beyond the tourist attractions.

They are in the park on Sunday, playing football or petanque. Or they are in the woods, on the Spree

Always on a Sunday

or Havel river, but still in Berlin. One third of the city is not developed at all. There are still farmers in the city. You can rent horses and ride out. You can sail through the woods all the way to the Glienicker Bridge and hike to Potsdam. But you don't have to. In the middle of the city, in the Tiergarten, practically at the base of the Goldelse, what Berliners call the "Siegessäule", or Victory Column, there is a boat hire. With Bellevue Palace in view, clouds of savoury smoke lace the air as Turkish families enjoy a Sunday barbecue, a Tai-Chi group performs its mimicked punches. A saxophonist has found a space where he can practise and an acrobat is warming up for tonight's performance at the Hackescher Markt...

Where to...

Despite its expanse, the sun-lit atrium of Quartier 206 on Friedrichstrasse (→ p. 54) has a cosy atmosphere.

Everything is possible: sleeping in a work of art or at the noble Hotel Adlon, having a fancy dinner or a quick snack, shopping for things you can't get at home or just going out on the town.

Accommodation

Luxurious or cosy, urban or rural? Berlin has a suitable option for everyone.

The reception hall of the legendary Hotel Adlon at the Brandenburg Gate (→ p. 54) has the luxurious flair of a world-class hotel.

Elegant buildings have lined the Gendarmenmarkt for a long time now, and there are new hotels opening up in both the Hackescher Markt and Prenzlauer Berg, where in the past none were actually needed. Potsdamer Platz and Leipziger Platz have been connected and are the preferred locations of international hotel chains. Nostalgia for the East is hardly in demand here. Even Kurfürstendamm has some new hotels.

Reservations and Information
Berlin Tourismus Marketing GmbH
Am Karlsbad 11, 10785 Berlin; tel. 0 30/ 25 00 25, fax 25 00 24 24; www.btm.de
Event ticket reservations may also be made when booking a partner hotel of Berlin Tourismus Marketing GmbH.

HOTELS ●●●●

Adlon ┄┄┄⟩ p. 137, F 8
For many in the roaring 1920s, the Adlon was the most beautiful hotel in the world, and at the time it was a breathtakingly modern establishment. It hosted prominent figures such as Charlie Chaplin and Thomas Mann. The restaurant here offers views of Brandenburg Gate, and local celebrities can sometimes be seen inside as well.
Unter den Linden 77; tel. 22 61 11 11, fax 22 61 22 22; www.hotel-adlon.de; S-Bahn: Unter den Linden; 401 rooms
●●●● CREDIT ⌭

Bleibtreu ┄┄┄⟩ p. 141, F 14
Nestled inconspicuously between an espresso bar and a florist, you could easily overlook the entrance to the beautiful courtyard of the Bleibtreu. The Italian furniture in this charming hotel has not been chemically treated. If you like, you may ask for a television wake-up call, and if you can figure it out, order breakfast in bed from the TV screen's menu.
Bleibtreustr. 31; tel. 88 47 40, fax 88 47 44 44; www.bleibtreu.com; U-Bahn: Uhlandstrasse; 60 rooms
●●●● CREDIT ⌭

Brandenburger Hof
┄┄┄⟩ p. 142, A 18
Hidden away from the noise and traffic down a side street in Wilmersdorf, an elegant Wilhelminian mansion houses this luxury hotel from the Relais & Chateaux chain. It features a piano bar, a large conservatory and a gourmet restaurant.
Eislebener Str. 14, Wilmersdorf; tel. 21 40 50, fax 21 40 51 00; www.brandenburger-hof.com; U-Bahn: Augsburger Strasse; 82 rooms
●●●● CREDIT ⌭

Grand Hyatt Berlin
┄┄┄⟩ p. 143, E 17
The first impression of this hotel may be a bit cool. Created by Spanish architect José Rafael Moneo and with interiors by Swiss designer Hannes Wettstein, the fine materials, distinctive colours and excellent service, however, quickly alter that impression into one of an oasis in a concrete jungle. High-speed Internet, a spa and fitness centre, and a view of the skyline from the pool are further enticements. Relaxing in the jazz club-style Vox Bar may be just the answer after a day's tour of the city.
Marlene-Dietrich-Platz 2; tel. 25 53 12 34, fax 25 53 12 35; www.berlin.grand.hyatt.com; U-Bahn: Potsdamer Platz; 342 rooms
●●●● CREDIT ♿

InterContinental ┄┄┄⟩ p. 142, B 17
Still one of the top addresses in the old West: great location, the gourmet restaurant "Hugo's" overlooking Berlin's rooftops, a pool and a Vitality Club.
Budapester Str. 2; tel. 2 60 20, fax 26 02 11 82; www.interconti.com; U-Bahn: Zoologischer Garten; 510 rooms ●●●● CREDIT ⌭

Savoy ┄┄┄⟩ p. 141, F 13
At this charming hotel near Ku'-damm, the historical flair is not only due to the resident literati. A new

Havanna Club has been added to the pleasant hotel bar.

Fasanenstr. 9–10; tel. 31 10 30,
fax 31 10 33 33; www.hotel-savoy.com;
U-/S-Bahn: Zoologischer Garten;
125 rooms●●●● CREDIT 🐾

The Regent   ⤳ p. 138, A 12
Pure luxury at the Gendarmenmarkt, and an oasis for relaxation.

Charlottenstr. 49; tel. 3 02 03 38, fax 30 20 33 61 19; www.regenthotels.com;
U-Bahn: Französische Strasse;
204 rooms ●●●● CREDIT 🐾

The Ritz-Carlton   ⤳ p. 143, E 17
This world-class hotel on Potsdamer Platz entices guests with an elegant, historical sense of charm including a bath butler who will draw and scent your bathwater, a relaxing tea lounge, antiques and a brasserie whose furnishings come from the French town of Mâcon.

Potsdamer Platz 3; tel. 33 77 77,
fax 3 37 77 55 55; www.ritzcarlton.com;

MERIAN Tip

🏅 Honigmond Garden

The street may seem bleak, but at number 122 a paradise awaits you in the big city. Chirping birds, croaking frogs, glimmering goldfish, a gurgling fountain and ancient ivy make this enchanting garden ideal for relaxing and daydreaming. The house was built in 1845, and it has been carefully restored. The old paintings and antique furnishings feel natural here. Garden sheds have been transformed into cosy guest cottages. Both Friedrichstrasse and the Museum Island are just 15 minutes away.

Invalidenstr. 122;
tel. 28 44 55 77, fax 28 44 55 88;
www.honigmond-berlin.de;
U-Bahn: Zinnowitzer Strasse ●● ▱
⤳ p. 137, F 6

U-Bahn: Potsdamer Platz; 302 rooms
●●●● CREDIT ♿ 🐾

HOTELS ●●●
Ackselhaus   ⤳ p. 139, D 10
One of the nicest hotels in Prenzlauer Berg is only a few minutes from Kollwitzplatz. Every room has a unique theme. You can sleep in Africa or slumber in Venice, or choose from the inexpensive apartments. They have a lovely garden as well.

Belforter Str. 21; tel. 44 33 76 33,
fax 4 41 61 16; www.ackselhaus.de;
U-Bahn: Senefelder Platz; 10 rooms
●●● MASTER VISA 🐾

Albrechtshof   ⤳ p. 137, F 7
Ideal for museum fans who want to be close to the theaters on Unter den Linden and Friedrichstrasse. Part of the Association of Christian Hotels, with a chapel and a pretty courtyard. Very tranquil location.

Albrechtstr. 8;
tel. 30 88 60, fax 30 88 61 00;
www.hotel-albrechtshof.de;
U-/S-Bahn: Friedrichstrasse;
100 rooms ●●● CREDIT 🐾

Ellington   ⤳ p. 142, B 17
By 1931, this address already had a unique history. It was the seat of the State Monopoly for Administration of Spirits, and its ballroom served as a venue for Duke Ellington and David Bowie. Only later did it become a modern city hotel with a fine restaurant near Ku'damm.

Nürnberger Str. 50–55;
tel. 68 31 50, fax 6 83 15 55 55;
www.ellington-Hotel.com;
U-Bahn: Wittenbergplatz;
285 rooms ●●● CREDIT ♿ 🐾

Hackescher Markt   ⤳ p. 138, B 11
The neighbouring streets are abuzz with activity both day and night, and the tram pulls up just round the corner, but the windows shield you from the noise regardless of which direction it comes from. The rooms are

decked in English fabric and the bathroom floor is heated. The bar gives off a definitively French air.

Grosse Präsidentenstr. 8;
tel. 28 00 30, fax 28 00 31 11;
www.hotel-hackescher-markt.de;
S-Bahn: Hackescher Markt; 31 rooms
●●● CREDIT 🐕

Hecker's Hotel ⸺⟩ p. 141, F 13

The lighting, the spacious foyer and the overall Italian flair has a magnetic effect. In addition, this hotel near Ku'damm was distinguished for its friendly service in 2003. Weekend arrivals are greeted with prosecco and a fruit basket, as if they had arrived in Tuscany or been sent back to colonial times. Bauhaus buffs will also find something to enjoy. If you want to stay longer, consider taking an apartment with a kitchenette and a walk-in closet.

Grolmannstr. 35; tel. 8 89 00,
fax 8 89 02 60; www.heckers-hotel.com;
S-Bahn: Savignyplatz; 69 rooms
●●● CREDIT ♿ 🐕

Residenz ⸺⟩ p. 142, A 18

Charming art-nouveau hotel just yards from Kurfürstendamm that has been admired as an historic film backdrop in the past.

Meinekestr. 9; tel. 88 44 30,
fax 8 82 47 26; www.hotel-residenz.com;
U-Bahn: Kurfürstendamm; 81 rooms
●●● CREDIT 🐕

Seehof am Lietzensee
⸺⟩ p. 140, B 13

Pleasant hotel with a large lakefront terrace and an indoor swimming pool.

Lietzenseeufer 11; tel. 32 00 20,
fax 32 00 22 51; www.hotel-seehof-berlin.de; U-Bahn: Kaiserdamm;
75 rooms ●●● CREDIT 🐕

HOTELS ●●
Bogota ⸺⟩ p. 141, E 14

This luxurious Berlin mansion from the turn of the 20th century hosted the young Benny Goodman in the

A modern oasis with style: the Grand Hyatt Berlin (→ p. 13).

1920s, and Helmut Newton completed his apprenticeship here. After a tour of the city, arriving back here is like coming home. The congenial atmosphere makes you feel like a visiting friend.

Schlüterstr. 45; tel. 8 81 50 01,
fax 8 83 58 87; www.hotelbogota.de;
U-Bahn: Adenauerplatz; 123 rooms
●● CREDIT 🐕

Frauenhotel Artemisia
⸺⟩ p. 141, D 15

Men are not allowed past the foyer in this "Women's Hotel" located in an old Berlin apartment building. Children stay for free. The rooms and public areas are decorated with famous women from Berlin's past.

Brandenburgische Str. 18;
tel. 8 73 89 05, fax 8 61 86 53;
www.frauenhotel-berlin.de;
U-Bahn: Konstanzer Strasse;
12 rooms ●● CREDIT

Gates ⸺⟩ p. 141, F 13

You would never guess that behind the Wilhelminian façade of this hotel, which has an historically listed staircase, is a high-tech facility with all the latest Internet technology at your disposal: flat-screen monitors and an unlimited high-speed connection. When you are finished, you'll retire to a hypo-allergenic bed, a pleasure that guests such as Harry Belafonte or Claudia Cardinale never even dreamed of back in 1957 when the establishment was called the Hotel Windsor. The online booking system calculates the room prices according to the current booking status.

Knesebeckstr. 8–9; tel. 31 10 60, fax 312 20 60; www.hotel-gates.com; U-Bahn: Ernst-Reuter-Platz; 100 rooms ●● CREDIT 🐾

Wittelsbach 🧒👶 ⸼⸼⸽ p. 141, E 15
Children and dogs are welcome here, and parents can leave their baby monitors and buggies at home. This hotel is furnished like a fairy tale and little guests are greeted by frogs, Rapunzel and a princess.

Wittelsbacher Str. 22; tel. 8 64 98 40, fax 8 62 15 32; U-Bahn: Konstanzer Strasse; 31 rooms ●● AmEx MASTER VISA 🐾

HOTELS ●
Die Fabrik ⸼⸼⸽ p. 145, F 22
This red-brick building in Kreuzberg, a hip, emerging neighbourhood, is located in a former telephone parts manufacturing facility. After being expanded and restored in 1995, it was equipped with a solar power system. High ceilings, large rooms with nice old furniture, pleasant pictures and lamps, a courtyard and a garden all make Die Fabrik an inviting space to stay or just plan your days. No television, no mini-bar, shared showers.

Schlesische Str. 18; tel. 6 11 71 16, fax 6 18 29 71; www.diefabrik.com; U-Bahn: Schlesisches Tor; 44 rooms ● ▱

Funk ⸼⸼⸽ p. 141, F 14
In Ku'damm's most elegant side street, where Danish actress Asta Nielsen lived from 1931 to 1937,

there is a pension where crystal chandeliers mingle with neon lamps, matt lacquer elements and Chippendale decor. The plush sofas and charming doilies of the 1920s served as the set for TV shows with actor Otto Sander.

Fasanenstr. 69; tel. 8 82 71 93, fax 8 83 33 29; U-Bahn: Kurfürstendamm; 14 rooms ● CREDIT 🐾

Motel One Berlin-Alexanderplatz ⸼⸼⸽ p. 138, C 11
This new (non-smoking) addition to the low-budget hotel chain for globetrotters is between Alexanderplatz and the Hackesche Höfe. Amenities include television, wireless LAN, Internet access and underground parking. Dogs cost an additional 15 €!

Dircksenstr. 36; tel. 20 05 40 80, fax 2 00 54 08 10; www.motel-one.com; U-/S-Bahn: Alexanderplatz; 202 rooms ● CREDIT ♿ 🐾

MERIAN Tip

⭐2 Künstlerheim Luise

A philosopher in the stairwell ponders the "fullness of the empty space" at this unique hotel in the government district. Guests have a choice of 48 dreamy works of art, also known as rooms, each designed by a different artist from Berlin, New York or even Uzbekistan. You can sleep like a starving poet or next to giant female statues, in spartan style or in luxury. Either way, you become a patron of the arts. A new construction in front of the train tracks reduces noise and makes for a nice courtyard, and bamboo flooring leads to the streets where it is only a short walk to the Brandenburg Gate.

Luisenstr. 19; tel. 28 44 80, fax 28 44 84 48; www.kuenstlerheim-luise.de; U-Bahn: Friedrichstrasse; 48 rooms ●● MASTER VISA   ⸼⸼⸽ p. 137, F 7

Food and Drink

Berlin: just the kebab capital? Far from it!
Gourmets enjoy new delicacies every day.

This hotspot with a high celebrity count offers the extraordinary creations of chef Philippe Lemoine: Borchardt (→ p. 22) at Gendarmenmarkt (→ p. 55).

Nobody refers to Berlin as a culinary wasteland any more. The gourmets' bible, Gault Millau, sends teams of eager testers to the city now, and in 2006 alone the people from Michelin awarded ten Berlin restaurants with stars. Seemingly unimpressed by all this, food culture in Berlin changes at its own gradual pace until the next trends are discovered. The good yet inexpensive restaurants near Kreuzberger Südstern are among the local favourites, while hungry customers queue up all around Kollwitzplatz in Prenzlauer Berg for modest but fresh Vietnamese fare. More trendy restaurateurs try to appease their regulars with restaurants that feature bars, dance floors and modern sounds.

Of course, you will also come across the ubiquitous "Currywurst", a curried sausage that is a Berlin speciality, but you'll need to know if you want them "with or without" (skin, that is) and if they should be firm or soft. You can even have them served on porcelain with a glass of bubbly.

Kebab Town with over 1,300 vendors? Indeed. And it is certainly convenient: pita bread, chopped meat, onions, lettuce, a little cabbage, maybe a dash of garlic sauce and off you go. If you can't find a Currywurst or kebab stand, a vendor with a basket of pretzels is sure to happen by at some point, either on the street, in the theatre or the jazz club, or in a bar or cinema. You'll never go hungry in Berlin, no matter the time of day.

Sauerbraten? There's that too, of course. You are more likely to find Italian cuisine though, from Emilia Romagna or Apulia or Sardinia. In an international city like Berlin, you will find food from all over the world: Austrian, Mexico, America, China, Korea, Japan, Indonesia or Thailand. If you're craving kangaroo, there are Australian places too. Or try East Prussian. And although French cuisine is suffering in popularity back at home, its popularity is on the rise in Berlin, from Schöneberg to Köpenick. Unfortunately, the Russian, Hungarian and Polish restaurants, of which there were so many in East Berlin during the days of the Wall, have now made way for other delights.

Breakfast all day long

But maybe your search is based on completely different criteria: quality or open-air or both? A late afternoon breakfast? Not a problem. Often even until 4 p.m. But at some point they have to call it quits.

And then there's the ever-spreading rumour that Berliners drink their "Molle" (glass of beer) with or without spirits or a "Berliner Weisse" with a spritzer, the latter being a sort of lager with a shot of either raspberry or woodruff syrup (and mostly enjoyed by tourists!). Micro breweries, such as in Spandau, brew tasty top-fermented ales. Dark ales have joined the palette too but the "Reinheitsgebot" (German Purity Law for beer) denies them the moniker "Beer". A bounty of new bars offer fancy cocktails as well, shaken or stirred.

With regard to wine, Berlin has quickly become a real bon vivant metropolis. At a rate of 28 litres per capita each year, Berlin drinks three times as much as other German cities. The senate's wine assessor is one of 70 civil servant wine experts in Germany, and, with over 15,000 visitors, the WEINmesse wine trade fair (www.weinmesseberlin.de) has now become the largest of its kind in the country. And although grapes grow in Neukölln and Kreuzberg, they are made into wine and bottled in traditional wine-producing areas.

In and around Charlottenburg and Kurfürstendamm

Ana e Bruno ┈┈⟩ p.134, B 4
Every Berliner, so the saying goes, has his favourite Italian. But for special occasions, they go to Ana e Bruno, where culinary surprises such as gnocchi with stinging nettle are proffered in a classic atmosphere. Cooking columnist, Wolfgang Siebeck, on their desserts: "heavenly".
Sophie-Charlotten-Str. 101;
tel. 3 25 71 10; S-Bahn: Westend;
Tue–Sat 6:30 p.m.–midnight ●●●● MASTER

Hugos ┈┈⟩ p. 142, B 17
The gourmet restaurant with the best view of Berlin. Head chef, Thomas Kammeier, earns the Michelin star and provides his guests with first-class specialities on the 14th floor of the Hotel Intercontinental.
Budapester Str. 2; tel. 26 02 12 63;
U-Bahn: Zoologischer Garten; Mon–Sat 6 p.m.–10:30 p.m. ●●●● CREDIT

Dal Buongustaio ┈┈⟩ p. 141, D 3
The Sardinian flatbread here is paper thin and the coarse home-made pork sausage is delicious. The Sardinians make a fine pizza as well.
Windscheidstr. 24; tel. 3 24 68 82;
S-Bahn: Charlottenburg; daily 6 p.m.–midnight ●●● ▱

Paris Bar ┈┈⟩ p. 141, F 13
This most famous of Berlin institutions is not renowned for its cuisine. The attraction here is the French-speaking men at the bar and the illustrious guests. Newly established next door: Le Bar du Paris Bar.
Kantstr. 152; tel. 3 13 80 52;
U-/S-Bahn: Zoologischer Garten;
daily noon–2 a.m. ●●● AmEx

Churascaria Brasil Brasiliero
┈┈⟩ p. 141, D 114
The speciality of the house is called "Rodizio Brasil Brasiliero". After appetisers from the buffet, meat-lovers can feast on lamb, kangaroo and beef, which will be delicately sliced off the skewer at your table, all accompanied by hot rhythms and cool waiters.
Kurfürstendamm 151; tel. 89 40 98 89;
U-Bahn: Adenauerplatz, Bus M 19,
M 29; Mon–Sat 5 p.m.–1 a.m.,
Sun 2 p.m.–1 a.m. ●● ▱

Diekmann ┈┈⟩ p. 142, A 18
This was once a colonial goods store. You can still tell by the shelving and plates. The food, however, is completely modern and perfect for an evening meal or a light lunch.
Meineckestr. 7; tel. 8 83 33 21; U-Bahn: Zoologischer Garten; Mon–Sat noon–1 a.m., Sun 4 p.m.–1 a.m. ●● CREDIT

Engelbecken ┈┈⟩ p. 140, C 13
Cuisine and wine are inspired by the Alps, and the beer is Bavarian. Pleasant spot for coffee and cake as well.
Witzlebenstr. 31; tel. 6 15 28 10; U-Bahn: Sophie-Charlotte-Platz; Mon–Fri 5 p.m.–1 a.m., Sat from 4 p.m., Sun from noon ●● MASTER VISA

Florian ┈┈⟩ p. 141, F 13
During the film festival, it's standing room only in this small restaurant, a celebrity spot without allures but with southern German cuisine. You can even order Nuremberg bratwurst after the kitchen is officially closed.
Grolmannstr. 52; tel. 3 13 91 84;
S-Bahn: Savignyplatz; daily 6 p.m.–3 a.m. ●● MASTER VISA

KaDeWe ┈┈⟩ p. 142, B 18
Of course there is the gourmet floor with foie gras and ocean fish varieties. But if you want to fill up at a fair price, without exotica but with a view over the roofs of Berlin, then try the meatballs, tender pork roast and hearty roast potatoes in the self-service restaurant of this famous department store. Afterwards, you can have a fabulous piece of cake with coffee. There is a sushi bar too.

Italian elegance dictates the interior of Sale e Tabacchi. One of the most influential designers of new Berlin, Swiss architect Max Dudler, crafted this space.

Tauentzienstr. 21–24; tel. 2 12 10;
www.feinschmeckeretage.de;
U-Bahn: Wittenbergplatz; Mon–Fri
11 a.m.–8 p.m., Sat 11 a.m.–4 p.m. ●●

Lubitsch ┉⟩ p. 141, F 13
Stucco decor, mirrors on the walls, and tasty modern cuisine all distinguish this venue from the "homey" atmosphere of its neighbours in this lively street near Ku'damm. Their pleasant boulevard terrace is open in summer.
Bleibtreustr. 47; tel. 8 82 37 56;
S-Bahn: Savignyplatz, U-Bahn:
Uhlandstrasse; Mon–Sat 10 a.m. –
1 a.m., Sun 6 p.m.–1 a.m.
●● AmEx MASTER VISA

Marjellchen ┉⟩ p. 141, E 13
Despite the fact that the owner is originally from Rome, his restaurant serves classic East Prussian cuisine including Königsberger meatballs, sorrel soup, Masurian roast, borscht and more. And it all comes in very hearty portions.
Mommsenstr. 9; tel. 8 83 26 76;
www.marjellchen-berlin.de; S-Bahn:
Savignyplatz; daily 5 p.m.–midnight
●● CREDIT

Le Piaf ┉⟩ p. 134, C 4
After visiting the castle in Charlottenburg, take a stroll down Schlossstrasse. At the weekend you may catch sight of a game of pétanque on the greens in the centre divider. You'll want to take a seat here, because the "Sparrow", as the name translates in English, serves consistently good Alsatian and French cuisine.
Schlossstr. 60; tel. 3 42 20 40; Bus 145;
Sun, Tue from 6 p.m.– and Wed–Sat
11 a.m.–midnight ●● CREDIT

San Giorgio ┉⟩ p. 141, D 13
There's an Italian restaurant every couple of steps in the former West. Over a dish pasta or pizza, lamb or rabbit, almost every regular here has spotted a well-known politician at a neighbouring table. Nobody would suspect them here and the food is just plain good.
Mommsenstr. 36; tel. 3 23 16 97;
U-Bahn: Wilmersdorfer Strasse;
Mon–Sat noon–midnight ●● CREDIT

XII Apostoli ┉⟩ p. 141, F 13
The most pleasant spot is in the garden in the summer, but the chapel

atmosphere of the interior is also conducive to savouring large, thin-crust pizzas or hearty pastas. Reservations required in the evenings.
Bleibtreustr. 49; tel. 3 12 14 33; S-Bahn: Savignyplatz; daily from 10 a.m. ●●

Soup Kultur   ┈┈⟩ p. 142, A 18
Guests jostle at the wooden counter standing over big porcelain bowls of soup. The concept was ridiculed at first but became quite a success.
Kurfürstendamm 224; tel. 88 62 92 82; U-Bahn: Kurfürstendamm; Mon–Fri noon–8 p.m., Sat noon–4 p.m. ●

Kreuzberg
Le Cochon Bourgeois
            ┈┈⟩ p. 144, C 23
Candlelight, cloth napkins, the delicate sounds of a piano, and delicious food reminiscent of France–all in the intimacy of a former three-room flat.
Fichtestr. 24; tel. 6 93 01 01; U-Bahn: Südstern; Tue-Sat from 6 p.m. ●●●

Grünfisch   ┈┈⟩ p. 144, A 24
Sicily and Vietnam join forces: seafood and refined vegetarian fare.
Willibald-Alexis-Str. 27;
tel. 61 62 12 52: U-Bahn: Gneisenaustrasse; Tue–Sun 6 p.m.–midnight
●● MASTER

Hartmanns   ┈┈⟩ p. 144, C 23
This restaurant is named after its chef. Classics and new dishes, but with definite Austrian tendencies. After years in Hamburg's "Canard" and Berlin's "Vau", Stefan Hartmann was quick to make a name with his romantic cellar restaurant.
Fichtestr. 31; tel. 61 20 10 03; U-Bahn: Südstern; daily 6 p.m.–midnight
●●

Osteria No. 1   ┈┈⟩ p.143, F 19
"Numero uno" has been the little Italian corner restaurant in Kreuzberg for over 25 years, and is always a favourite among Italophiles. Whether

MERIAN Tip

③ Bocca di Bacco
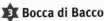

Tables set in white and bright-red paintings on the wall create a sitting room atmosphere and an appetite for whatever the ›mouth of the God of wines‹ has to offer. This elegant Italian restaurant undoubtedly belongs to the culinary highlights at the Gendarmenmarkt. Ravioli with goat cheese, liver with sage, grilled monkfish wrapped in bacon, all served with wine from many of the known Italian vineyard regions. The smoking section has a view of the wine while non-smokers get to watch Friedrichstrasse–in the unlikely event their eyes leave their plates, that is.

Friedrichstr. 167/168; tel. 20 67 28 28; U-Bahn: Französische Strasse; Mon–Sat noon–midnight, Sun 6 p.m.–midnight ●●●●
AmEx MASTER VISA   ┈┈⟩ p. 138, A 12

you like pasta, polenta, pizza, lamb or fresh fish, the palm trees in the garden, the natural stone floors and the garlic in the air all create a fitting atmosphere for a summer night. Just as welcoming in the colder season. Reservations recommended.
Kreuzbergstr. 1; tel. 7 86 91 62; U-Bahn: Mehringdamm; daily noon–2 a.m., dinner from 4 p.m. ●● AmEx MASTER VISA

Sale e Tabacchi   ┈┈⟩ p. 144, A 21
This elegant Italian bistro is a mix of osteria and wine bar, pub and café. The kitchen's fresh creations are listed on large blackboards. Sale e Tabacchi is located on the ground floor of the building of the German daily newspaper, taz. The signs from Arezzo in Tuscany are originals.
Kochstr. 18; tel. 2 52 11 55; U-Bahn: Kochstrasse; Mon–Fri 8 a.m.–midnight, Sat and Sun noon–midnight
●●● MASTER VISA

Mitte and Prenzlauer Berg

Margaux ⤑ p. 137, F 8
Berliners may mock the "expense account" atmosphere, but not only professional epicureans' eyes light up at Margaux–and that's before the food even arrives. Avant-garde and imaginative, this is a culinary star on Pariser Platz.
Unter den Linden 78; tel. 22 65 26 11; S-Bahn: Unter den Linden; Mon–Sat 7 p.m.–10:30 p.m. ●●●● CREDIT

VAU ⤑ p. 138, A 12
Hamburg's famous chef, Josef Viehhauser, has set himself up quite nicely at the Gendarmenmarkt. Chef de cuisine is Kolja Kleeberg. It feels more like Paris than Berlin at VAU. Looking for a multi-course delight? Precious creations at accordingly expensive prices.
Jägerstr. 54/55; tel. 2 02 97 30; www.vau-berlin.de; U-Bahn: Französische Strasse; Mon-Sat noon-2:30 p.m., 7 p.m-10:30 p.m. ●●●●

Borchardt ⤑ p. 138, A 12
This former congregation hall for Huguenots now provides a dignified bistro dining atmosphere with many politicians and members of the media from the area. Reservations recommended. Inexpensive set lunch.
Französische Str. 47; tel. 81 88 62 62; U-Bahn: Französische Strasse; daily 11:30 a.m.–1 a.m. ●●● AmEx MASTER VISA

Entrecôte ⤑ p.144, A 21
This French restaurant is hidden away near Checkpoint Charlie. It features not just mussels, oysters and sea bream but unusual items like duck confit on sauerkraut with roast potatoes. Good selection of wines.
Schützenstr. 5; tel. 21 06 54 96; U-Bahn: Kochstrasse; Mon–Fri 10 a.m.–1 p.m., Sat, Sun noon–1 a.m. ●●● CREDIT

Horvath ⤑ p. 145, D 23
Bresse hen, duck Nantaise, tongue of veal. Or perhaps Alsatian leek torte and pike-perch? For a real taste of the creations of this gourmet chef from Baden, order an Amuse Bouche set menu (five to ten appetizer courses).
Paul-Lincke-Ufer 44a; tel. 61 28 99 92; U-Bahn: Kottbusser Tor; Tue–Sat noon–1 a.m. ●●● CREDIT

shiro i shiro ⤑ p. 138, C 11
A fine dining experience is pretty much guaranteed here. Extravagance is pursued not only in the food but also in the blue and white interior by Hyun Jung Kim and in the mother-of-pearl tables shining in the light of the open kitchen. The celebrity factor is high: Mick Jagger and Sharon Stone have been guests.
Rosa-Luxemburg-Str. 11; tel. 97 00 47 90; U-Bahn: Rosa-Luxemburg-Platz; daily from 6:30 p.m. ●●● CREDIT

Diekmann im Weinhaus Huth
⤑ p. 143, E 17
Blood sausage in crêpe batter. Or vegetarian and fish dishes. Sometimes French, then Italian, then German. Inexpensive business lunch in the "last house on Potsdamer Platz".
Alte Potsdamer Str. 5; tel. 25 29 75 24; U-Bahn: Potsdamer Platz; daily noon–1 a.m. ●● MASTER VISA

Ganymed Brasserie ⤑ p. 137, F 7
At the time of the Wall, VIPs from East and West met next to the Berliner Ensemble (a renowned theatre), and this restaurant often served as salon to the stars and starlets from the theatre. Now, with music from Adamo to Piaf, it has started again as a brasserie. Among the specialities from the new chef these days are oysters and crustaceans or else Alsatian choucroute.
Schiffbauerdamm 5; tel. 28 59 90 46; U-Bahn: Friedrichstrasse; daily 11:30 a.m.–2 a.m. ●● CREDIT

Hasir ⤑ p. 138, B 11
The largest and nicest member of the famous Turkish restaurant group.

The gourmet restaurant VAU, near Gendarmenmarkt (→ p. 55), offers first-class culinary delights in an elegant French atmosphere.

Regulars–including countrymen of the chef–rate the starters especially highly. No dogs allowed.
Oranienburger Str. 4; tel. 28 04 16 16; S-Bahn: Hackescher Markt; daily noon–1 p.m. ●● AmEx MASTER VISA

Kadima ⋯⋙ p. 138, A 11
A very special restaurant has established itself next to the new synagogue. Every table is dedicated to a famous Jewish personality. Israeli, non-kosher and Russian cuisine alternate on the menu. Lovely courtyard for summer dining.
Oranienburger Str. 28; tel. 27 59 42 51; S-Bahn: Oranienburger Strasse; Mon–Sat 5 p.m, Sun noon–1 a.m. ●● CREDIT

Maedchenitaliener ⋯⋙ p. 138, C 10
Fans of Italian cuisine will find a few surprises as well as standard fare.
Alte Schönhauser Str. 12; tel. 40 04 17 87; U-Bahn: Weinmeister-strasse; ; daily from 5 p.m.
●● MASTER VISA

Maultäschle ⋯⋙ p. 144, A 21
Despite the name, homesick folks from Germany's Swabia region will have to prepare themselves for some exotic variations on the theme of their traditional ravioli-like pasta dish, Maultaschen. The owner's Turkish wife really mixes things up with fillings such as porcini mushrooms or minced lamb. Connoisseurs praise both the Southern German and the Anatolian cuisine.
Charlottenstr. 79/80; tel. 22 48 86 00; U-Bahn: Kochstrasse; Mon–Fri 8 a.m.–8 p.m. ●● MASTER

Maxwell ⋯⋙ p. 138, A 10
An elegant bistro nestled into a neo-Gothic brick building in one of Berlin's loveliest courtyards. The two-level converted restaurant in the former Josty Brewery has a beautiful terrace. The dishes are inspired by Mediterranean and Asian cuisine, and the chef seldom buckles to modern styles. Ingredients are organic and guests often come from the art and film scenes.
Bergstr. 22; tel. 2 80 71 21; U-Bahn: Rosenthaler Platz; daily from 6 p.m.
●● CREDIT

Pan Asia ⋯⋙ p. 138, B 11
Guests are seated at long wooden tables here and the friendly staff quickly prepares tasty Vietnamese, Thai and Chinese dishes.

Rosenthaler Str. 38; tel. 27 90 88 11;
S-Bahn: Hackescher Markt; daily noon–
2 a.m., bargain lunches noon–3 p.m.
●● CREDIT

Reinhard's   ⇢ p. 138, B 12

The Mata Hari salad is excellent in
this restaurant in the central Nikolai
district. Artists' photographs create a
comfortable atmosphere.
Poststr. 28; tel. 2 42 52 95; U-/S-Bahn:
Alexanderplatz; daily 9 a.m.–1 a.m. ●●

Salumeria Culinario   ⇢p.138, A 10

In the raised ground floor behind the
Heckmann Höfe, ministers of state
mingle with tourists over afternoon
soup and salad. The glass case contains prosciuto de Parma, the likes
of which one does not often come
across in Berlin. Reservations recommended on weekends.
Tucholskystr. 23; tel. 28 09 67 67;
S-Bahn: Oranienburger Strasse;
Mon–Sat from 10 a.m., Sun from 1 p.m.
●● CREDIT

Samâdhi   ⇢ p. 137, F 8

Vegetarians and vegans find refuge in
this meat-free zone. Savoury tofu is
prepared with coconut milk, chilli and
herbs based on recipes from various
Southeast Asian countries.
Wilhelmstr. 77; tel. 22 48 88 50; U-Bahn:
Mohrenstrasse; Mon.–Fri. 10 a.m.–
11 p.m., Sun. Brunch 10 a.m.–3 p.m.
●● CREDIT

Sarah Wieners Speisezimmer
⇢ p. 137, F 6

Known by many Germans from her
time as cook in a reality television
show set in the 1900s, Sarah Wiener
has three restaurants in Berlin. Her
cakes are served at the Arts Academy
on Pariser Platz and she oversees the
Bistro am Hamburger Bahnhof. She
also has an international catering
business. This popular breakfast and
lunch location has, in the meantime,
become a full-fledged restaurant with
a beer garden.

Chausseestr. 8 (courtyard); tel.
70 71 80 20; U-Bahn: Oranienburger Tor;
Mon.–Fri. 10 a.m.–11 p.m., Sun. brunch
10 a.m.–3 p.m. ●●/●●● CREDIT

Schinkel-Klause   ⇢ p. 138, A 12

In the basement of the Prinzenpalais,
under the Operncafé, fans of traditional German–and Berlin–cuisine are
served hearty soup terrines or
Königsberger meatballs. Vegetarian
fare is also available.
Unter den Linden 5; tel. 20 26 84 50;
S-Bahn: Unter den Linden; daily from
11 a.m. ●● CREDIT

Theodor Tucher   ⇢ p. 137, F 8

Coffee house, dining chamber and
reading room–depending on the time
of day. Pleasant atmosphere, inexpensive set lunches.
Pariser Platz 6 a; tel. 22 48 94 64;
S-Bahn: Unter den Linden; daily
9 a.m.–1 a.m. ●● AmEx MASTER VISA

Ishin   ⇢ p. 138, A 12

Fast and fresh, this is a popular place
for a sushi lunch. There's even time to
spare for a cup of green tea.
Mittelstr. 24; tel. 20 67 48 29;
U-Bahn: Friedrichstrasse; Mon-Fri 11
a.m.-8 p.m., Sat 11 a.m .- 6 p.m.
●/●● ▭

Zur letzten Instanz   ⇢ p. 138, C 12

When the Wall came down, this site
next to the ruins of the medieval city
wall was an insider's tip. Probably
the oldest tavern in Berlin, dating
from 1621, you can sit next to the
famous majolica tiled stove as
Napoleon or Charlie Chaplin did
before you. As the place's name
would imply (roughly, "final appeal")
your goulash, pig's knuckles or meatballs may be called "Sühneversuch"
("Clemency appeal") or "Kreuzver-
hör" ("Cross examination"), after
events in the nearby former city court.
The tiled stove in this tavern has been
famous through film and television–
a real tourist attraction.

Waisenstr. 14–16; tel. 2 42 5528;
www.zurletzteninstanz.de; U-Bahn:
Klosterstrasse; Mon–Sat noon–1 a.m.,
Sun noon–11 p.m. ●/●●
AmEx MASTER VISA

Kellerrestaurant im Brecht-Haus ⤳ p. 137, F 6

Next to the Bertolt Brecht memorial,
this restaurant serves rustic dishes
such as lentil stew or herring made
according to the recipes of his Viennese companion, Helene Wiegel.
Chausseestr. 125; tel. 2 82 38 43;
U-Bahn: Oranienburger Tor; Sun–Fri
noon–midnight, Sat 6 p.m.–midnight
● AmEx DINERS MASTER

Konnopke ⤳ p. 138, C 9

This sausage stand under elevated
rail tracks has attained cult status.
Even strangers to the place know the
name of Berlin's most famous "Currywurst" vendor. The meat patties are
worth the temptation.
Schönhauser Allee 44 a/Ecke
Kastanienallee; U-Bahn: Eberswalder
Strasse; Mon–Fri 6 a.m.–8 p.m. ●

Splendid ⤳ p. 137, F 7

Three words describe this delicat-
essen's fare: fresh, regional, organic.
Regional here means all over Germany: prawns from the North Sea,
cheese from the Allgäu or sausage
from Ruegen. The fresh dairy products, fruit and vegetables come from
Brandenburg. Not everything is take-
away. Try the potato soup, Swabian
Maultaschen or Brandenburg buffalo
mozzarella for a quick snack.
Dorotheenstr. 37; tel. 92 12 72 47;
U-Bahn: Friedrichstrasse; Mon-Sat 9:30
a.m.-8 p.m., lunch Mon-Sat from 11:30
a.m. ● CREDIT

Tiergarten
Tizian ⤳ p. 143, E 17

Not just Hyatt hotel guests get to
enjoy the hearty classics from the
undisputably best restaurant on
Potsdamer Platz.

Marlene-Dietrich-Platz 2; tel.
25 53 17 64; U-Bahn: Potsdamer Platz;
daily 11 a.m.–11 p.m. ●●● CREDIT

Zehlendorf
Remise Schloss Glienicke
⤳ p. 140, southwest A 16

Pike-perch and catfish from the Havel
river and Lake Müritz with an Austrian touch grace the plates at this fine
establishment in a palace park. Veni-
son dishes are also available.
Königstr. 36; tel. 8 05 40 00;
S-Bahn: Wannsee, then Bus 116;
Wed-Sun noon-11 p.m. ●●● MASTER

BEER GARDENS, OPEN-AIR SPOTS AND SHIPS

Putting tables and chairs out despite
dust, smoke and construction noise
has long been common practice in
Berlin. But those looking for a quiet,
idyllic spot under an old tree at the
water's edge won't have any difficulty in the capital city.

Altes Zollhaus ⤳ p. 144, B 22

Very good home cooking with quality
ingredients in an old half-timbered
house that one might not expect to
find in this Kreuzberg neighbourhood. For a special evening. Reservations recommended.

MERIAN Tip
4 Thai Inside

Consistently good food here, so the
tables are quickly taken by the many
people who work in the area. In the
evening this plain, almost spartan
establishment comes alive with
fancy cocktails and elegant dishes
served in baskets or even pineap-
ples. The clientèle is international
and early reservations are definitely
recommended.
Dircksenstr. 37; tel. 24 72 43 71; S-
Bahn: Hackescher Markt; daily noon–
midnight ●● CREDIT ⤳ p. 138, C 11

Prince Carl of Prussia commissioned Karl Friedrich Schinkel to remodel Schloss Glienicke (→ p. 68) in 1824. The carriage house is now a restaurant (→ p. 25).

Carl-Herz-Ufer 30, Kreuzberg;
tel. 6 92 33 00; U-Bahn: Prinzenstrasse;
Tue–Sat 6 p.m.–11 p.m. ●●● CREDIT

Blockhaus Nikolskoe
····⟩ p. 140, southwest A 16
There is indeed space here for 600 guests at this historical tavern, but not all of the seats offer you breathtaking views of the Havel River and the Pfaueninsel (Peacock Island), or St. Peter and Paul. With dishes such as pork knuckles and asparagus, the fare is reliably traditional.
Nikolskoer Weg, Zehlendorf;
tel. 8 05 29 14; S-Bahn: Wannsee, Bus 216; May–Oct, Fri–Wed noon–10 p.m., Nov–April noon–8 p.m. ●● ▱

Café am Neuen See ····⟩ p. 136, B 8
A Biergarten in the Tiergarten, away from the hustle and bustle of it all. There are two areas: one with Italian food and service, and another with self-service salads and snacks. Boats are also available for hire.
Lichtensteinallee 2, Tiergarten;
tel. 2 54 49 30; Bus 100; daily 10 a.m.–midnight in summer, only weekends in winter

Café am Ufer ····⟩ p. 145, D 22
Casseroles, salads and fish, served on the Landwehrkanal of the Spree.
Paul-Lincke-Ufer 42/43, Kreuzberg;
tel. 6 12 28 27; U-Bahn: Kottbusser Tor; daily 10 a.m.–1 a.m.

Café der Schwartz'schen Villa
····⟩ p. 141, south F 16
Dine under shade trees in this romantic villa's enchanting garden.
Grunewaldstr. 54/55; tel. 7 93 79 70; U-Bahn: Rathaus Steglitz; daily 10 a.m.–midnight MASTER VISA

Capt'n Schillow ····⟩ p. 135, F 4
Café and restaurant boat for long, summer nights or Sunday brunches. The evening standard is fish.
Strasse des 17. Juni; tel. 31 50 50 15; U-Bahn: Ernst-Reuter-Platz; Mon–Sat 11 a.m.–midnight, Sun 10 a.m.–midnight ● ▱

Freischwimmer ····⟩ p. 145, F 22
In the beginning, over 80 years ago, these were floating piers. The boathouse and storage rooms were converted to kitchen and bar, and now it's the guests who sway on the planks.

Vor dem Schlesischen Tor 2, Kreuzberg;
U-Bahn: Schlesisches Tor

Kastanie ⋯⋙ p. 134, C 4
The lovely Schlossstrasse, whose
centre strip is used to play boules, is
also home to a little garden where,
besides the beer, organic meals,
soups and juices are served.
Schlossstr. 22; tel. 3 21 50 34;
U-Bahn: Sophie-Charlotte-Platz;
daily noon–2 a.m.

Klipper ⋯⋙ p. 145, east F 24
After plying the Ijsselmeer, the Klipper anchored for good between Plän-
ter Wald and Treptower Park on the
Spree. Boats pass beneath weeping
willows. Occasionally, the bright red
seaplane takes off on an excursion.
On the Insel der Jugend, young parents lie in the sun while children play,
and music drifts past every now and
then. Fish fans can order the "Kapi-
tänsteller" or "Captain's plate". They
serve late breakfasts and the cakes
come highly recommended.
Bulgarische Strasse; tel. 53 21 64 90;
S-Bahn: Treptower Park, then 15 min.
walk along the riverbank; daily
10 a.m.–1 a.m. ●/●●

Prater ▒▒ ⋯⋙ p. 138, C 9
This restaurant opened in 1837, outside the city walls. These days, it is
surrounded by the buildings of Prenzlauer Berg. In the last few years they
have made it possible again to sit
under the trees outside. Open-air
dancing on Wednesdays, and popular
stage performances on occasion.
Kastanienallee 7–9; tel. 4 48 56 88;
U-Bahn: Eberswalder Strasse;
Mon–Fri 4 p.m.–midnight, Sat, Sun
noon–midnight

Van Loon ⋯⋙ p. 144, B 22
Start the day with prawns and scram-
bled eggs on a boat in this urban port.
Carl-Herz-Ufer 5, Kreuzberg;
tel. 6 92 62 93; U-Bahn: Prinzenstrasse;
daily 10 a.m.–1 a.m.

Zillemarkt ⋯⋙ p. 141, F 14
A garden just a few minutes from Kurfürstendamm and, what's more, one
of the few remaining traditional pubs
in the area to go for a proper meal.
Bleibtreustr. 48 a, Charlottenburg;
tel. 8 81 70 40; S-Bahn: Savignyplatz;
daily 10 a.m.–1 a.m. ●

Zollpackhof ⋯⋙ p. 137, E 7
Between central station and Parliament, walk down the new promenade
along the Spree river to a beer garden
with old trees and a view of the Chancellor's building.
Alt Moabit 143–145, Mitte;
tel. 33 09 97 20; S-Bahn: Hauptbahn-
hof/Lehrter Bahnhof; daily from 11 a.m.
in summer, in winter Wed–Sat 11
a.m.–11 p.m., Sun 10 a.m.–10 p.m.

CAFÉS AND TEAROOMS
**In and around Charlottenburg and
Kurfüstendamm**
Arc ⋯⋙ p. 141, F 14
When it seems like the train is rolling
directly above the breakfast table,
then you know you're in the big city.
In this case, it also means breakfast
until 4 p.m. The kitchen here always
has new surprises.
Fasanenstr. 81; tel. 3 13 26 25;
U-/S-Bahn: Zoologischer Garten;
daily 8 a.m.–midnight

Café Aedes ⋯⋙ p. 141, F 13
The adjacent architecture gallery
seems to provide for new guests
and conversation over red wine and
an espresso.
S-Bahnbogen 599; Savignyplatz;
tel. 3 12 55 04; S-Bahn: Savignyplatz;
daily 8 a.m.–midnight

Café Einstein ⋯⋙ p. 142, B 17
A piece of old Berlin in the former villa
of actress Henny Porten. You'll need
to know the difference here between
a "melange" and a "Kleiner Brauner"
when ordering your coffee if you
don't want to provoke the staff.

Kurfürstenstr. 58; tel. 2 61 59 96;
Bus 100; daily 10 a.m.-2 a.m.

TTT ⟶ p. 142, C 19
Over 140 types of tea, poetically described and served in fine English
porcelain with an hourglass in a
smoke-free atmosphere.
Goltzstr. 2; U-Bahn: Eisenacher Strasse;
Mon-Sat 8:30 a.m.–midnight, Sun from
10 a.m.

**Wintergarten Café im
Literaturhaus** ⟶ p. 141, F 14
A short walk to the Literaturhaus
leaves the bustling Ku'damm behind.
The large café here is relaxing, whether you're in for breakfast, to read
the paper or enjoy a tasty snack. The
menu changes daily here and offers
few but fine dishes, either vegetarian
or with free-range organic meats.
Fasanenstr. 23; tel. 8 82 54 14; U-Bahn:
Uhlandstrasse; daily 9:30 a.m.–1 a.m. ●●

Kreuzberg
Bergmann 103 ⟶ p. 144, A 23
Spread over multiple levels, with sub-
stantial breakfast and daily menus.
After a lavish Sunday brunch you can
move on to the long list of cocktails.
Try the "Flammkuchen" (Tarte Flam-
bée), an Alsatian treat.
Bergmannstr. 103; tel. 6 94 83 23;
U-Bahn: Mehringdamm; daily
9 a.m.–1 a.m.

Café Adler ⟶ p. 144, A 21
Regulars at this Checkpoint Charlie
venue enjoyed a bit of history with
their coffee during German reunification. Back then they served bubbly
and the Statue of Liberty hung above
the construction site. Today they look
on as new office spaces fill up–or not.
Friedrichstr. 206/Zimmerstrasse;
U-Bahn: Kochstrasse; Mon–Fri 10 a.m.–
1 a.m., Sat and Sun from 11 a.m.

Café Milagro ⟶ p. 144, A 23
Organic food in a relaxed environment. Sidewalk seating in summer.

Bergmannstr. 12; tel. 6 92 23 03;
U-Bahn: Gneisenaustrasse; daily
9 a.m.–1 a.m.

Flammende Herzen ⟶ p. 145, D 22
Kitsch is king at this address in the
once infamous district of SO 36.
Oranienstr. 170; tel. 6 15 71 02;
U-Bahn: Kottbusser Tor; daily
from 11 a.m.

Mitte and Prenzlauer Berg
Cinema Café ⟶ p. 140, B 11
If Laurel and Hardy weren't standing
guard outside, you'd probably over-
see this narrow café decorated with
GDR film props in this otherwise tren-
dy new area.
Rosenthaler Str. 39; Tel. 2 80 64 15;
S-Bahn: Hackescher Markt; daily from
noon

Operncafé ⟶ p. 138, A 12
As the name might indicate, the
Operncafé offers you a bit of 19th
century, a bit of ritz, and an exquisite
selection of pastries. The illuminated
terrace allows for long summer
evenings.
Unter den Linden 5; tel. 2 04 22 69;
U-Bahn: Stadtmitte; daily 9 a.m.–
midnight

Schall & Rauch
⟶ p. 138, north C 9
A great place for late breakfast in
the afternoon, with a very tempting
brunch buffet at the weekend.
Gleimstr. 23; tel. 4 48 07 70; U-/S-Bahn:
Schönhauser Allee; Mon–Fri
10 a.m.–3a.m., Sun 9 a.m.–3 a.m.

Tadschikische Teestube
⟶ p. 75, a 2
Lounging on cushions between thick
carpets, tea is brought to you in
Russian style, with rum raisins and
vodka.
Palais am Festungsgraben 1 (behind
the Neue Wache); tel. 2 04 11 12; Bus
100; Mon–Fri 5 p.m.–midnight, Sat and
Sun 3 p.m.–midnight

Shopping

Kitsch, creativity and cuisine: Much about Berlin makes shopping a journey of discovery.

France in the middle of Berlin: the Galeries Lafayette Berlin (→ p.31) is the only branch of the famous Parisian department store outside of France.

Trash or treasure? For some there is no difference. It could be a Berliner bear or a miniature Brandenburg Gate, a beer stein or a simple t-shirt. Almost every one of the countless tourists here takes home some sort of souvenir.

Beyond the mundane mementos, however, the capital has countless other, higher quality temptations to lure the cash from your pocket: precious designer porcelain from a formerly royal manufactory, hand-sewn Budapest shoes, comical and colourful cardboard furnishings, and lamps that could be more aptly named luminary objects. Or perhaps an enshrouded Parliament building autographed by Christo and Jean-Claude, fantastic objects from still unknown artists, filigree glass hummingbirds, a wooden tie or some fine millinery. Or under-the-counter books from the times in the GDR when they were forbidden and now serve as unique documents of contemporary history.

Shop opening times vary, of course. While many businesses in the outer districts close between 6 p.m. and 7 p.m., you can typically shop in the stores in the centres of the East and West until at least 8 p.m. On special occasions the shops are open Sundays as well, and on one long shopping night in fall, businesses around Ku'damm and Tauentzien are open until midnight.

AMPELMÄNNCHEN   ⸱⸱⸱⸱⸱⸱⸱⸱> p. 138, B 11
Only Berlin is home to two different "Ampelmännchen", or "Little traffic-light men", with top hats who tell you to cross when green and stop when red. Of course, only the East Berlin originals deserve the name, but they were able to prevent his complete removal from the system, and now he competes with the Berlin Bear for space on lamps, t-shirts and myriad other souvenirs. Since 1990, the production plant in Wildenfels near Zwickau has had its hands full because the little man is not only officially protected in Berlin. He has gained popularity all over the country. Since his 40th birthday, a gallery has even been devoted to him in the Hackesche Höfe, and every once in a while the traffic psychologist, Karl Peglau, his inventor, autographs souvenir versions of him.
Rosenthaler Str. 40, Hof V

ANTIQUES
There are about 250 antiques shops in Berlin, with their main concentration on the Suarezstrasse in Charlottenburg (⸱⸱⸱⸱⸱> p. 140, C 13). About 30 dealers are there. U-Bahn: Sophie-Charlotte-Platz (⸱⸱⸱⸱⸱> p. 134, C 4).

Bärenstark   ⸱⸱⸱⸱⸱> p. 138, A 11
The hearts of young and old will be touched by the new, oversize and older teddy bears available at this shop, "Strong as a Bear".
S-Bahnbogen 201, Mitte;
U-/S-Bahn: Friedrichstrasse

Echte alte Lampen   ⸱⸱⸱⸱⸱> p. 141, F 15
A full range of the original lamps from the beginnings of electrical wiring, art deco and art nouveau.
Pfalzburger Str. 12, Wilmersdorf;
U-Bahn: Hohenzollerndamm

Golem   ⸱⸱⸱⸱⸱> p.138, B 11
This small entreprise specialises in the traditional manufacture of glass ceramic tiles, mainly used to replace old ones in art nouveau buildings. Orders for the Hundertwasser Column in Vienna and for Harrods Place in London have been filled here too.
Rosenthaler Str. 40/41, Hof VII, Mitte;
S-Bahn: Hackescher Markt

Lehmanns Kolonialwaren
      ⸱⸱⸱⸱⸱> p. 141, F 13
Leather trunks, pith helmets, hat boxes, dividing screens – all the travel necessities of colonial times.
Grolmannstr. 46, Charlottenburg;
S-Bahn: Savignyplatz

HOUSEWARES

Kapula Candles ⋯⋯⋟ p. 138, A 12
The candles sold here are made in South Africa and each is a unique work of art painted with non-toxic pigment colours.
Friedrichstr. 68 (Quartier 205);
U-Bahn: Französische Strasse

Küchenladen ⋯⋯⋟ p. 141, F 14
Nothing shoddy here. The wares in this shop are good, useable and a tad up-scale. You can find suitable recipes here as well.
Knesebeckstr. 26, Charlottenburg;
S-Bahn: Savignyplatz

DEPARTMENT STORES

Berlinomat ⋯⋯⋟ p. 139, east F 12
T-shirts from hasipop, sneakers from Zeha, jeans from HOTINAF, sunglasses from ic!Berlin and more. The one thing connecting all the labels in this store: all 30 designers are from Berlin (www.berlinomat.com). Everything is innovative here, from the furniture and fashion to the accessories and jewellery. In the lounge you can have a coffee or just wait to see which object will be awarded Product of Berlin status.
Frankfurter Allee 86, Friedrichshain;
U-Bahn: Frankfurter Allee

Galeries Lafayette ⋯⋯⋟ p. 138, A 12
France in the Friedrichstrasse. It is primarily a curiosity for locals, but in the event that shopping is not the real objective, the architecture alone, with its glass pyramid affording views of the other floors, makes this attractive edifice designed by star architect Jean Nouvel much more than a department store. Of course, fashion and other extravagances are on offer as well as a French bookshop. Besides the fine porcelain for sale in the basement, you can also purchase gourmet delicacies or try them on the spot with a glass of champagne.
Friedrichstr. 76–78, Mitte;
U-Bahn: Französische Strasse

KaDeWe ⋯⋯⋟ p. 142, B 18
Founded in 1907, the Kaufhaus des Westens (Department Store of the West) was, with its surplus of just about everything, the showcase for capitalistic West Germany during the Cold War. Now, especially after ramping up to handle Parisian competition from the East, it amazes many a rural visitor to the capital with its splendour and abundance. The food, or more accurately, the epicurean hall on the 6th floor, inspires boundless consumer passion with 1,800 types of cheese, 1,000 types of sausage, ham and pâtés, wine, and champagne–simply everything from everywhere.
Tauentzienstr. 21–24, Schöneberg;
www.kadewe.de; U-Bahn: Wittenberg-platz

Naturkaufhaus
⋯⋯⋟ p. 141, south F 16
Cushions from India, fancy rubber boots, warm pullovers, pretty clothes for body, bed and table.
Schlossstr. 101 (Galleria), Steglitz;
U-Bahn: Rathaus Steglitz

Stilwerk ⋯⋯⋟ p. 141, F 13
The Conran Shop (now "zene") was for many people the most exciting of the 58 shops in the 63,000 square feet of the 5-floor interior design centre "Stilwerk", which opened in November 1999. It's smart and simple, just like in London, Tokyo, New York and Hamburg, and the exclusive brand names for furniture, jewellery, porcelain, fabrics, carpets and pianos range from Alessi and Bechstein to La Ventana and Zeitlos.
Kantstr. 17; U-/S-Bahn: Zoologischer Garten; Mon–Fri 10 a.m.–8 p.m., Sat 10 a.m.–4 p.m.; viewing only on Sun noon–6 p.m.

Viethaus ⋯⋯⋟ p. 138, B 12
With 50,600 square feet of space, this is the largest Vietnamese store outside of Vietnam. Offering quality

products including porcelain, ceramic, rattan furniture, coffee and tea, they also offer a restaurant where cooks from Hanoi serve a range of specialties. Vietnamese art and travel advice can also be found here.
Spittelmarkt, Mitte; U-Bahn: Spittelmarkt

COOKING
Kochlust ····> p. 138, C 10
Sometimes the recipes in those fancy cookbooks just don't quite seem to work at home. Kochlust not only offers the book, but also the chance to watch cooks at work, then make a meal and dine with them. Things at home should go more smoothly then.
Alte Schönhauser Str. 36/37, Mitte; tel. 24 63 88 83; www.kochlust-berlin.de; U-Bahn: Weinmeisterstrasse

ARTISANS
Kunstreich ····> p. 138, A 11
This tiny shop almost directly across from the Pergamon Museum is full of fanciful works of ceramic, leather, glass, paper and felt. They always have new exhibits as well.
Am Kupfergraben 6, Mitte; U-Bahn: Friedrichstrasse; Tue–Sun 11 a.m.–7 p.m.

MARKETS
Markt der Kontinente is the name of this unusual market event in the Dahlem Museums at weekends during the Advent period. Dealers, galleries, artists and clubs sell arts and crafts from all over the world: African fabrics, Indian jewellery, Mexican toys, Brasilian hammocks, Christmas ornaments and musical instruments from every continent. To top it off, there are cultural events and it is a perfect opportunity to have a look around the Museum of Asian Art and the Ethnological Museum.
Lansstr. 8; U-Bahn: Dahlem-Dorf; Sat and Sun 11 a.m.–7 p.m.

Grosser Berliner Kunst & Trödelmarkt ····> p. 135, F 4
An established flea market, yes, but actually more like an antiques market with prices to match. Half the space is taken up by Berlin artists who produce fashion goods and jewellery or paintings and sculptures.
Strasse des 17. Juni, Charlottenburg; U-Bahn: Ernst-Reuter-Platz; Sat and Sun 10 a.m.–4 p.m.

FASHION
Many of the best fashion boutiques are on Kurfürstendamm, Schlüterstrasse or on Bleibtreustrasse in the Charlottenburg district. If you're looking for big name designers like Jil Sander, Escada, Féraud, Max Mara, Versace, Sonia Rykiel or Yves Saint Laurent you'll have to explore the section between Kurfürstendamm Adenauerplatz. Shopping activities in the Steglitz area are focused on Schlossstrasse; in Schöneberg on Akazienstrasse and Goltzstrasse; in Prenzlauer Berg on Kastanienallee; in Kreuzberg on Bergmannstrasse; and in the Mitte district look on Friedrichstrasse. The hippest boutiques will probably be around the Hackescher Markt.

Claudia Skoda Level ····> p. 138, C 10
Offbeat knitwear.
Alte Schönhauser Str. 35; U-Bahn: Weinmeisterstrasse

MERIAN Tip

⑤ Türkenmarkt

The name of this market ("Turks Market") is really meant to imply the boisterousness and abundance at this, the most colourful of Berlin's bazaars. Find everything your heart desires, from foods and fabrics to porcelain and clothing.

Maybachufer, Kreuzberg; U-Bahn: Kottbusser Tor;Tue and Fri noon–6p.m. ····> p. 145, D 23

The collections from Respectmen guarantee an individual outfit.

Daniel Rodan ····⟩ p. 142, A 17
Bright red and velvety, embroidered and painted, bell-shaped and ruffled, underwear or ball gown–you can't imagine the myriad forms leather can take on. Worth a visit for inspiration alone. A tailored item can be sent by post, or look for a bargain at a Sunday afternoon fashion show.
Kurfürstendamm 29; www.rodan.de;
U-Bahn: Kurfürstendamm

Departmentstore ····⟩ p. 138, A 12
Not only is the architecture impressive (Pei, Cobb, Freed & Partner), but the haute couture as well (Donna Karan, Manolo Blahnik, etc.)–for men, women and even dogs.
Friedrichstr. 71, Mitte;
U-Bahn: Französische Strasse

Durchbruch Moden ····⟩ p. 141, E 13
Established in the 1980s, this shop offers extravagant items that do not require their hosts to be overly bold. Fitting jewellery as well.
Schlüterstr. 54, Charlottenburg;
S-Bahn: Savignyplatz

Femme ····⟩ p. 141, F 14
Exquisitely fine, delicate and above all tempting lingerie.

Fiona Bennett ····⟩ p. 138, B 11
Extravagant design from this well-known milliner.
Grosse Hamburger Str. 25, Mitte;
U-Bahn: Weinmeisterstrasse

Hautnah ····⟩ p. 141, F 13
Eccentricities in latex, leather, and patent leather. Under and outerwear.
Uhlandstr. 170, Charlottenburg;
U-Bahn: Uhlandstrasse

Kaufhaus Schrill ····⟩ p. 141, F 13
This shop is like the costume storage room at a theatre: feather boas, sequined vests and rattling neckties.
Bleibtreustr. 46, Charlottenburg;
S-Bahn: Savignyplatz

Respectmen ····⟩ p. 138, B 10
Three expert designers create elegant, youthful men's clothing from the finest fabrics.
Neue Schönhauser Str. 14, Mitte;
U-Bahn: Weinmeisterstrasse

Tagebau ····⟩ p. 138, B 10
Six designers presenting fashion, jewellery, furniture and accessories.

Creative and unsual.
Rosenthaler Str. 19, Mitte;
U-Bahn: Weinmeisterstrasse

Yoshiharu Ito ····⟩ p. 138, A 10
Purist/avant-garde design from this
Japanese artist who is said to be one
of the most innovative in Berlin.
Auguststr. 9, Mitte, U-Bahn:
Oranienburger Tor

MUSIC
Cantus 139 ····⟩ p. 141, E 13
This smaller successor to the leading
specialist music store Bote & Bock
has a large assortment of notes for
all musical interests, music books
and international works. A true treasure trove.
Kantstr. 139, Charlottenburg;
S-Bahn: Savignyplatz

Grammophon-Salon
····⟩ p. 142, C 19
You can have your really old phono-
graph records repaired here, or you
can buy and sell them. Replacement
parts for gramophones are also no
problem.
Eisenacher Str. 11, Schöneberg;
tel. 21 47 46 40; U-Bahn: Eisenacher
Strasse; open Thu and Fri

Platten Pedro ····⟩ p. 134, C 2
Probably the largest antique record
shop in the world. Looks and actual-
ly is more like a library.
Tegeler Weg 100, Charlottenburg;
U-/S-Bahn: Jungfernheide

Soultrade ····⟩ p. 145, D 23
Specialised in black American music
of all kinds. Everything from new un-
derground recordings out of New
York to forgotten soul classics.
Sanderstr. 29, Neukölln;
U-Bahn: Schönleinstrasse

JEWELLERY
Lalic ····⟩ p. 141, F 13
Designer jewellery for those who
like it a bit more eccentric.

Bleibtreustr. 47, Charlottenburg;
S-Bahn: Savignyplatz

Schmuckwerk ····⟩ p. 138, B 11
This shop has gold and mountain
crystal, from subtly stylish to outra-
geous. Sabine Dubbers also takes
commission work.
Rosenthaler Str. 40/41, Mitte;
S-Bahn: Hackescher Markt

SHOES
Toscanini ····⟩ p. 141, south F 16
Handsome shoes, but only in slightly
unusual sizes. Ladies' European sizes
from 32 to 35 and 42 to 46. Men's
European sizes 38 to 39 and 46 to 52.
Schlossstr. 119, Steglitz;
U-Bahn: Schlossstrasse

SOAP
Seifroh ····⟩ p. 138, B 11
Chocolate soaps, cake soaps–not to
eat, of course–perhaps you prefer
the Berlin television tower, Alexander, to soap up with. The imagination
evidently has no boundaries here.
Sophienstr. 7, Mitte;
S-Bahn: Hackescher Markt

MERIAN Tip

⑥ Trippen

In the middle of the Hackesche
Höfe, scattered around a lovely
courtyard with a fountain, a number
of young entrepreneurs have set up
businesses and revived the work-
shop-in-store tradition. Most of the
items on sale are made by the shop-
keepers themselves. One of the
nicest of the shops is the shoemaker
Trippen. The prototypes from the
shop's first collection adorn the tiles
as a sort of relief. You can even have
your own shoes tailor made here.
Rosenthaler Str. 40/41, Hof 3, Mitte;
S-Bahn: Hackescher Markt
····⟩ p. 138, B 11

Toys
Spielbrett ····⟩ p. 144, C 23
No PlayStations here. Instead, a large selection of board games and wooden toys for both young and old.
Körtestr. 27, Kreuzberg;
U-Bahn: Südstern

Zauberkönig ····⟩ p. 145, D 24
Basic equipment for up-and-coming magicians, or just cunning gimmicks to amuse the parents.
Hermannstr. 84–90, Neukölln;
U-Bahn: Hermannplatz

Sport
Globetrotter
Europe's largest outdoor recreation shop? Possibly so, and with its 46,000 square feet it is at the very least breathtaking and informative for clients who want to test the Arctic durability of their sleeping bag: wind blows, and the thermometer shows minus 25 degrees Celsius. Hiking shoes can be tested on the treadmill and then on other surfaces. Then it's back to the cooling chamber to test the trekking jacket. The boat goes in the pool, and you yourself go onto the climbing wall. Water-resistant zippers, concealable hoods and forearm ventilation are the new standards in hiking. If they don't have the outdoor gear you are looking for here, then it doesn't exist. 12,000 items are on offer, along with a variety of events such as slide shows, exhibitions and introductory climbing courses.
Schlossstr. 78–82, Steglitz;
tel. 8 50 89 20, www.globetrotter.de;
U-Bahn: Rathaus Steglitz

Fabric
Handweberei
Angela Binroth-Gierke
····⟩ p. 138, B 11
Table cloths, foulards, jackets and dresses in beautiful colours.
Sophienstr. 16, Mitte;
S-Bahn: Hackescher Markt

A department store in extra-large: KaDeWe (→ p. 31) on Tauentzienstrasse.

Sweets
Confiserie Melanie ····⟩ p. 141, F 13
Unique delectables like cherries from Ventoux, France, preserved in vinegar and Provence honey.
Goethestr. 4, Charlottenburg;
S-Bahn: Savignyplatz

Fassbender & Rausch
····⟩ p. 138, A 12
Chocolate, chocolate, chocolate. Apparently, you can make anything with it: bears, Brandenburg Gates or Parliament buildings. And you can cook with it too. Courses offered.
Mohrenstrasse/Ecke Charlottenstrasse, Mitte; U-Bahn: Stadtmitte

Bags
Penthesileia ····⟩ p. 138, A 11
Designers, Anke Runge and Sylvia Müller, make novel handbags and rucksacks out of leather.
Tucholskystr. 31, Mitte;
S-Bahn: Oranienburger Strasse

Bedroom
Schlafwandel ····⟩ p. 141, F 14
Sundry items for the dream bedroom.
Grolmannstrasse at the corner of Kudamm, Charlottenburg; U-Bahn: Uhlandstrasse

Nightlife

Where Berliners go to dance, listen to jazz, rock out or just have a beer.

Neu im April

15.04.	Triton/Brand New Bag
18.04.	Na Zemlje
28.04.	Mann ist Mann

The Schaubühne theatre on Lehniner Platz (→ p. 41) celebrated its 40th anniversary in 2002. The typical rotunda construction was erected by world-renowned architect Erich Mendelsohn in the 1920s.

Three major opera houses, one smaller stage, 31 theatres in total, 29 vaudeville venues, 18 children's theatres, and 15 cabarets. On top of that, there are 130 bars and dance clubs, and countless open-air events in the summer. No wonder it's difficult to decide where to go when you are spoilt for choice like this. And if you can't decide, you can try one of the 242 cinemas in town.

The capital's cultural budget encourages creative rivalries. Traditional theatres rework their repertoires while fringe theatres that play host to the big names at weekends become rehearsal rooms during the week for new plays and players. Wednesday is "experimental" day, but some experiment daily.

BARS/NIGHTCLUBS

Bar am Lützowplatz ····⊱ p. 142, C 17
At nearly 100 feet, it is probably the longest bar in town. A dozen different champagnes and 100 different cocktails are on offer here. Frequented by the "see and be seen" crowd.
Lützowplatz 7, Schöneberg; U-Bahn: Kurfürstenstrasse; daily 5 p.m.-3 a.m.

CSR-Bar ····⊱ p. 139, F 12
In the historically listed Zuckerbäcker-Allee in Friedrichshain, the former offices of Ceskoslovensko Aeroline are achieving new fame these days. Architects rave about the purist combination of nostalgic old East and post modernism. Try a gin fizz at the white counter.
Karl-Marx-Allee 96, Friedrichshain; tel. 29 04 47 41; U-Bahn: Weberwiese; daily from 8 p.m.

Harrys New York Bar
····⊱ p. 142, C 17
Seated in red leather furniture, budding investors, media people and the occasional artist enjoy tasty cocktails, extravagantly mixed by head bartender Andreas Lanninger and his crew. Much praised service.

Grand Hotel Esplanade, Lützowufer 15, Tiergarten; tel. 2 54 78 86 33; U-Bahn: Wittenbergplatz; daily from noon

Riva ····⊱ p. 138, B 11
Soccer fans know the Sardinian, Luigi Riva, after whom this bar is named. But to imagine a certain atmosphere because of this connection would be hasty. In addition to the colourful decor, an exquisite crowd of cocktail drinkers adorns the premises.
Dircksenstrasse, Bogen 142, Mitte; tel. 24 72 26 88; www.riva-berlin.de; S-Bahn: Hackescher Markt; daily from 8 p.m.

Saphire-Bar ····⊱ p. 139, north F 9
Autumn in Peking, Mummies on Ice, and Scarlett O'Hara are some of the names of the cocktails that have replaced the usual Caipirinhas, Cosmopolitans or Mai Thais–all in an elegant 70s style.
Bötzowstr. 31, Prenzlauer Berg; tel. 25 56 21 58; S-Bahn: Greifswalder Strasse; ; Sun-Thu 8 p.m.-2 a.m., Fri, Sat until 4 a.m.

Victoria Bar ····⊱ p. 143, D 18
Bartender Stefan Weber was selected by Gault Millau as champion of the year in his field, both for classic and new creations. The best part for exhausted clients: starting at 6 p.m. people sidle up to the bar or sink into the sofas for the three-hour Happy Hour. Small food selection.
Potsdamer Str. 102, Tiergarten; tel. 25 75 99 77; www.victoriabar.de; U-Bahn: Kurfürstenstrasse; Sun-Thu 6:30 p.m.-3 a.m., Fri/Sat until 4 a.m.

Zur weissen Maus ····⊱ p. 141, F 14
The atmosphere: jazz in the air and Otto Dix on the walls, Planter's Punch in muted lighting and men with ponytails who you could swear you've seen somewhere before.
Ludwigkirchplatz 12, Wilmersdorf; tel. 88 67 92 88; U-Bahn: Hohenzollernplatz; daily 8 p.m.–4 a.m.

Windhorst   ⤑ p. 137, F 7
For many this is the best bar in Mitte, and still an insiders' tip, but it is concealed by the adjacent U.S. Embassy's barricades until at least July 2008. A small venue with excellent cocktails and fine snacks.
Dorotheenstr. 65, Mitte; tel.
20 45 00 70; S-Bahn: Unter den Linden;
Mon–Fri from 6 p.m., Sat from 9 p.m.

CABARET, VAUDEVILLE,
MUSICAL, REVUE

Admiralspalast   ⤑ p. 138, A 11
For over 100 years it has been a point of interest in Berlin: first as an ice-skating arena with Russian-Roman thermal baths, then as an operetta house, and since 2006, after its renovation as a landmark, there's honky-tonk, theatre, a café, and the in-house salt spring baths are planned for reopening.
Friedrichstr. 101; Mitte; tel. 47 99 74 99;
www.admiralspalast.de;
U-Bahn: Friedrichstrasse

Bar jeder Vernunft   ⤑ p. 141, F 14
A mirrored tent over the rooftop parking at the Musical Theater, where many German stars of stage and sound started their careers. After a show there is music, and at the weekend there are the legendary night shows. You'll find a larger version, "Tipi das Zelt", in the Tiergarten next to the Federal Chancellery (Grosse Queralleee, Tel. 0180/3 27 93 58).
Schaperstr. 24, Wilmersdorf; tel.
8 83 15 82; www.bar-jeder-vernunft.de;
U-Bahn: Kurfürstendamm; from 8:30 p.m., bar from 7 p.m.

Berliner Kriminaltheater
                              ⤑ p. 139, F 11
Since 2001, Agatha Christie's "The Mousetrap" has been performed more than 300 times here. When the theatre moved from Wilmersdorf to the Umspannwerk Ost in the Friedrichshain district, they took the "Mousetrap" with them.

Palisadenstr. 48, Friedrichshain;
tel. 47 99 74 88; U-Bahn: Weberwiese

Chamäleon   ⤑ p. 138, B 11
Comedy and satire, artists and verbal acrobats. A perfect show is rare, and the toy vendor always comes by with her tray of curiosities.
Hackesche Höfe, Rosenthaler
Str. 40/41, Mitte; tel. 2 82 71 18;
www.chamaeleonberlin.de;
S-Bahn: Hackescher Markt

KulturBrauerei   ⤑ p. 138, C 9
Alternating programme of readings, cabaret, music, open discussions.
Schönhauser Allee 36/39,
Prenzlauer Berg; tel. 4 41 92 69;
U-Bahn: Eberswalder Strasse

Radialsystem V   ⤑ p. 145, E 21
Beautiful dance and music hall in an old pumping station on the Spree. The offerings range from older music to contemporary dance. In the summer, you can spend the intermission on the terrace by the water.
Holzmarktstr. 33, Mitte;
tel. 2 88 78 85 88; ww.radialsystem.de;
S-Bahn: Ostbahnhof

Stars in Concert
                      ⤑ p. 145, south F 24
The live shows in the Festival Center of the Estrel, the largest hotel in Germany with 1,125 rooms, easily rival Las Vegas–by their own accounts, anyway. Mega-stars (or at least their doubles) regularly appear here.
Estrel Festival Center, Sonnenallee 225,
Neukölln; tel. 68 31 68 31;
S-Bahnhof: Sonnenallee

Wintergarten   ⤑ p. 143, D 18
Glittering vaudeville re-established by André Heller and Bernhard Paul has become a real attraction for fans of light entertainment. Billing top entertainers.
Potsdamer Str. 96, Schöneberg;
tel. 23 08 82 30; U-Bahn: Kurfürsten-strasse

CINEMAS

Behind the 95 official addresses for cinema houses, you'll find 231 movie theatres, screen stages and other venues throughout the city. You can see films in their original language (the abbreviation for this in German is: OMU) in the Sony Center or in the Hackesche Höfe. The programmes can be found in the Thursday newspapers or in event schedule magazines, on advertising pillars or at www.berlinonline.de/kulturorte.

READINGS

Readings of all kinds occur daily in salons, on theatre stages and in taverns around town. Quality of venue and text varies, of couse. The Alte Kantine in the KulturBrauerei serves as a meeting place for various readings every Saturday. Most of the presenters are unknown (outside of Berlin)–young people with trendier texts. The odd career as an author started like this. Event programmes, for instance in the dailies (→ p. 132), can help you make a choice.

MUSIC VENUES

Constantly changing events make for a variety of opening times. Find out what is on by looking in the events programmes (→ Newspapers, p. 132).

A-Trane ⤍ p. 141, F 14
Classic and austere. Modern jazz or swing, occasionally blues.
Bleibtreustr. 1, Charlottenburg;
S-Bahn: Savignyplatz; daily
9 p.m.–2a.m., Fri, Sat open end;
concerts begin at 10 p.m.

B-Flat ⤍ p. 138, B 10
Jazz, swing revival, and a chance for newcomers. The 30-something audience is expected to dance.
Rosenthaler Str. 13, Mitte; U-Bahn:
Weinmeisterstrasse; daily from 8 p.m.,
events 9 p.m.; Fri, Sat, Sun live jazz,
Wed swing, Thu, Sun tango (not live)

Junction Bar ⤍ p. 144, A 23
Mixture of bar and club. Jazz concerts Monday to Friday beginning at 9 p.m.
Gneisenaustr. 18, Kreuzberg;
U-Bahn: Gneisenaustrasse

Quasimodo ⤍ p. 141, F 13
The most popular venue for jazz and blues can be found beneath the Delphi-Kino cinema, and with a little luck you'll be privy to a spontaneous star-studded session.
Kantstr. 12 a, Charlottenburg;
U-/S-Bahn: Zoologischer Garten

Parkhaus ⤍ p. 145, southeast E 24
This club offers rock music from the old East, with an ambience that has not been seen for a while in the West.
Puschkinallee 5, Treptow;
S-Bahn: Treptower Park

Yorckschlösschen ⤍ p. 143, F 19
Traditional jazz bar, ennobled with plush and patina.
Yorckstr. 15, Kreuzberg; U-Bahn:
Mehringdamm; live concerts Wed, Sat
from 9 p.m., Sun 2 p.m.–6 p.m.

CASINO

Spielbank Berlin ⤍ p. 143, E 17
Roulette, baccarat, blackjack and slot machines.
Marlene-Dietrich-Platz 1; tel. 25 59 90;
U-/S-Bahn: Potsdamer Platz; machine
hall, daily 10:30 a.m.-2:30 a.m.; classic
gaming casino 3 p.m.-3 a.m.

DANCE CLUBS

The venues hosting clubs, parties and concerts usually open around 7 p.m. Some are open daily, some only at weekends. Public parties in living rooms have become a permanent fixture in this transient scene, especially in Friedrichshain. Before midnight you'll be too early at just about all of these events, but you'll rarely be too late. Free schedules like the one in the city magazine, "30", and current flyers can be found in many cafés and bars.

Clärchens Ballhaus ⋯⟩ p. 138, A 10
After 91 years, the premises have been modestly refurbished and now it's almost like old times again. New to the establishment are the music, the tinsel and RotKäppchen champagne, and the younger crowd that mingles with the older regulars. Another innovation is the nice garden for a tasty lunch or afternoon coffee.
Auguststr. 24, Mitte; U-Bahn: Oranienburger Tor; Tue–Sun from noon

Kaffee Burger ⋯⟩ p. 138, B 10
Home to Berlin's famous "Russendisko". Otherwise, a bar with an unaffected retro look and readings.
Torstr. 60, Mitte; tel. 28 04 64 95; U-Bahn: Rosenthaler Platz

Roter Salon ⋯⟩ p. 138, C 10
Next to the Volksbühne theatre, the Red Salon offers varying music in a 1950s-style salon. Wednesday tango night from 9:30 p.m.
Rosa-Luxemburg-Platz, Mitte; tel. 24 06 58 06; U-Bahn: Rosa-Luxemburg-Platz

Sage Club ⋯⟩ p. 139, D 12
As good as in New York: imaginative, classy interior, well-dressed clientèle, good cocktails, three bars, a lounge, two dance floors, and a chill-out zone.
Brücken-/Köpenicker Strasse, Mitte; tel. 2 78 98 30; U-Bahn: Heinrich-Heine-Strasse; Fri–Sun from 11 p.m.

Watergate ⋯⟩ p. 145, F 22
For some, this club is the best in Berlin. With reflections of silos on the Spree river, you can choose from 80 different cocktails and two dozen types of whisky at the glamorous bar in this former warehouse. Occasional guest DJs from the UK.
Falckensteinstr. 49, Kreuzberg; tel. 61 28 03 94; U-Bahn: Schlesisches Tor; Thu, Fri from 11 p.m., Sat from midnight

THEATER, OPERA AND CONCERTS

Berliner Ensemble ⋯⟩ p. 137, F 7
Director Claus Peymann considers it the finest theatre in Berlin. The stuffiness of the past has been eliminated, Brecht and Heiner Müller are now a thing of the past.
Bertolt-Brecht-Platz 1, Mitte; tel. 28 40 81 55; U-Bahn: Friedrichstrasse

Deutsches Theater ⋯⟩ p. 137, F 7
Since its founding in 1883, the Deutsches Theater has been making

The dazzling vaudeville evenings in Chamäleon (→ p. 38) are reminiscent of old films and draw consistently large crowds.

MERIAN Tip

🔟 The Neuköllner Oper

Berlin's smallest opera house is a bit out of the way but it has made a name for itself with a programme of sensational performances. With six to eight première per season, connoisseurs do not have to wait long for a world première, and there is no permanent ensemble. Being that it's all about the high art of intelligent entertainment here, there is no need for tuxedo and evening gown. The show, after all, is on the stage and not in the audience.

Karl-Marx-Str. 131–133, Neukölln;
tel. 68 89 07 77; U-Bahn: Karl-Marx-Strasse ⤳ see the front jacket

history. Max Reinhardt laid the foundation here for what was to be a modern director's theatre, and it was with him in 1895 that the theatre began its ascent to international prestige.
Schumannstr. 13, Mitte; tel. 28 44 12 25;
U-/S-Bahn: Friedrichstrasse

Komische Oper ⤳ p. 138, A 12
The name comes from the French "Opéra comique", in which the dialogue replaced the recitative and, in contrast to aristocratic opera, the pieces were about ordinary citizens.
Behrenstr. 55/57, Mitte;
tel. 47 99 74 00; U-Bahn: Französische Strasse

Maxim-Gorki-Theater ⤳ p. 75, a 2
Predominantly visiting directors present Russian-authored and currently critical pieces.
Am Festungsgraben 2, Mitte;
tel. 20 22 11 15; U-/S-Bahn: Friedrichstrasse

Philharmonie ⤳ p. 143, E 17
Headquarters of the Berlin Philharmonic Orchestra, the building was opened in October of 1963 with a show conducted by Herbert von Karajan. It was designed by architect Hans Sharoun.
Matthäikirchstr. 1, Tiergarten; tel.
25 48 81 32; U-/S-Bahn: Potsdamer Platz

Schaubühne am Lehniner Platz
⤳ p. 141, D 14
Under the direction of Peter Stein and Claus Peymann, this theatre evolved in the 1970s and 1980s to become the most stylistically influential stage in Germany. At the time, Sascha Waltz was the star, now Ostermeier and Hillje direct this famous house.
Kurfürstendamm 153, Charlottenburg;
tel. 89 00 23; U-Bahn: Adenauerplatz

Sophiensäle ⤳ p. 138, B 11
In 1997, with his successful piece, "Allee der Kosmonauten", choreographer Sasha Waltz opened one of the most prestigious venues for free projects in the performing arts in this historic location.
Sophienstr. 18, Mitte; tel. 2 83 52 66;
S-Bahn: Hackescher Markt

Staatsoper
Unter den Linden ⤳ p. 138, A 12
Under chief conductor Daniel Barenboim, the "Linden Opera" has emerged as Berlin's leading temple of muses, with first-class international productions on offer.
Unter den Linden 5–7, Mitte;
tel. 20 35 45 55; U-Bahn: Französische Strasse

Volksbühne ⤳ p. 138, C 10
After the fall of the Wall, Frank Castorf transformed this theatre into the most exciting stage in Berlin. Following spectacular performances of the classics, the diverse programme is now dominated by socially critical works, young visiting directors and dance theatre.
Rosa-Luxemburg-Platz, Mitte;
tel. 24 06 57 77; U-Bahn: Rosa-Luxemburg-Platz

Festivals and Events

The best of the best. There's always something on in Berlin.

Performers from at least 80 countries do their thing at the Carnival of Cultures (→ p. 44) in May.

When thousands of people are rocking, singing and dancing in the streets from noon to nightfall; when samba, soca and steelbands provide the infectious rhythms; and when colourful costumes flutter, thrilling masks protrude from the crowd, and dancers move to unique choreography, then you know it's Pentecost in Berlin and you're at the Carnival of Cultures.

Yes, it may rain on this endless parade of about 4,000 participants, but when more than 100 formations from 80 countries present a piece of their culture–from Africa, Asia or Latin America–with music, dancing, masks and props, then Berliners just add their umbrellas to the colourful mix. They certainly don't stay home because of it! The **Carnival of Cultures** is not just a fair-weather friend, but a bit of sunshine obviously doesn't hurt either.

The performers prepare all year long for the three-day festival, when they finally stage their show and inspire veteran and first-time visitors alike with their incredible energy. Blücherplatz turns into a melange of tents, booths and games galleries. You can listen to a female percussion band from Brasil, or songs from Nicaragua; watch dance from Chile, or hear music from Peru; enjoy a lyrical Russian ballad or a Yakut shaman chant. Children learn the drums, while storytellers relate tales from 1,001 Nights. Who knew that there was such a thing as ballet from Angola and the Congo or hip-hop from the Orient?

The **Love Parade**, a big, colourful and loud event, initially attracted ravers and other young people from around the globe, but has now moved elsewhere. In its place are other events that have become tradition. Art and cultural happenings in summer and autumn, meant to bring a bit of flair to the divided city, now entertain Berliners and visitors in both East and West alike. The **Allied folk festivals** have survived as an enduring sign of friendship. New events have found their way to town, such as the **Classic Open Air** and the **Musik-Biennale**, which only took place in East Berlin from 1967 until German reunification.

A number of small trade fairs have joined the big ones, promoting products from the East and from the Baltic Sea regions, but not all of them have a permanent place in the annual schedule. When the museums stayed open until midnight over the Easter weekend, as a trial run for a new idea, that became an annual event tradition as well. Other cities in Germany have even followed suit with their own museums.

JANUARY
International Green Week
This is actually an international agricultural fair, but Berliners flood the fairgrounds by the thousands to get a taste of what other countries eat and drink.

Long Night of the Museums
Theatre, music and of course art until midnight in most of the museums. Information at www.lange-nacht-der-museen.de. Takes place in August.

Six-Day Race
International cycling stars kicked off the 86th "Six Days" in the brand new velodrome with its 250-metre Siberian spruce track in the Landsberger Allee. Novice spectators are a bit disappointed: The racers don't really cycle day and night. But the old sport palace tradition has been revived.

FEBRUARY
International Film Festival
It started in 1951, and since 1956, the signature gold and silver Bears have been awarded annually here. Sometimes only a few stars find their way to the capital, but more and more

visitors take their seats in festival cinemas, where film submissions from around the world are screened. Since 2001 on Potsdamer Platz, which seems made for the event.

MARCH
ITB - International Travel Fair
The world's largest travel fair with exhibitors from countries whose names you might have never heard. Lots of colourful brochures to take home while branch professionals hold conferences on stimulating future growth in the industry.

MAY
Carnival of Cultures 👫
With international costumes, traditions and dance, this festival makes the Kreuzberg area into what everyone would imagine: a colourful mixture of local immigrants and guests.

Ladies German Open
International women's tennis championship in the courts of the "Rot-Weiss" tennis club in Grunewald.

JUNE
Jazz across the Border
International jazz festival in the House of World Cultures.

Christopher Street Day
Gay and lesbian parade and party around the Nollendorfplatz.

Theatertreffen (Berlin Theatre Days)
From among all the productions from Germany, Austria and Switzerland, a jury chooses roughly ten to be part of the competitive exhibition of German-speaking theatre. Followed by the Theatertreffen der Jugend (Youth Theatre Days).

JULY
Classic Open-Air
Music, music and more music on the finest outdoor stages in the city: in

front of the concert hall at Gendarmenmarkt, at the Waldbühne, in the English Garden (in the Tiergarten), and even at the nicest horse racing track, the Hoppegarten.

Bach Days Berlin
Bach only: international soloists and ensembles play music from the maestro and his sons as well as other important Baroque works. Charlottenburg Palace is one of the venues.

International Hurdy-Gurdy Festival
Wonderful, large-scale barrel organs are the highlight of this bi-annual festival with a parade on Kurfürstendamm.

AUGUST
Internationale Funkausstellung
Since 2006, the world's largest annual consumer electronics fair presents international innovations from all areas of information technology. Representatives from radio and television can be found in their "glass" studios and the celebrities are closer than ever.

International Dance Festival
Top dance companies from the international avant-garde put common club-goers to shame with performances in places like the Komische Oper, the Hebbel Theater, the Theater am Halleschen Ufer and the Podewil centre.

SEPTEMBER
Berlin Festival Weeks
Two months of concerts, theatre, musical theatre, dance and discussions with a new theme every year: that's how the largest event of the Berliner Festspiele describes itself. Young artists are the focal point here and they are meant to be experienced in as varied a spectrum as possible. First nights and world première show how things are evolving in other

countries. There's almost always a theme-oriented exhibit in the Martin-Gropius-Bau.

Popkomm
Roughly translated, the organization behind this event is the "International Music and Entertainment Business Platform". In other words, a trade fair for the music business. Part of this is a festival that sends waves through the whole city: "400 acts from more than 30 countries and 30 official Popkomm venues" were announced for 2007, and for three days Berlin was stage and backstage all in one.

Clubs United
One ticket lets you hop from club to club through Berlin's music scene. Special buses provide transportation free of charge.

Berlin Marathon
42.195 kilometres through Berlin. The largest international marathon in Germany begins at the Victory Column on the Strasse des 17. Juni, and the finish line is the Brandenburg Gate. The past events have seen many a record broken. The run attracted over 40,000 athletes in 2007.

OCTOBER
Art Forum Berlin
If it can be done in Cologne, then Berlin can do it better. The international fair for contemporary art attracts art lovers from around the world and the jury of specialists, which changes every year, chooses the galleries to be included. In 2003, there were 101 exhibitors displaying everything from video works, photography and painting to sculpture, installations and works on paper. Virtually all of the artistic media of the 21st century is represented, and anyone looking to get an update on the current arts scene is in the right place here. Rest areas, cafés, restaurants, the fair library, a reading room and a

discussion forum, diverse performances and receptions of all kinds complete the picture.

NOVEMBER
International Boat Show
Nowhere is it more apparent that Berlin is by the water.

JazzFest Berlin
It's not just about jazz here, but other kinds of musical and performing arts as well. Folklore, theatre and sometimes even magic are displayed in ways that are influenced or interact with jazz. There is often a regional or thematic emphasis. The most traditional jazz festival in the country has inspired some competition, though.

DECEMBER
Christmas Markets 👨‍👧
There are indeed several, but the prettiest ones are at Breitscheidplatz and at the Gendarmenmarkt. Near the Ku'damm you can have a traditional "Feuerzangenbowle" punch with your sweets from the Altberliner Mandelbrennerei (sugar-coated almonds). Authenticity and an original assortment are priority at the Gendarmenmarkt where an historic backdrop is incorporated into the market, artists and artisans offer unusual crafts and selected culinary specialties are on offer. One of the smallest Christmas markets in Berlin is on Richardplatz in Neukölln: very nostalgic, without electrical lighting, but with wooden toys and a carousel.

New Year's Eve Party
Over one million Berliners and guests ring in the new year between the Brandenburg Gate and the Victory Column. If you didn't bring it yourself, you can buy from one of numerous food and beverage vendors, while live music is being played on various stages and DJs spin the latest tunes. The new year is greeted with spectacular fireworks.

Tips for Families and Kids

Science, stages, sea lions and more: exciting things for kids to do in Berlin.

Medieval taxi: In the Museumsdorf (outdoor museum) Düppel (→ p. 49), Willibald the ox pulls a wooden cart around the old square.

It all begins with the unusual scent of camels at **Zoo Station**, and before the bushes become too thick with green leaves in springtime you can see why. There is a second **zoo in Friedrichsfelde**. And next to the **Märkisches Museum**, in the middle of town there is a compound at the Köllnischer Park with three bears: Maxi, Schnute and Tilo.

In the **Ufa-Fabrik** in the Tempelhof district, not only can you observe loads of animals but you can also watch children practising their skills at a school for acrobatics. At weekends in the summer you can go with a tour guide to explore underground vaults and secret passageways in an old fortress from the 1800s at **Fort Hahneberg** in Spandau.

You can go for a swim the **Havel River** as well as in the **Wannsee** and **Müggelsee** lakes. The latter offers solar boat rides, and boat hire is also available at the Neuer See in the Tiergarten. There are children's films and theatre to see every day in Berlin, and a lot of museums are particularly interesting for children. Two observatories are available for gazing at the heavens.

If that's still not enough for you, pay a visit to **Loretta im Garten** in the Lietzenberger Strasse and ride the Ferris wheel, or discover the unknown in the exciting labyrinth at the Children's Museum. Boredom is also a foreign concept in the **Wuhlheide** recreational centre, located in an expansive wooded area in the south-eastern part of the city.

Aquarium in the Zoologischer Garten ⋯⟩ p. 142, B 17

Giant sea turtles and hammerhead sharks, moray eels and gobies. It's a fascinating underwater experience here at the aquarium in the Zoologischer Garten, one of the largest of its kind on the planet. The dim lighting is a necessity, so the fish can feel comfortable and "at home".

Zoologischer Garten, Budapester Strasse, next to the Elephant Gate; U-/S-Bahn: Zoologischer Garten; daily 9 a.m.–6 p.m.

CineStar IMAX ⋯⟩ p. 143, E 17

At this exciting cinema, 3D glasses with liquid crystal lenses are handed out at the entrance before visitors take their places in one of more than 500 luxury seats and await the spectacular presentation on 588 square metres of screen. The programme changes every hour here: fish splash around in the ocean at what seems to be arm's length, you duck when a tiger pounces, and feel like you're floating during a walk on the moon.

Potsdamer Platz, Tiergarten; tel. 26 06 64 00; U-Bahn: Potsdamer Platz

Berliner Bonbonmacherei
⋯⟩ p. 138, A 11

A sweet haze floats over a bubbling cauldron as the blue liquid ("Bosnian Plum") flows into a concoction of sugar, water and glucose syrup. The hot brew is then cooled on a metal table, cut apart with scissors and pressed into yard-long lumps. And then? Well, have a look for yourself. Bonbons in flavours like woodruff, orange or lemon, like they used to make them in many a Berlin kitchen.

Oranienburger Str. 32, Mitte (Heckmann-Höfe); S-Bahn: Oranienburger Strasse; Wed-Sat noon–8 p.m.

Der Spielball ⋯⟩ p. 141, south F 16

Café for kids with a cosy corner, ball basin and tumbling course.

Lefèvrestr. 20, Schöneberg; U-Bahn: Walter-Schreiber-Platz; Mon–Fri 10 a.m.–6 p.m., Sun sightseeing

FEZ Wuhlheide
⋯⟩ p. 139, southeast F 12

Recreation and leisure park with a railway, open-air stage, indoor swimming pool, a greenhouse designed for children, a small zoo, a few playgrounds, a fun palace with three floors for sports as well as games, pottery, and computer rooms.

Eichgestell, Köpenick; tel. 53 07 10;
S-Bahn: Wuhlheide, U-Bahn: Tierpark,
then tram 26, 61, 67; daily from 9 a.m.

Grips-Theater ····➔ p. 136, B 7

Sometimes with performances for adults but primarily offerings for people "from 6", "from 13" or "from 16" years of age. Berlin's best-known children's and youth theatre presents exciting plays about ordinary neighbourhood people, hippie grannies, civil courage and much more.

Altonaer Str. 22, Tiergarten;
tel. 3 91 40 04; www.grips-theater.de;
U-Bahn: Hansaplatz

Kinderinsel ····➔ p. 138, A 10

When the parents are too busy, have an urgent appointment or just want to discover Berlin on their own, the kids will find individual offers for a variety of age groups and nationalities in the field of experiential learning. The little archaeologists make their way to excavations, while others explore museums. For some, a good-night story is enough (from €10 per child per hour).

Eichendorffstr. 17, Mitte;
tel. 41 71 69 28; www.kinderinsel.de;
U-Bahn: Oranienburger Tor

Labyrinth ····➔ p. 137, northwest E 5

This children's museum in a former factory is ideal for both four-year-olds and even playful 40-year-olds. With changing themes, the concept here is discovery and participation. You can boogie to your own music when little wooden triangles emit different tones, or discover your own heartbeat. The exhibitions are always in flux, and inspire both young and old to play and learn.

Because of their contemporary plays and solid productions, the Grips-Theater is known well beyond Berlin. Here, a scene from "Linie 1", a work that has become a classic over the years.

Osloer Str. 12, Wedding; tel. 49 30 89 01; U-Bahn: Osloer Strasse; Tue–Sat 1 p.m.–6 p.m., Sun 11 a.m.–6 p.m.

Machmit-Museum

┈┈⟩ p. 139, north D 9
For almost 100 years this was a church, the Eliaskirche. Now, at the "Participation Museum", the old altar has been converted into a stage, there are two wood labyrinths in the nave, and the steeple serves as a fitting room for costumes. Six- to 12-year-olds will have a lot of fun joining in and trying out all of the different activities.

Senefelderstr. 6, Prenzlauer Berg; tel. 74 77 82 00; S-Bahn: Prenzlauer Allee; Tue–Fri 9 a.m.–6 p.m., Sun 10 a.m.–6 p.m.

Museumsdorf Düppel

┈┈⟩ p. 140, southwest A 16
At this medieval village, spinning wool, baking bread, woodworking, and shaping clay and iron into utensils is part of the daily operation. Barefoot men and women with costume scarves and felt hats work in gardens where medicinal herbs and mangold are planted. They look the part, and the sheep look just as small as in the Middle Ages. You can experience how life was 800 years ago at this original site, and Willibald the ox pulls children around the village square in a wooden cart.

Clauertstr. 11, Zehlendorf; S-Bahn: Zehlendorf, Bus 115; April–Oct, Sun 10 a.m.–5 p.m.

Puppentheater-Museum

┈┈⟩ p. 145, southeast D 24
Rumpelstiltskin awaits your arrival at the entrance. Puppeteer Nikolaus Hein shows the little guests how to make the devil dance while dragons and princes watch.

Karl-Marx-Str. 135, Neukölln; tel. 6 87 81 32; U-Bahn: Karl-Marx-Strasse; Mon–Fri 9 a.m.–4 p.m., Sat and Sun 11 a.m.–18 p.m.

MERIAN Tip

⑧ Deutsches Technik-museum Berlin

You can see it from a distance: a plane from the Airlift (C 47 Skytrain) perched on the roof, and it really looks as if it is steering towards Potsdamer Platz. Aircraft like this one carried all of life's necessities into West Berlin in 1948 and 1949 when the city was blockaded by the Soviets. The attractions continue too. In a still-functional television studio from 1958, you can watch yourself—of course in black and white—on the screen. Or you can explore steam engines, classic cars, locomotives, train carriages, ships and even airplanes. There are also windmills and watermills, blacksmiths and breweries on display in the museum's park. But even more exciting, even for the parents, is the Science Center Spectrum next door, where you can conduct your own experiments. There are answers to the craziest questions here, like why the sky is blue, how a battery works or how an organ pipe produces tones...and much more.

Trebbiner Str. 9, Kreuzberg; tel. 90 25 40; U-Bahn: Gleisdreieck; Tue–Fri 9 a.m.–5:30 p.m., Sat, Sun 10 a.m.–6 p.m.; adult admission € 4.50, children € 2.50   ┈┈⟩ p. 143, E 18

Junior-Museum

┈┈⟩ p. 140, south B 16
Germany's only children's museum for ethnology leads eight- to twelve-year-olds through accessible interactive experiential landscapes. They'll visit Aborigines in Australia and Tuaregs in Africa.

Ethnologisches Museum, Arnimallee 23, Dahlem; U-Bahn: Dahlem-Dorf; Tue–Fri 1 p.m.–6 p.m., Sat and Sun 11 a.m.–6 p.m.

Out and about in Berlin

The Hackesche Höfe (→ p. 55) is a favourite destination for art lovers and shoppers to take a break in one of the open-air cafés.

Construction on Unter den Linden and Leipziger Platz, where cranes rotate and the museums transform. Looking for Old Berlin? You don't have to stay around Ku'damm to find it.

Sights

Some change can be charming, but many of
Berlin's beloved sights are still around.

*Potsdamer Platz (→ p. 57), once a traffic intersection, has now become a city
within the city. The TV tower appears much closer than it is.*

Visitors to Berlin have the chance to discover things that will never be mentioned in any travel guide, if for no other reason than the things that are here today may indeed be gone tomorrow. Gone like the Wall, the symbol of a divided city that is now barely visible. And is that forgotten watchtower still there? Does the Tacheles cultural centre still exude its morbid charm, or will a construction site soon unveil a modern building in its place? Is Prenzlauer Berg still the fabled successor to the alternative neighbourhood of Kreuzberg, or has the scene already moved on to Friedrichshain?

Of course, the Berlin of yesteryear has not disappeared. The effects of its inertia can be seen in the furnishings of the lakeside terraces at the Tegeler See, where the locals still go out to shake a leg like in the old days; in the tranquillity of Peacock Island in summer; in the solitude of ice fishers on Müggelsee; and even in the slightly morbid charm of the East Block at some of the local neighbourhood bars (just not on Oranienburger Strasse).

The monuments and sights that tell the capital's story are naturally spread all over town, and can only give a true picture of this multi-facetted metropolis when seen in their totality. The huge construction sites, such as at Mediaspree, and the gigantic events arena O2-World, between the Spree and Ostbahnhof, are all part of that bigger picture.

It would seem that, along with the Bear, the city has found a new symbol in the bulldozer. Berlin is constantly reinventing itself these days. The mobility, the ever-changing potpourri, and the unimagined possibilities should all be taken advantage of when you make a trip to Berlin. And make use of its cultural diversity, where the array of choices is most noticeable.

New trends that have barely hit the streeets tend to disappear as fast as they came into being, like the living-room and basement clubs, just flashes in the pan of a party scene that was itself previously referred to as a club scene. Nowadays, the parties are on the rooftops overlooking the city. These unpredictable elements, these here-today-and-gone-tomorrow trends, are yet another of Berlin's endearing qualities.

New museums and buildings grow old at an astounding pace. The same place with a queue around the block yesterday, is perfect for a solitary viewing today. Thankfully, "old" does not always mean "out".

MITTE

Until 1860, Berlin included what is now just the Mitte district (without Tiergarten and Wedding), only 1.2 percent of the total area of the city today. It is where the towns of Berlin and Cölln were settled at the beginning of the 13th century, and after construction of the palace in 1470, Berlin became the residence of Brandenburg's elector princes. By 1709 it was the seat of its kings.

Alexanderplatz   ⋯⟩ p. 138, C 11
Berliners can tell who is from the East or from the West merely by the way they pronounce the name of this square, named after Tsar Alexander I in 1805 upon his visit to Friedrich Wilhelm III.

Once a marketplace and parade ground, the largest traffic junction in the East of Berlin was nothing but rubble after World War II before being redesigned as a pedestrian zone in the 1960s. A massive and somehow inhospitable square, punks and vagabonds wait for better times here, beer can in hand. The "Little Manhattan" promised in the adverts after the Wall is not likely to materialise, but new temples to consumerism like the city hall arcades and the pink Alexa have sprung from construction pits, and hotels are not far behind. The 33-foot **World Clock** tells the time around the globe. The real eye-catcher here is of course the iconic **TV tower** 🏨🏨, "Alex", Berlin's highest edifice at over 1,200 feet. In 40 seconds the lift whisks visitors to the 680-foot-high rotating Tele-Café (viewing deck Mar–Oct daily 9 a.m–1 a.m., Tele-Café daily 10 a.m.–1 a.m., Nov–Feb deck and café daily 10 a.m.–midnight). From here you get a beautiful view of churches and cranes and Berlin's copious greenery and parks. If you stay seated for half an hour, then you'll have seen everything.

The **Neptunbrunnen** (Neptune Fountain) by Reinhard Begas (1891, restored in 1969), originally in the courtyard of the Berlin Palace, is reminiscent of Bernini's Fontana dei Quattro Fiumi in Rome: It has four picturesque neo-baroque female figures representing the Elbe, the Vistula, the Oder and the Rhine rivers, all taking their places around Neptune.
U-/S-Bahn: Alexanderplatz

Berliner Dom   ⸬⸬⸬⸭ p. 138, B 11
Commissioned by Wilhelm II as a sepulchral church for the Hohenzollern family, it was built from 1894 to 1905 in Wilhelminian style based on disputed designs by city architect Julius Raschdorf. It was to be the "mother church of Prussian Protestantism in Berlin". Imposing, with cupolas and towers, the cathedral houses 95 sarcophagi of the ruling dynasty. The edifice, heavily damaged during and after the war, underwent renovations until 1993.
Lustgarten; Bus 100; church: Mon–Sat 9 a.m.–8 p.m., Sun noon–8 p.m., winter to 7 p.m.; Imperial Staircase and dome panorama: daily 9 a.m.–8 p.m., Oct–Mar 9 a.m.–5 p.m.; Admission €1,50; dome and royal crypt: Mon-Sat 9 a.m.–7 p.m., Sun noon–7 p.m.; cathedral maintenance fee for all areas €5, reduced €3, children under 14 free

Berliner Rathaus   ⸬⸬⸬⸭ p. 138, C 11
The "Red Town Hall", the mayor's seat in Berlin, is only called this for the colour of brick used in 1869 to replace its medieval predecessor. The relief on the frieze beneath the windows of the main floor is a stone chronicle of the city.
Spandauer Strasse; U-/S-Bahn: Alexanderplatz

Brandenburg Gate   ⸬⸬⸬⸭ p. 137, F 8
The last of 14 town gates, the symbol of a divided city from 1961 to 1989, and since then the icon of a reunified Germany, this gate opens onto the grand Prussian boulevard Unter den Linden and leads directly to the palace. Carl Gottfried Langhans based the structure (1788-1791) on the Propylaeum atop the Acropolis in Athens, and Johann Gottfried Schadow crowned it with the Quadriga in 1793, complete with chariot and goddess of peace, Irene. Napoleon absconded with the Quadriga to Paris in 1806, Marshal Blücher got her back in 1814, and Karl Friedrich Schinkel transformed the lady with the iron cross and oak wreath into a goddess of triumph – Victoria. The GDR had it removed, considering it a symbol of militarism, and it was replaced during restoration in 1991.
Pariser Platz; S-Bahn: Unter den Linden

Friedrichstrasse
      ⸬⸬⸬⸭ p. 138/144, A 10–22
Nearly 2.2 miles long and extending all the way from Oranienburg Gate to Mehringplatz at the Hallesches Tor, the most interesting portion of Friedrichstrasse is the two hundred yards to the left and right of Unter den Linden. This is where the history of the former Imperial street can be found, and the designs of modern international architects have already manifested themselves in stone and glass here. The slightly nondescript exteriors make the area around the Parisian department store **Galeries**

Lafayette all the more exciting. At Checkpoint Charlie, at Zimmer and Schützenstrasse, you'll find information on the history of the area and its transformation into a business park along the former path of the Wall.
U-/S-Bahn: Friedrichstrasse

Gendarmenmarkt   ⤳ p. 138, A 12
The square is named after the "Gens d'Armes", the regiment of "Soldier King" Friedrich Wilhelm I. During his reign, stables ringed this space. One of Germany's most important neoclassical ensembles, the Gendarmenmarkt's focal point is the **Schauspielhaus** theatre, built from 1818 to 1821 according to plans by Karl Friedrich Schinkel on the foundations of Langhans' National Theatre, which had been destroyed by a fire. The pediment figures were done by Christian Friedrich Tiek, and the steps to the atrium, with its Ionic columns, was accessible only to members of the royal court at the time. In 1821, Carl Maria von Weber's opera, "Der Freischütz", had its world première here. In December 1932, Gustaf Gründgens played Mephisto in Goethe's "Faust" on this stage, and in 1934 he became artistic director of the National Theatre. The SS set fire to the building at one point. Leading East German politicians decided on its restoration in 1976, along the lines of Schinkel's aesthetic: in white, red and gold. And in 1984 it was re-opened as a concert hall. It now provides the backdrop for the Classic Open Air (→ p.44) every summer. The **Schiller Memorial** by Reinhold Begas was erected here in 1871 here.

The names **German Cathedral** and **French Cathedral** were eventually accepted for the two churches on the square, built from 1780 to 1785 by Carl von Gontard with matcing domes. The latter was used by the Huguenot community, to which a museum is devoted here (Tue–Sat noon–5 p.m., Sun 11 a.m.–5 p.m.; admission 1€). A carillon plays daily at noon, 4 and 7 p.m.

The German Cathedral hosts a permament exhibition on the development of parliamentary democracy in Germany. The architect Pleuser made the different epochs of construction recognisable in the interior (Tue 10 a.m.–10 p.m., Wed–Sun 10 a.m.–6 p.m.; admission free).
U-Bahn: Stadtmitte

Hackesche Höfe   ⤳ p. 138, B 11
Just after the turn of the 19th century, a clever real estate speculator created an ensemble of eight

The Classic Open Air takes place every year in July at Gendarmenmarkt.

Nefertiti and other exhibits await a new home in the Egyptian Museum and Papyrus Collection.

spacious courtyards between Rosenthalerstrasse and Sophienstrasse. In 1995, after years of renovation, the first scaffolding came down and a priceless jewel was revealed. The builder, Kurt Berndt, had nearly all the façades in the entire structure clad in stucco. And for the largest interconnected residential and business complex in Europe, he commissioned avant-garde artist August Endell (1871 – 1925) with the design of the ballroom and the first courtyard. Endell's intention was to use colourfully glazed bricks for the façades to create the dynamic of a moving space and thus extend the street into the courtyard.

In the Schwarzenberg house next door, things still looks like they did just after the fall of the Wall, and it's supposed to stay that way. The Otto Weidt workshop for the blind, where some Jewish citizens found shelter during the war, has been also converted to a museum.
Rosenthaler Str. 40/41;
S-Bahn: Hackescher Markt

Holocaust Memorial ⋯⋯⟩ p. 137, F 8
With 2,711 concrete slabs on 4.7 acres in the middle of the city, American architect Peter Eisenman created this monument for the six million murdered Jews of Europe. The memorial is accessible 24 hours a day and is illuminated at night. The underground musuem portion contains four rooms with information about the fates of different families and extermnination camps.
Ebertstrasse; Bus 100; Ort der Information Tue–Sun 10 a.m.–8 p.m.; Guided tours in German English, Polish, Russian, French, Italian, Hebrew, sign language

Marx-Engels-Forum ⋯⋯⟩ p. 138, B 11
A piece of real socialism in the middle of town: larger-than-life bronze versions of the philosophers Karl Marx and Friedrich Engels are seated on the banks of the Spree river. They were done by Ludwig Engelhard.
Bus 100

Museumsinsel ⋯⋯⟩ p. 138, B 11
Conceived by Schinkel to resemble an ancient temple complex, five major museums form a unique historical ensemble on an island in the Spree. Since 1992, the museums have been merged with West Berlin collections to become the National Museums of Berlin, part of the Prussian Cultural Heritage Foundation. At this point, it will take another couple of years before all of the works have found their proper places, and the location itself is certainly still in need of repair, but the ensemble of museums is striking.

The **Altes Museum** (Old Museum) at the Lustgarten (1825-1830) is de facto Berlin's oldest museum today. It was directly across from the palace, and the king had paid for it, but it was open to the public, which was a sensation at the time. The staircase, flanked by the spectacular Amazon fighting a tiger (August Kiss, 1842) and an anonymous lion fighter (Albert Wolff, 1858), leads up to the atrium, which is supported by 18 Ionic columns. The great granite basin in front of the museum was created in 1830 by stonecutter Christian Gottlieb Cantian. Works of late antiquity have been on view here since 1998, and the **Ägyptisches Museum** (Egyptian Museum) has also taken up temporary residence here: Nefertiti and other important exhibits that are waiting for a permanent home have been on display since August of 2005.

The **Neues Museum** (New Museum), commissioned by Frederich Wilhelm IV in 1841, heralded the beginning of Berlin's development into a reputed art centre. The edifice, designed by Schinkel's apprentice Friedrich August Stüler, was almost completely destroyed during World War II. Renovations are to be completed by 2009.

The **Alte Nationalgalerie** (Old National Gallery; entrance on Bodestrasse), designed by Stüler and built between 1866 and 1876, stands like a Corinthian temple on a high foundation. The equestrian monument to Friedrich Wilhelm IV above the rounded arch entrance was created by Alexander Calandrelli. Since its reconstruction, the works of the Charlottenburger Galerie der Romantik have been housed here.

The **Bode Museum**, named after its long-time director, Wilhelm von Bode, was originally the Kaiser-Friedrich-Museum. Renovation of the neo-baroque building, erected from 1898 to 1904 by Ernst von Ihne, was completed in October 2006.

The **Pergamon Museum** 🏛🏛 was built in neoclassical style between 1910 to 1930 according to plans by Alfred Messel and Ludwig Hoffmann

to house the west façade of the Pergamon Altar. It was one of the first architecture museums in the world (more information → p. 76).
Bodestr. 1–3; S-Bahn: Hackescher Markt

Nikolaiviertel ⋯⋙ p. 138, B 10–C 12
The oldest core of Berlin was empty until, under the direction of Günter Stahn, it was reconstructed in time for the celebration of Berlin's 750th anniversary in 1987. Now narrow cobblestone alleys, taverns (→ Reinhard's, p. 24), cafés and exclusive shops cluster around the **Nikolai Church** with its double steeples. The "historical" façades are really just modern East German concrete. The oldest parts of this place of worship are medieval, and during reconstruction,
St Nikolai was given the form it possessed in 1878. Hardly anyone knows that Tetzel, the infamous seller of indulgences, preached here. The interior houses a division of the Märkisches Museum with exhibits illustrating Berlin's history (Tue–Sun 10 a.m.–6 p.m.).

Still intact, but moved roughly 40 feet, Berlin's most beautiful bourgeois private home, the **Ephraim-Palais** from the 18th century, is back on Poststrasse. Diagonally opposite is the **Knoblauch-Haus** (1759/60), with its tendrilled early neoclassical décor. It provides information on the Knoblauch family, which owned the house until 1928, as well as general information about the daily life of the middle classes in the 19th century.

The equestrian statue of St. George with the dragon, by August Kiss, was a gift from the artist to King Wilhelm I in 1865 and stood in the courtyard of the Stadtschloss.
U-/S-Bahn: Alexanderplatz

Potsdamer Platz ⋯⋙ p. 143, E/F 17
Long nothing more than a spectacular construction site, Potsdamer Platz

celebrated 10 years of being a "city within the city" in 2008. The platz was actually never a public square in the sense of a piazza. It was more a giant intersection with such dense traffic that it was the site of Europe's first traffic light. Old photos show the city in the 1920s, when it was an entertainment district with hotels. The goal of the projects here was to reconnect with that era by adding a gigantic service centre. Plazas and hotels emerged along with a casino and a theatre, a film museum, cinemas and restaurants, all with car parks, subways and tunnels below them. The glass Sony Center with its floating pavilion roof is one of the highlights of the new capital city architecture (→ walking tours, p. 80).
U-/S-Bahn: Potsdamer Platz

Sea Life Center   ····⟩ p. 138, B 11
Visitors walk inside a glass tunnel through the aquarium, wildlife swirling around them. The Spree river flows through 30 basins from its source through the Spree forest, continues in the Havel river to the Elbe, into the North Sea and finally into the Atlantic. Sturgeons and rudds swim in Wannsee lake, and you can actually find red-tailed trout in the Hamburg Harbour basin. Children can touch starfish. The show-stopper comes at the end when visitors ride in a panorama lift through the world's largest aquarium, the Aquadome (Info-Hotline: tel. 99 28 00).
Spandauer Str. 3; U-/S-Bahn: Alexanderplatz; daily 10 a.m.–6 p.m.; admission adults €13.50, children €10

Schlossbrücke   ····⟩ p. 138, B 12
Commissioned by King Friedrich Wilhelm III, Karl Friedrich Schinkel built this bridge between 1819 and 1824 to replace the old and dilapidated Hundebrücke (dog bridge), named as such because hunters used it on their way out of town with the hounds. The bridge's ornamentation was meant to exude national pride, but Schinkel died in 1841 and the figures were not mounted until the reign of Friedrich Wilhelm IV.

Distance between important sights and with public transport*
(in minutes on foot).

	Potsdamer Platz	Unter den Linden	Hackesche Höfe	Savignyplatz	Nikolaiviertel	Kaiser-Wilhelm-Gedächtniskirche	Schloss Charlottenburg	Waldbühne	Botan. Garten	Reichstag
Potsdamer Platz	–	20	10*	25*	20*	15*	45*	40*	35*	10*
Unter den Linden	20	–	10–15	20*	20*	15*	35*	45*	35*	5–15
Hackesche Höfe	10*	10–15	–	20*	25	20*	40*	35*	45*	20
Savignyplatz	25*	20*	20*	–	25*	25	20*	15*	45*	20*
Nikolaiviertel	20*	20*	25	25*	–	25*	60*	45*	60*	30
Kaiser-Wilhelm-Gedächtniskirche	15*	15*	20*	25*	25*	–	20*	25*	40*	15*
Schloss Charlottenburg	45*	35*	40*	20*	60*	20*	–	40*	50*	30*
Waldbühne	40*	45*	35*	15*	45*	25*	40*	–	35*	25*
Botan. Garten	35*	35*	45*	45*	60*	40*	50*	35*	–	35*
Reichstag	10*	5–15	20	20*	30	15*	30*	25*	35*	–

Travelling through France?
Make sure Michelin is with you!

MICHELIN
A better way forward

The themes of the corner elements include: the winged goddess of victory, Nike, teaching a boy heroic sagas (Emil Wolff, 1847); crowning the victor (Friedrich Drake, 1853); caring for the wounded (Ludwig Wichmann, 1853); and carrying a fallen warrior to Olympus (August Wredow, 1847). The centre elements show a boy being instructed in the use of weaponry, and the warrior finally receiving weapons, being led to battle and being protected. Berliners were originally scandalised by the immoral nudity of the figures.

The statues were removed during World War II, but West Berlin eventually traded them with East Berlin in 1981 in exchange for the archives of the royal porcelain manufactory.
Bus 100

Schlossplatz → p. 138, B 12
Not a palace, but a temporary art space fills the gap where the East German Palast der Republik once stood. Some of the debris has been removed from the palace cellars, and the limestone foundations of the Hohenzollern residence surfaced in 1996, including ruins of the Münzturm, built in 1573. It has been decided that the Hohenzollern castle from over 500 years ago will be reconstructed, the postwar ruins of which were ordered destroyed by Walter Ulbricht in 1950. After all, it once set the standard for the city as a sort of museum of architecture. A palace mockup from 1993 made this clear. The Humboldt Forum is to be built behind palace walls. The view of the Friedrichswerder Church, now the Schinkel Museum (Tue–Sun 10 a.m.–6 p.m.), is still unimpeded.
Bus 100

Unter den Linden
→ p. 137/138, F 8 – B 12
This grand boulevard was once the cultural centre of Berlin. In 1647, the Great Elector had six rows of linden trees planted along the bridle path leading from the palace to the Tiergarten, but prestige first came to the street under Friedrich I and Friedrich the Great, whose equestrian statue by Christian Daniel Rauch stands in front of the Wilhelm-Palais. The **Forum Fridericianum** was built based on plans by Georg von Knobelsdorff and spans the entire Bebelplatz. It is crowned by the Opera, the Prinz-Heinrich-Palais (Humboldt University), the Alte Bibliothek and St. Hedwig's Cathedral.

The **Zeughaus**, at Unter den Linden 2, was started in 1695 by Johann

The skyline of "the West": (from left) Kaiser Wilhelm Memorial Church (→ p. 62), Europa-Center (→ p. 62) and a building at the Kantdreieck.

Arnold Nehring and remained a weapons arsenal until 1875. It then became a military museum with the largest weapon collection in Europe, until 1944. After reconstruction in 1952, it functioned as the central historical museum of the GDR until 1990, when it was finally converted to the **German Historical Museum** (p. 72). The courtyard of the most beautiful baroque building in northern Germany is adorned by 22 highly expressive masks of dying warriors (Andreas Schlüter, 1696) and occasionally plays host to live concerts. Since 2003, the original building is linked to a new building by a glass arbour (designed by I.M. Pei, architect of the pyramid at the Louvre in Paris).

The **Opernpalais** (Unter den Linden 5) is a reconstruction (1962/63) of the Palace of Princesses, built in 1733 for the Prussian finance minister and serving as home to the royal princesses from 1810. It is connected by a bridge to the **Kronprinzenpalais**, where the Treaty for German Unification was signed in 1990. The noble Operncafé (p. 28), a lovely terrace and two restaurants serve as rest stops for visitors.

The **Neue Wache** (New Watchhouse), built from 1816 to 1818 by Schinkel as his first Berliner edifice with a neoclassical, Doric-columned portico, was the royal watchhouse for 100 years. Then it was a soldiers' memorial from 1931, and in 1960 it was converted to a monument for the victims of fascism and militarism (with an eternal flame protected by plexiglass). A Pietà by Käthe Kollwitz, enlarged to four times life-size and sometimes called the "fat mother", adorns the room. As of 1993, the square has served as the **central memorial space of the Federal Republic of Germany.**

The **Maxim-Gorki-Theater**, behind the Neue Wache (Am Festungsgraben 2), was built by Schinkel apprentice Carl Theodor Ottmer for the director of the Choral Society, Carl Friedrich Zelter. It was famous at the time for its excellent acoustics and for the fact that men and women were allowed to sing together in this secular choir. After the war it was converted into a theatre. The adjacent Palais am Festungsgraben, built from 1751 to 1753, was the seat of the Prussian Minister of Finance and later the residence of Baron vom und zum Stein. Today, Sotheby's holds auctions here, a marionette theatre presents shows, and the only memory of its former function as the House of German-Soviet Friendship is the Tajik Tearoom (p. 28).

Humboldt University was built from 1748 to 1753 on designs by Johann Boumann as a residence for Friedrich the Great's brother, Prince Henry. However, at the urging of Wilhelm von Humboldt, the building was allocated to the university in 1809. The founding rector was Johann Gottlieb Fichte, and university life began here with 300 students.

The most beautiful building on this street is the **German State Opera**, commissioned by Friedrich the Great and built from 1741 to 1743 based on plans by Knobelsdorff in the style of a Corinthian temple. Destroyed during the war, then reconstructed and modernised again in 1986, it is Berlin's most important opera house today. Take a peak inside during opening hours for ticket sales.

The Pantheon in Rome was the inspiration for **St. Hedwig's Cathedral** on Bebelplatz. Built between 1747 and 1773 on designs by Friedrich the Great and Jean Legeay as an icon of religious tolerance, it was destroyed by bombings in the war but rebuilt from 1952 to 1963 as the bishop's church of the Archdiocese of Berlin.

Surrounded by austere neoclassical architecture, the high-baroque style of the **Alte Bibliothek** (1780) does stand out on Bebelplatz. The curved façade, reminiscent of Viennese styles, led to its nickname, "The Commode". Indeed, Georg Christian Unger did imitate the Michael Wing of the Hofburg Imperial Palace in Vienna in his designs. The building was gutted by fire in 1945, but reconstructed from 1967 to 1969.

In 1995, an underground library with empty shelves was built by Micha Ullman below the centre of the square with a glass cover. It serves as a reminder of May 10, 1933, when National Socialists burned more than 20,000 books here.

The glorious **equestrian statue of Friedrich the Great**, Christian Daniel Rauch's most famous sculpture, was erected in 1851. It was never fully destroyed, but it has disappeared a couple of times. The bronze work was hidden at Sanssouci Palace, and Erich Honecker's demand that it be "repatriated" to the GDR was an international scandal. Now "der Alte Fritz", or "Old Fritz", as the Germans call him, is back in his original location.
Bus 100

CHARLOTTENBURG
Europa-Center ⤳ p. 142, A/B 17
This former symbol of West Berlin was built in 1963. Grouped around a courtyard are about 100 shops, bars, cafés and offices. A 46-foot-tall Mercedes star rotates on the roof, and the cabaret "die Stachelschweine (the Porcupines)" is in the cellar. Inside, time flows through a 43-foot-tall water-clock. During the week, Ahmet Tecimen shines shoes. The Budapester Strasse exit leads to the Tourist Information Centre. On Breitscheidplatz, water spills over the globe fountain designed by Joachim Schmettau (1983): a world split between north and south. A weekly market is planned to replace the slightly less than ideal atmosphere of street urchins, panhandlers and dealers on the square.
Breitscheidplatz; U-/S-Bahn: Zoologischer Garten

Funkturm ⤳ p. 140, A 13
Like the Eiffel Tower, you can see the Radio Tower from some distance when it's illuminated at night. Berlin's iconic landmark was erected in 1926 for the third German Radio Show on the edge of the fair grounds as an observation tower, restaurant (180 feet high), a radio mast and a light tower for air traffic.

The adjacent **Deutschlandhalle** is the largest and only remaining event hall from pre-World War II times. It was built in 1935 for the 1936 Olympic Games.
Messedamm 22;
S-Bahn: Messe Nord/ICC

Kaiser-Wilhelm-Gedächtnis-Kirche ⤳ p. 142, A 17
Wilhelm II had this memorial church built in 1895 to honour his grandfather. After being destroyed in the war, it now stands with Egon Eiermann's memorial church, from 1961, at the centre of Ku'damm. It represents a conflict between the Wilhelminian need for prestige, the scars of war and a postwar urge to replace everything that was destroyed. The newer church is a bit dull at first glance, but when illuminated in the evening the blue interior is of breathtaking beauty when the light falls through the glass bricks from Chartres, France.
Breitscheidplatz; U-/S-Bahn:
Zoologischer Garten

Kurfürstendamm/Ku'damm
⤳ p. 140–142, B 15–A 17
The Parisian Champs-Elysées provided the inspiration here. In the grand style of that boulevard, Bismarck had the old 16th-century causeway connecting the Stadtschloss with the Grunewald royal hunting lodge redesigned to form an avenue over two miles long and 175 feet wide. This led the emancipated bourgeoisie of the day to resettle here at the end of the 19th century, where they built grandiose houses with decorative

façades. Behind them lived Berlin's artists in so-called "garden houses", small one- or two-room apartments, but those days are long gone. Prices rise as you go toward Olivaer Platz, and Kurfürstendamm is a shopping street with nothing but high-rent properties. The new steel and glass structure on the Kranzlereck corner makes the famous Café Kranzler look like a forgotten doily–a new era has indeed begun for Ku'damm.

U-/S-Bahn: Zoologischer Garten

Olympia Stadium

⟶ p. 134, west A 4

On the eve of the 1936 Olympic Games, brothers Walter and Werner March built the first stadium on the continent intended to accommodate all sporting disciplines of the time. This classic piece of modern sports arena architecture was renovated for World Cup 2006 and can be visited, unless Herta BSC is playing, when you'll have to buy a ticket. The field is 400 feet below the entrance, which makes the stadium appear smaller than it actually is, despite dimensions of 985 x 755 feet and seating for 96,000 spectators. The aquatics stadium to the north was modernised in 1978 for the world championships.

The Maifeld to the west is an areal with space for 70,000 spectators. The 250-foot belltower, which was removed due to war damage, was replaced in 1962.

Olympischer Platz; U-Bahn: Olympiastadion

Savignyplatz

⟶ p. 141, F 13

Despite being cut off by the Kantstrasse, this 19th-century jewel was preserved. With benches under old trees, exclusive shops of all kinds, and dozens of restaurants along side streets that radiate in a star shape from the square (walking tours, p. 84) the area has an urban feel that is hard to find elsewhere in Berlin. The painter Georg Grosz lived here, and

The Neue Wache (→ p. 61) became a memorial for the victims of fascism. Particularly impressive is the bronze sculpture "Mother with dead Son" by Käthe Kollwitz.

the writer Mascha Kaleko lived on Bleibtreustrasse. A sign on a fence reveals that Walter Benjamin went to school here.

S-Bahn: Savignyplatz

Schloss Charlottenburg

⟶ p. 134, C 3

The most important historical edifice in the western part of the city, Charlottenburg was originally planned as Lietzenburg Castle (1695–1699, after the village of Lietzow) by Johann Arnold Nering. It was later renamed for its first resident, Queen Sophie Charlotte, after her death. The baroque central structure of this **Summer Palace** was expanded by Friedrich Eosander von Göthe, after Prince Elector Friedrich III was crowned King Friedrich I of Prussia in Königsberg in 1701. After the structure was expanded again in 1713, with the **Orangerie** and a **cupola tower**, Friedrich the Great commissioned Georg Wenzeslaus von Knobelsdorff with the eastern addition (the New Wing). After completion of the **Schlosstheater** in 1791 under Friedrich Wilhelm III, the building had grown to a total length of over 1,650 feet. After an air raid in 1943, the palace was almost completely gutted by fire. It took decades of work to restore. Today, the premises and its changing exhibitions are open to the public. The former palace theatre is now a museum for early and pre-history.

The **equestrian monument to the Great Elector** in the cour d'honneur (Andreas Schlüter, 1696/97)–located until the war on the Rathausbrücke in the Mitte district–was supposed to be brought here by barge for safe-keeping but the barge sank in Tegel harbour. The statue wasn't retreived until 1950 and was erected again two years later.

Local residents stroll through the **French baroque gardens,** and the **English landscape garden** is pleasant for summer rest and relaxation. An avenue lined with fir trees leads to the **Mausoleum of Queen Louise,** designed as a Doric temple by Schinkel. Paintings and sculptures occupy the **Schinkel Pavillon,** while the **Belvedere,** a three-storey tea-house beyond the main bridge (de-signed by Langhans in 1788), has a collection of Berlin porcelain from the 18th and 19th centuries.
Luisenplatz; Bus 145; Tue–Fri 9 a.m.–5 p.m., Sat and Sun 10 a.m.–5 p.m.

Waldbühne ⛺⛺ ⸺⸽ Front cover
While parents listen to the music, children make their way down the colossal bowl to the front of the stage covered by a giant double-peaked pavilion roof. Built in a depression in the Murelle hills. it is considered one of the largest open-air stages in Europe with seat-ing for 20,000 spectators. It was designed by Werner March as a Nazi-era cult and event venue reminiscent of a Greek theatre. It now hosts rock and pop concerts, film and jazz events and opera performances.
S-Bahn: Pichelsberg

Zoologischer Garten ⛺⛺
⸺⸽ p. 142, A/B 17
Alexander von Humboldt, Peter Joseph Lenné and natural scientist Martin Lichtenstein founded the first zoological gardens in Germany, which opened in 1844. Among the 91 surviving animals from the origi-nal 10,000 were the hippopotamus "Knautschke" and an elephant. At one point, the zoo was supposed to be moved to Grunewald, but dur-ing her term as zoo director from 1945–1956, Katharina Heinroth pushed for its reconstruction on the original site. Today 19,000 animals from about 1,400 species live in this 35-hectare areal. The Aquarium, founded by Alfred Brehm, houses 10,000 more creatures.
Hardenbergplatz 8; U-/S-Bahn: Zoolo-gischer Garten; Mar 15–Oct 14 daily 9 a.m.–6:30 p.m., mid-Jul–mid-Sep until 9 p.m. (from 6:30 p.m. entrance at Elephant Gate, Budapester Str. 34), Oct 15–Mar15, 9 a.m.–5 p.m.; zoo ad-mission €12, children €6, with aquarium €18, childen €9

KÖPENICK
Berlin's largest district, (⸺⸽ p. 139, southeast F 12) has the most lakes and wooded areas and is the most sparsely populated. Located in the south-east, some of its neighbour-hoods still seem rural. Until traces of settlements from the 12th century were found in the Mitte district in the spring of 1997, Köpenick was con-sidered the oldest settlement in the Spree Valley. The narrow and winding historic core has been under renova-tion for years.

The **town hall,** built in 1904 in northern German neo-Gothic brick style, was the scene of a veritable coup in 1906 when the shoemaker Wilhelm Voigt, in the guise of "Cap-tain von Köpenick", made his way

The Brandenburg Gate (→ p. 54) represents consummate Berlin neo-classicism at the end of the 18th century. Carl Gotthard Langhans created Berlin's world-famous landmark.

into the history books. Having been denied a return to middle-class life by the government, Voigt disguised himself as a captain using second-hand uniforms, assigned 12 infantrymen to his command, arrested the mayor and demanded the city treasury. His antics earned him not only permanent exile from the city, but a permanent exhibit in the town hall 👥👤 and a monument by Spartak Babajan that was cast in the Schöneiche foundry and unveiled in 1996 to commemorate him. His story was made into a popular play as well. The Maxim-Gorki-Theater (→ p. 61) has the work in its repertoire, and every summer the event is re-enacted in the "Köpenicker Summer".

Köpenick Castle, built by Rutger van Langerveld from 1677 to 1683 in Dutch baroque style, became a historical site in 1730 when Hans Hermann von Katte, close friend of Crown Prince Friedrich–later Friedrich II–was court-martialled for assisting in the prince's desertion and sentenced to death. The palace has been an arts and crafts museum since 1963. Schlossinsel; S-Bahn: Köpenick; Tue–Sun 9 a.m.–5 p.m.

STEGLITZ
Botanischer Garten 👥👤
⋯⋗ p. 141, south F 16
Countries with colonies in Africa were obliged to research tropical agricultural crops. The first small botanical gardens in Berlin were thus moved from the Lustgarten (1897 –1903) to the grounds on the edge of Steglitz, where approximately 20,000 plants from around the globe can be viewed on 43 hectares of land. Besides the famous botanical-geographical section, there is also a scent and touch exhibit for visually impaired visitors, a moorland and a waterfall in the tropical house. During the "long night" in January, when museums are open until midnight, the guests can visit the awakening rainforest.

The **Botanical Museum** is an important research centre with a large speciality library and general herbarium with more than two million pepared plant samples.
Königin-Luise-Str. 6 and Unter den Eichen 5–10; S-Bahn: Botanischer Garten; Nov–Jan daily 9 a.m.–4 p.m., Feb 9 a.m.–5 p.m., Mar,Oct 9 a.m.–6 p.m., Sep 9 a.m.–7 p.m., Aug 9 a.m.–8 p.m., May–Jul 9 a.m.–9 p.m.

In the summer, the Waldbühne (→ p. 64) serves as an idyllic setting for concerts of all kinds as well as film festivals.

SPANDAU

Zitadelle 🏰👤   ⤳ p. 134, west A 1

The formidable citadel north of where the Spree flows into the Havel is the oldest secular edifice in the city. The circular keep, also known as the Julius Tower, dates from the 12th century and was later renamed in 1584 after the Duke of Braunschweig-Wolfenbüttel. Napoleon barricaded himself in the citadel in 1813 as the Prussians and Russians approached. In the 19th century the imperial war treasury was hidden here and, as the museum documents, the Nazis tested toxic gases in the laboratories here. Today, the citadel hosts concerts and exhibitions. Some unusual visitors use the citadel in winter: thousands of bats hang from the dark corridor ceilings. A research team of outdoor biologists from the Freie Universität Berlin leads tour groups through the vaults (registration tel. 79 70 62 67).

Am Juliusturm; U-Bahn: Zitadelle; Tue–Fri 9 a.m.–5 p.m., Sat and Sun 10 a.m.–5 p.m.; admission €4.50, children €2.50, audio guide in German, English and Italian

TIERGARTEN

Haus der Kulturen der Welt
⤳ p. 137, D 7

A contribution from the USA to Interbau in 1957 (p. 109), this city landmark is commonly referred to as " the pregnant oyster". American architect Hugh A Stubbins, assistant to Walter Gropius at Harvard, designed it as a convention centre, but increasing oxidation of the steel girders led to the collapse of the roof in 1980. It was re-opened seven years later as the "House of World Cultures" for ambitious events and exhibitions. Future demands were kept in mind for the renovations in August 2007. A pier allows for Spree cruises in the summer. The water basin in front of the hall holds the Henry Moore sculpture "Two Forms". The almost 140 foot high carillon (→ p. 103) sounds daily at noon and 6 p.m.

John-Foster-Dulles-Allee; Bus 100

Kulturforum   ⤳ p. 143, D 17

In 1960, at the end of the western world, today Potsdamer Platz, Hans Scharoun began construction of an architecturally striking space around

August Stüler's **St. Matthäus-Kirche** (1846): the golden, shimmering plastic facing of the Berlin **Philharmonie**, with its magnificent acoustics, chamber music hall, a museum of musical instruments and a copperplate printing room. The **National Library** on the east side of Potsdamer Platz continues the flow of the Philharmonie building, and Mies van der Rohe threw an additional "hall per se", as he called it, into the configuration with his **New National Gallery** (1965-1968). With the opening of the **Gemäldegalerie** ("paintings gallery") the forum is now complete.

Matthäikirchplatz; Bus 142, 148, 248; museums: Tue–Sun 10 a.m.– 6 p.m., Thu to 10 p.m., admission €8, children and youths under 16 free (→Admission prices, p. 71)

Reichstag　　　⋯⋯⋗ p. 137, E 7

Built between 1884 to 1894 according to designs by Paul Wallot, the structure may have been at its most beautiful while it was covered in fabric for Christo's sensational veiling in 1995. The magnificent edifice was to symbolise the size and strength of the German Empire, hence the Emperor's refusal of the inscription "To the German People" as too democratic. It wasn't until 1916 that the words were added to the pediment. Two years later, parliamentarian Scheidemann declared the Weimar Republic from here, which lasted until Hitler's appointment as Chancellor. The burning of the building on the night of February 28, 1933, paved the way for a National Socialist majority, and on April 30, 1945, Soviet soldiers hoisted the red flag from the roof.

The building now has a glass dome designed by Lord Foster to represent the transparency of democracy, and on April 19, 1999, the German Parliament (Bundestag) once again took up residence here.

Platz der Republik; Bus 100; dome open daily 8 a.m–10 p.m.

Schloss Bellevue　　⋯⋯⋗ p. 136, C 8

Berlin's first early neoclassical palace from the time of Friedrich the Great was designed by Philipp Daniel Boumann in 1785, on a sizable piece of property where mulberry trees had been cultivated for silkworm breeding. After being destroyed in World War II, the castle underwent reconstruction until 1959 and now serves as the President's house. Only a few steps away is the Office of the Federal President, erected in 1998 on an elliptical floor plan according to designs by architects Martin Gruber and Helmut Kleine-Kranebur. The environmentally-friendly thermo façade has a dark gleam. Solar panels on the roof provide half of the energy required for the offices.

Spreeweg 1; S-Bahn: Bellevue

Siegessäule (Victory Column) 👫

⋯⋯⋗ p. 136, C 8

The winged Victoria is more then 27 feet tall, weighs roughly 35 tons and is made of gold-plated bronze. Designed by Friedrich Drake, and nicknamed "Goldelse" or "Golden Lizzy" by Berliners, the statue was inaugurated by Emperor Wilhelm I in 1873 as a symbol of Prussia's triumphant campaign against Denmark in 1864, against Austria in 1866 and against France in 1870/71. It was originally located in front of the parliament building. An observation platform is accessible via spiral staircase with 285 steps.

Grosser Stern; Bus 100; Apr–Oct daily 9:30 a.m.–6:30 p.m., Nov–Mar to 5:30 p.m.; admission €1.20, children up to 8 years of age are free

Tiergarten-Dreieck　　p. 142, C 17

A green ribbon of 4,000 adjustable copper slats snakes around five Nordic embassies (Norway, Denmark, Sweden, Finland, Iceland), which all surround a park with a pond in the Rauchstrasse that is meant to symbolise the Baltic Sea. Some smaller

Central American countries are looking to follow suit. The Mexican Embassy, with 40 columns of marble-concrete, is situated directly across the street.
Bus 100

Treptow
Sowjetisches Ehrenmal
⋯⃗ p. 137, E 8
Planned for eastern Berlin by city parks director Gustav Mayer and completed in 1882 in the style of an English landscape garden, Treptower Park was used by Emperor Wilhelm II in 1896, during the Berlin Industrial Exhibition, to demonstrate the growing military power of the Empire. Between 1946 and 1949, a colossal monument was built on a 12-hectare memorial site for the approximately 5,000 Soviet soldiers killed in and around Berlin. Using debris from the destroyed Reich Chancellery, red marble flags and stone sarcophagi were made for each of the former 16 republics of the union. On top of a mausoleum, a nearly 40-foot-high Soviet soldier holds a child in one arm and a sword pointing towards a destroyed swastika in the other.

Another monument can be found on the Strasse des 17. Juni, where 2,500 Soviet soldiers are buried.
S-Bahn: Treptower Park

Weissensee
Jüdischer Friedhof
⋯⃗ p. 139, northeast F 9
With 15,000 graves, the Jewish Cemetery, one of four here, is the largest in western Europe and the most important of its kind. Publishers R. Mosse and Samuel Fischer, Theodor Wolff, Alex and Doris Tucholsky, and department store founder Hermann Tietz rest here.
Herbert-Baum-Str. 45; Tram 2, 3, 4;
Summer: Sun–Thu 8 a.m.–5 p.m., Fri
8 a.m.–3 p.m., Winter: Sun–Thu 8 a.m.–
4 p.m., Fri and before Jewish holidays
8 a.m.–3 p.m.

Zehlendorf
Glienicker Brücke ⛪⛪
⋯⃗ p. 140, southwest A 16
Spies were exchanged on this bridge in the early 1960s. On November 9, 1989, the barriers were raised, and today Potsdam is only a step away. The first bridge was built here back in 1660 so that the Great Elector could reach his best hunting grounds more easily. Its successor, made of iron and steel and still standing today, was opened in 1907.
Bus 116

Pfaueninsel (Peacock Island) ⛪⛪
⋯⃗ p. 140, southwest A 16
At the end of the 18th century, Friedrich Wilhelm II decided to build a small romantic castle (→Excursions, p. 90) for himself and his mistress, Countess Wilhelmine von Lichtenau, but he died just after its completion. However, his son, King Friedrich Wilhelm III, and his wife Louise took a liking to the castle and used it as a summer residence. Peter Joseph Lenné set up a menagerie here that later became the basis for the zoo and transformed the island into an English-style landscape park.
Pfaueninselchaussee; Bus 116, 216,
ferry; castle visits: Tue–Sun 10 a.m.–
12:30 p.m. and 1:30 p.m.–4:30 p.m.

Schloss and Park Klein-Glienicke ⛪⛪
⋯⃗ p. 140, southwest A 16
Summoned by Friedrich Wilhelm III, young landscape gardener Peter Joseph Lenné joined master architect Schinkel and his pupil Ludwig Persius in 1824 to conjure up a structure worthy of antiquity on the Havel river: a neoclassical palace emerged, with Italian charm and a delightful landscape. Embedded in the outer walls are sculpture fragments collected by Prince Carl of Prussia on his travels in Italy in 1822.
Königstrasse; S-Bahn: Wannsee,
Bus 116

DISCOVER HEIDELBERG'S SECRETS.

MERIAN *live!*

Heidelberg

ENGLISH EDITION

Wine taverns – cuisine and lifestyle in Baden • MERIAN special: student life, yesterday and today

8-page street atlas

NEW removable city map

MERIAN *live!*
The pleasure of travelling

Museums and Galleries

Old Masters from East and West meet the young artists from Berlin and the rest of the world.

Skewed slit windows are a design feature of Daniel Libeskind's Jewish Museum (→ p. 74).

The highlight of Berlin's museum scene is certainly the Museums-insel (Museum Island). With five historic buildings, the island has been listed since 1999 as a UNESCO World Heritage site. Since its inception in 1957, the Prussian Cultural Heritage Foundation has taken over the direction of 17 state museums. While renovation of the Neues Museum should be completed in 2009–it is scheduled to be re-opened along with the Egyptian Museum and Papyrus Collection in the same year–the next project is already underway: the new central entrance hall on Museum Island. British architect David Chipperfield designed a graceful, transparent structure that, as a soaring temple of slender columns on a raised foundation, will meld elegantly with the existing buildings. Simultaneously, a colonnade court is planned for the space between the Neues Museum and the entrance hall as a continuation of the colonnade by Stüler between the Neues Museum and the Old National Gallery. Construction begins in 2010.

The well-informed Berliner will answer "170" when asked the number of museums in town, but that number seems to be rising. A Kennedy Museum opened on Pariser Platz and Madame Tussauds Wax Museum opened on Unter den Linden. The Nolde Foundaton Seebüll opened a two-storey extension at Jägerstr. 54/55 on Gendarmenmarkt, and a couple of doors down, in the renovated coach house no. 51, information on the Mendelssohn family in Berlin is on offer. After being closed for five years, the Museum of Things (Werkbund-Archiv) has moved into new premises at Oranienstrasse 25.

In southeastern Berlin, in the Schöneweide district, some of the old industrial buildings on the Spree are morphing into new exhibition halls and a centre for contemporary art where, in addition to a renowned private collection, 15 galleries and a branch of the Museum of Modern Art in Frankfurt am Main will be moved in 2009. The issue of a low-cost interim solution for the Schlossplatz as an art space is still being debated while construction on the Humboldt Forum has begun behind the castle walls.

More than 4,000 artists from around the world work in Berlin, often presenting their creations in the art quarters around Linienstrasse and Auguststrasse, in the railway arches along the Spree in Holzmarktstrasse, on Invalidenstrasse and on Zimmerstrasse. The studios and off-art spaces in Neukölln and Wedding are innumerable–many being interim occupants of empty shops. And since the art dealers follow the artists, the first art trade fair, Art Forum Berlin, was a success back in 1995. Notable galleries from the Rhineland moved to Berlin some time ago as well. In 2007, Michael Janssen moved to Kochstrasse 60, which in turn has attracted the MK Galerie of Rotterdam. Düsseldorf art lover Axel Haubrok's voluminous collection can be seen in the former "Haus des Kindes" at Strausberger Platz 19. Gallery event calendars are available in hotels, restaurants and museums.

Admission prices

The various public museums (see www.smb.museum) offer "Standort-karten" (site tickets) for their permanent exhibitions, in lieu of tickets for single museums. Museum Island (Alte Nationalgalerie, Altes Museum, Bode Museum, Pergamon Museum) €12 (disc. €6); Charlottenburg (Museum of Pre- and Early History, Museum Berggruen, Museum für Fotografie–Helmut Newton Foundation) €6 (disc. €3); Dahlem (Ethnologisches Museum, Museum of European Cultures, Museum for Asian Art) €8 (disc. €4); Kulturforum Potsdamer Platz with the Gemäldegalerie (paintings of the old masters), Kunstbiblio-

MERIAN Tip

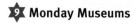

💎 Monday Museums

You only have a long weekend, and the museums are closed on Monday? Not in Berlin. Many museums are open daily, or close on other days of the week. Some of those open on Monday are: the Altes Museum, Bauhaus Archive, Berlinische Galerie, Bode Museum, Brücke Museum, the German Historical Museum, Jewish Museum, Liebermann Villa and the Pergamon Museum.

thek (art library), Museum of Decorative Arts Tiergarten and Köpenick, Museum of Prints and Drawings, Neue Nationalgalerie (excluding special exhibits) and the Museum of Musical Instruments, €8 (disc. €4). The Three-Day Ticket costs €15. Admission is free for children up to 16 years of age. The museums open until 10 p.m. on Thursday charge no admission for the last four hours.

MUSEUMS

Alte Nationalgalerie ⤳ p. 75, b 1
This temple to German culture, built in 1876, was re-opened in December 2001 after extensive renovations. The highlight of this collection of 19th-century paintings are the French Impressionists.
Bodestr. 1–3, Mitte; Tel. 20 90 55 77; S-Bahn: Hackescher Markt; Tue–Sun 10 a.m.–6 p.m., Thu to 10 p.m.; admission €8

Bauhaus Archive –
Museum for Design ⤳ p. 142, C 17
Modern design from Gropius to Alessi. The collection comprises architectural models, paintings, furniture, drawings, industrial and handcrafted products–all based on Bauhaus concepts. One of the most important art institutes of the 20th century. Clearly structured building from 1979.

Klingelhöferstr. 14, Tiergarten; Tel. 2 54 00 20; U-Bahn: Nollendorfplatz; Bus 100, M29; Wed–Mon 10 a.m–5 p.m., admission Sat–Mon €7, Wed–Fri €6

Berlin Wall Documentation Center
⤳ p. 138, A 9
Initiated on November 9, 1999, the 10th anniversary of the fall of the Berlin Wall, this ensemble features the Wall Monument (corner of Bernauer and Ackerstrasse), the Chapel of Reconciliation and other exhibitions recalling life in the shadow of the Wall.
Bernauer Str. 111; S-Bahn: Nordbahnhof; Apr–Oct Tue–Sun 10 a.m.–6 p.m., Nov.–Mar 10 a.m.–5 p.m.

Berlinische Galerie ⤳ p. 144, B 21
A former glass depot was refurbished to house this collection devoted to 20th century art made in Berlin.
Alte Jakobstr. 124–128, Kreuzberg; Tel. 78 90 26 00; U-Bahn: Hallesches Tor, Bus M29, M41, 240; Wed–Mon 10 a.m.–6 p.m.; admission €6

Bode Museum ⤳ p. 138, A 11
The wonderfully restored building itself is worth a visit, but the real attraction is one of the largest collections of sculpture, ranging from the early Middle Ages to the end of the 18th century, as well as Byzantine art.
Bodestr. 1–3; Tel. 20 90 55 77; S-Bahn: Hackescher Markt; daily 10 a.m.–6 p.m., Thu to 10 p.m, admission €8

Brecht-Weigel Memorial
⤳ p. 137, F 6
From Bertholt Brecht's last apartment and studio, you can see directly into the Dorotheenstadt cemetery where he rests. Visits to the late neoclassical house only by guided tour.
Chausseestr. 125, Mitte; Tel. 2 83 05 70 44; U-Bahn: Zinnowitzer Strasse; Tue, Wed, Fri 10 a.m.–11:30 a.m., Thu 10 a.m.–noon and 5 p.m.–6:30 p.m., Sat 9:30 a.m.–1:30 p.m., Sun 11 a.m.–6 p.m.

The Pergamon Museum (→ p. 76), with its famous altar, offers a spectacular collection of antiquities–a must in Berlin.

Brücke Museum

····> p. 140, west A 16

A collection of Expressionist works from the Dresden art group "Die Brücke" ("The Bridge"), founded in 1905. Members included artists such as Erich Heckel and Ernst Ludwig Kirchner. Karl Schmidt-Rottluff donated the house.
Bussardsteig 9, Zehlendorf;
Tel. 8 31 20 29; Bus 115; Wed–Mon 11 a.m.–5 p.m.; admission €4

Das verborgene Museum
(The Hidden Museum)

····> p. 141, E 13

A documentation of art and photography by women.
Schlüterstr. 70, Charlottenburg;
Tel. 3 13 36 56; S-Bahn: Savignyplatz;
Thu and Fri 3 p.m.-7 p.m., Sat and Sun noon-4 p.m.; admission €5

DDR Museum ····> p. 137, F 6

Sit in an East German car, watch their TV shows, test their jeans and look through their kitchen drawers–an exploration of daily life. Even try out the secret-police (Stasi) wiretap device.
Karl-Liebknecht-Str. 1 (opposite the Berliner Dom on the Spree), Mitte; Tel. 8 47 12 37 31; U-Bahn: Alexanderplatz;

Mon–Sun 10 a.m.–8 p.m., Sat 10 a.m.–10 p.m.; admission €5

Deutsches Guggenheim Berlin

····> p. 138, A 12

Over 5,000 sq ft for art from classic modern to contemporary at the Berlin branch of this renowned gallery.
Unter den Linden 13–15, Mitte;
Tel. 2 02 09 30; S-Bahn: Unter den Linden; daily 11 a.m.–8 p.m., Thu to 10 p.m.; lunch lectures Wed 1 p.m.; Mon admission free, otherwise €3

Deutsches Historisches Museum

····> p. 138, B 12

This former arsenal presents objects from the Romans to the GDR. The extension is the work of star architect Ieoh Ming Pei.
Unter den Linden 2, Mitte; Tel. 20 30 40; Bus 100; daily 10 a.m.–6 p.m.; admission €5

Film and Television Museum 👫

····> p. 143, E 17

This film house with German cinematheque was opened in 2000 as a museum of German film history.
Filmhaus am Potsdamer Platz;
Tel. 3 00 90 30; S-Bahn: Potsdamer Platz; Tue–Sun 10 a.m.–6 p.m., Thu to 8 p.m.

Gemäldegalerie im Kulturforum
→ p. 67   ⋯⟩ p. 143, D 17

Gedenkstätte Berlin Hohenschön-
hausen   ⋯⟩ p. 139, northeast F 9
This memorial in the formerly prohibited military zone tells visitors about
the history of political persecution,
from the special internment camps
run in the Soviet Occupation Zone
(SBZ) to the remand prisons of the
GDR. Some of the tours are guided by
former prisoners.
Genslerstr. 66; Tel. 98 60 82 30 ; Tram
M5, M6, M17, Bus 256; only per guided
tour Mon-Fri 11 a.m. and 1 p.m., Tue-
Thu again at 3 p.m., Sat, Sun hourly
10 a.m.- 4 p.m.; admission €4

Hamburger Bahnhof –
Museum für Gegenwart
⋯⟩ p. 137, E 6
Following the modern art collection
in the Stüler edifice opposite Charlottenburg Palace and the Neue Nationalgalerie, the "Hamburger Railway Station" opened in 1996 as the
third space with contemporary are of
the 20th century. The collection of
Erich Marx, with works by Joseph
Beuys, Andy Warhol and Anselm
Kiefer, forms the core. The Christian
Friedrich Flick Collection (Bruce Nau-
mann, Pippilotti Rist) opened in 2004.

Invalidenstr. 50, Tiergarten; Tel.
39 78 34 12; S-Bahn: Hauptbahnhof/
Lehrter Bahnhof; Tue–Fri 10 a.m.–6 p.m.,
Sat 11 a.m.–8 p.m., Sun 11 a.m.–6 p.m.

Haus am Checkpoint Charlie
⋯⟩ p. 144, A 21
The focus of this museum "against
forgetting" is the Wall, erected on
August 13, 1961, and the history of
Berlin as the centrepoint of the
division and as Europe's bridge. Documents, photographs, objects, paintings from international artists, and
films and lectures tell the story.
Friedrichstr. 43–44, Kreuzberg; U-Bahn:
Kochstrasse; daily 9 a.m.–10 p.m.

Heinrich-Zille Museum
⋯⟩ p. 138, C 12
A house for the art of famous Berlin
illustrator Heinrich Zille, with photographs, drawings and sculptures of
daily life in working class Berlin at
the turn of the 20th century.
Propststr. 11; Tel. 24 63 25 00;
www.heinrich-zille-museum.de;
U-Bahn: Alexanderplatz; daily
10 a.m.–8 p.m., Nov–Mar 11 a.m.–
p.m.; admission €4,50

Jewish Museum   ⋯⟩ p. 144, A 22   **8**
Between 1999 and its official opening, thousands had already visited

*The Bauhaus-Archiv (→ p. 72), with its narrow, white, shed-roofed towers, is a cult
site for classic modernist architecture and design.*

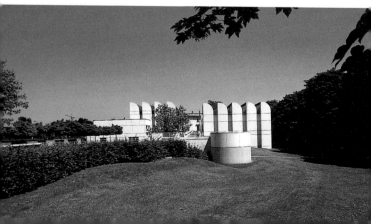

Museumsinsel and Nikolaiviertel

© MERIAN-Kartographie

this still-empty museum. Designed by architect Daniel Libeskind, the building is poisitioned like a burst Star of David in a residential area, with skewed window slits and angles. Opened on September 11, 2001, the day the World Trade Center was destroyed, expectations of the project were great. Tours, exhibitions and events make the museum a living cultural centre.

Lindenstr. 9–14, Kreuzberg; Tel. 25 99 33 00; U-Bahn: Hallesches Tor, Bus M29; daily 10 a.m.–8 p.m., Mon 10 a.m.–10 p.m.; closed Yom Kippur, Rosh Hashanah (Sep/Oct) and Christmas Eve; admission €5

Käthe-Kollwitz Museum

·····⟩ p. 141, F 14

Socially critical and political graphics and the complete sculpture works of this Berlin artist (1867-1945). Special exhibits twice a year.

Fasanenstr. 24, Charlottenburg; Tel. 8 82 52 10; www.kaethe-kollwitz.de; U-Bahn: Kurfürstendamm; Wed–Mon and holidays 11 a.m.–6 p.m.; admission €5

Liebermann Villa on Wannsee

·····⟩ p. 140, southwest A 16

This summer house of the painter and president of the Prussian Academy of Arts (until 1933) was built in 1909. He designed the garden, which was renovated in 2006, and painted more than 200 works there. The house is a gallery for his paintings of Wannsee.

Colomierstr. 3, Wannsee; Tel. 30 80 58 38 30; S-Bahn: Wannsee, Bus 114; Apr–Oct Wed–Mon 11 a.m.– 6 p.m., Thu to 8 p.m., Nov–Mar to 5 p.m.; admission €8

Martin-Gropius-Bau ┄┄⟩ p. 143, F 17
Named after the uncle of Bauhaus founder Walter Gropius, this house was opened as a museum of applied arts in 1881, evidenced by the façade ornamentation. Since its renovaton and re-opening in 1981, the building with its unique atrium plays host to rotating large-scale exhibitions.
Niederkirchner Str. 7, Kreuzberg; Tel. 25 48 60; U-/S-Bahn: Potsdamer Platz; Wed–Mon 10 a.m.–8 p.m.

Museum Berggruen ┄┄⟩ p. 134, C 4
Significant works from Picasso and contemporaries like Klee, Cézanne and the cubists Braque and Laurens.
Schlossstr. 1, Charlottenburg; Tel. 32 69 58 15; S-Bahn: Sophie-Charlotte-Platz, Bus 145; Tue–Sun, holidays 10 a.m.–6 p.m.; admission €6

Museum für Fotografie
┄┄⟩ p. 142, A 17
The first two levels of this Wilhelminian building contain works from the Helmut Newton Foundation, on permanent loan from the famous photographer to his hometown.
Jebensstr. 2, Charlottenburg; Tel. 31 86 48 25; U-/S-Bahn: Zoologischer Garten; Tue–Sun 10 a.m.–6 p.m., Thu to 10 p.m.

Museum für Naturkunde
┄┄⟩ p. 137, F 6
From archaeopteryx to the common head louse–30 million objects are on display here at Germany's largest natural history museum. Renovations were completed in 2007 on almost 70,000 sq ft of space.
Invalidenstr. 43, Mitte; Tel. 20 93 85 91; U-Bahn: Zinnowitzer Strasse; Tue–Fri 9:30 a.m.–5 p.m., Sat, Sun 10 a.m.–6 p.m.; admission €5, children €3

Pergamon Museum
┄┄⟩ p. 138, A 11; p. 75, a 1
Berlin's most sensational stairs lead upwards between gods and giants to the Pergamon Altar, where sacrifices were made to the gods 2000 years ago. The oldest architecture museum in the world was built here between 1910 and 1930 to house exclusively the 118-foot-wide west façade of the Pergamon Altar (180-160 B.C.) excavated by C. Humann between 1878 and 1886. The glorious Ishtar Gate and the Processional Way of Babylon are also sites to behold. 6,000 years of art are shown in 14 different collections.
Bodestr. 1–3, Mitte; Tel. 20 90 55 77; S-Bahn: Hackescher Markt; Tue–Sun 10 a.m.–6 p.m., Thu to 10 p.m.; admission €8

Schwules Museum ┄┄⟩ p. 144, A 23
Temporary exhibitions present the history of homosexuals in Germany.
Mehringdamm 61, Kreuzberg; Tel. 69 59 90 50; U-Bahn: Mehringdamm; Wed–Mon 2 p.m.–6 p.m., Sat 2 p.m.–7 p.m.; admission €5

MERIAN Tip

⑩ New Synagogue/ Centrum Judaicum

With space for 3,000, what was once the Germany's largest synagogue sustained relatively minimal damage during the pogrom of November 9, 1938, but was ultimately destroyed in 1943 while being used as a storehouse by the Wehrmacht. Reconstruction in moorish-oriental style was completed on May 8, 1995, the 50th anniversary of the war's end. Since then, parts of the synagogue are open to the public, with tours, exhibitions, concerts and readings.

Oranienburger Str. 28, Mitte; Tel. 88 02 83 00; S-Bahn: Oranienburger Strasse; Apr–Sep Sun, Mon 10 a.m.– 8 p.m., Tue–Thu 10 a.m.–6 p.m., Fri 10 a.m.–5 p.m., Mar/Oct Fri 10 a..m.– 2 p.m., Nov–Feb Sun–Thu 10 a.m.– 6 p.m., Fri 10 a.m.–2 p.m.

┄┄⟩ p. 138, A 11

The Story of Berlin
⋯⟩ p. 141, F 14
Over 800 years of city history in a multimedia time travel format through rooms with a variety of themes. There is even a real nuclear fallout shelter. Entertaining as it is, the tour takes time: at least 1.5 hours.
Kurfürstendamm 207–208;
Tel. 88 72 01 00; U-Bahn:
Uhlandstrasse; daily 10 a.m.–8 p.m.
(admission until 6 p.m.); admission
€9.80, children €3.50

GALLERIES

Akademie der Künste ⋯⟩ p. 137, F 8
Temporary exhibitions at the Academy of Arts, with changing themes, drawings, photography.
Pariser Platz 4; Tel. 20 05 70; S-Bahn: Unter den Linden; ; Tue–Sun 11 a.m.–8 p.m.

Bereznitsky ⋯⟩ p. 138, A 10
Ludmila Bereznitsky, a young gallery owner from Kiev, exhibits young talent from the Ukraine–practically without competition in Berlin.
Linienstr. 144, Mitte; U-Bahn: Oranienburger Tor; Mon–Sat 11 a.m.–6 p.m.

Brusberg ⋯⟩ p. 141, F 14
Renowned mega-gallery on Uhlandstrasse with great masters (Botero, Max Ernst, Altenbourg, Heisig) and new discoveries in painting, etching and sculpture.
Kurfürstendamm 213, Charlottenburg;
Tel. 8 82 76 82; U-Bahn: Uhlandstrasse;
Tue–Fri 10 a.m.–6 p.m., Sat
10 a.m.–2 p.m.

Contemporary Fine Arts
⋯⟩ p. 138, B 11
David Chipperfield built Heiner Bastian's noble house of art on Museum Island. The famous gallery, with fine presentations of select works of art, was deemed an appropriate tenant.
Am Kupfergraben 10, Mitte; Tel.
2 88 78 70; U-Bahn: Friedrichstr.;
Tue–Sat 10 a.m.–6 p.m.

Eigen + Art ⋯⟩ p. 138, A 10
Fresh non-conformists like Neo Rauch discoverd by Harry Lybke.
Auguststr. 26, Mitte; Tel. 2 80 66 05;
U-Bahn: Oranienburger Tor; Tue–Sat
11 a.m.–6 p.m.

Kunst-Werke ⋯⟩ p. 138, A 10
This epicentre of the new art district, in a beautifully renovated margarine factory, always shows exciting contemporary works. Artists live and work in the side wings. A glass-encased café completes the picture.
Auguststr. 69, Mitte; S-Bahn: Oranienburger Strasse; Tue–Sun noon–7 p.m., Thu to 9 p.m.; admission €6

Neu ⋯⟩ p. 137, F 6
Keep your eyes peeled for the company logo, otherwise you'll miss this gallery. Located in the former stables of the Veterinary Institute of Charité, it has now become a home for free project artists.
Philippstr. 13, Mitte; Tel. 2 85 75 50;
U-Bahn: Zinnowitzer Strasse; Tue–Sat
2 p.m.–6 p.m.

Neuer Berliner Kunstverein
⋯⟩ p. 137, F 6
The rotating exhibitions of contemporary art here include artists from beyond Berlin. Film, video and photography shows change approximately every two months.
Chausseestr. 128/129, Mitte;
Tel. 2 80 70 20; U-Bahn: Oranienburger Tor; Tue–Fri noon–6 p.m., Sat, Sun
2 p.m.–6 p.m.

Singuhr-Hörgalerie
⋯⟩ p. 139, D 9/10
After ten years of sound art in the Mitte district, this unique sound gallery has moved to the historic water cisterns in Prenzlauer Berg and thus into the ideal space for acoustic art, kinetic sculpture and sound chambers.
Belforter Strasse, Prenzlauer Berg; Tel.
24 72 44 65; U-Bahn: Senefelderplatz

Walking Tours and Excursions

*Pack your swimsuit! There are a number of lovely lakes in and around Berlin.
Pictured here: Grosser Müggelsee (→ p. 47) with sun worshippers.*

Walkers gather at Potsdamer Platz, Ku'damm, Prenzlauer Berg or in Grunewald; history buffs make their way to Potsdam; and bookworms head to Buckow.

4 Potsdamer Platz: high-tech modernity in glass and steel

Features: The largest urban construction site for decades in the Western world was meant to emerge as THE city of the 21st century. Thousands come here daily just to see what's new. **Duration:** 15 minutes or two hours, depending on your curiosity. **Refreshment:** Tizian (→ p. 25), the Ritz-Carlton (→ p. 14). **U-/S-Bahn:** Potsdamer Platz and Mendelssohn-Bartholdy-Park; **Map:** → p. 143, E/F 17

Not just high-tech: a street performer on Potsdamer Platz.

Berlin's largest construction site is now over at Leipziger Platz. Potsdamer Platz is finished. Is it really a plaza or a city within a city? It doesn't have a name, really. It seems to have just sprouted from the earth as Europe's largest urban construction feat at the site known until the war as Potsdamer Platz. Before that, it was just a field where rabbits played next to the one surviving house–the Weinhaus Huth–in the shadow of the Berlin Wall.

Now, Renzo Piano's Daimler City building, with its narrow streets, terracotta facades, brooks and passages where bamboo sways in the wind stands opposite Helmut Jahn's glass Sony City, with a canopy roof floating above the spacious plaza below. At the fountain you can look down into the subterranean Kinowelt (cinema world). The Kaisersaal (Emperor's Hall), from the old Hotel Esplanade, was actually moved here on air cushions and provides a link to the past with its stucco elements amidst the glass and steel. It is now an upscale restaurant. By contrast, futuristic will come to mind as you ride the glass elevator to the film museum.

To summarise: the cornerstone was laid here in October, 1994. Daniel Barenboim choreographed the dancing construction cranes for the completion festivities in 1996. In 1998, 10 new streets and 17 new buildings were opened. In February 2000, the red carpets were rolled out for the film festival. In December 2000, the red Infobox, which had served as a viewing platform for millions of visitors to watch the project unfold, was auctioned off bit by bit and finally fully dismantled at the beginning of 2001. Now, you can get an overview from the high-rise at Potsdamer Platz 1.

Prenzlauer Berg: visiting a legend

Features: Revisit a myth? No longer possible. The cradle of resistance against the constraints of the GDR, with its grey buildings and crumbling tile balconies, is in a state of constant evolution as one of the hippest neighbourhoods in the centre.
Duration: 2-3 hours; **Refreshment:** Prater (→ p. 27), Schall & Rauch (→ p. 28);
U-/S-Bahn: Senefelderplatz; **Map:** ⤳ p. 82

Prenzlauer Berg begins after Torstrasse. The city once ended at this former district, and only with increasing industrialisation at the end of the 19th century did it see much growth. Factory workers came from all corners of the Empire and in 1920, over 300,000 people lived on 10 square kilometres. The prime real estate was fully utilised and courtyards emerged between blocks of five-storey apartment buildings. They were tiny, only 17 square feet each–just enough for the fire brigade trucks to turn around. This building style can still be seen in Kreuzberg and Neukölln, but many of the courtyards have been gutted and filled with vegetation over the course of massive renovations. In 2001, the area was incorporated into the borough of Pankow. Referred to as Prenzlberg for quite some time now, the name comes from the postal abbreviation »Prenzl.Berg«. Our stroll begins at the U-Bahn stop **Senefelderplatz**. A **monument to Alois Senefelder**, the inventor of lithography, can be found here. It was created in 1892 by Rudolf Pohle. As with his invention, the lithograph, his name is written by cupids in mirrored script on the foundation, one of them originally holding a–long missing–looking glass. Next to the yellow brick house with the police station, built from 1883 to 1887 as a nursing home to serve the Jewish community here, you'll find the first squatters' house in East Berlin. Many demonstrators from October 1989 were arrested here.

The adjacent **Jewish Cemetery** was originally placed beyond the city walls in 1827. More than 5,000 Jewish citizens are buried here, among them the musician Giacomo Meyerbeer (d. 1864), the publisher Leopold

The old Jewish Cemetery on Schönhauser Allee is the final resting place for many renowned Berlin personalities like Liebermann and Ullstein.

Ullstein (1899) and the painter Max Liebermann (1935). During the imperial era, the cemetery was on the path leading from the palace to the summer residence, Niederschönhausen. As a result, Jewish funeral processions were detoured down an alternate "path for Jews" on the rear side of the cemetery so as not to sour the sovereign's mood. The path is barely discernable today.

Jewish Cemetery
···> Husemannstrasse

Via **Kollwitz** and **Belforter Strasse** you can reach the water tower, in use as such from 1877 to 1915 before being converted to a living space. The cellar is notorious for its use by the National Socialists as a torture chamber, but now serves the Singuhr sound gallery as a venue for performances. Around the corner, tables

and chairs are set out by little restaurants in the summer, creating one big open-air café.

The only **synagogue** in Berlin that was not destroyed by the Nazis in 1938 is in the courtyard at Rykestrasse 53. Stormtroopers turned it into stables instead. Repairs were done in 1953, and renovations completed in August 2007 returned it roughly to its original 1904 state. It is now the largest and most beautiful synagogue in Germany, with seating for 1,200 people.

Knaackstrasse brings you up to **Kollwitzplatz**, named after the artist Käthe Kollwitz, who lived here for more than 50 years with her husband Karl Kollwitz, a physician for the needy. Gustav Seitz' statue of her from 1958 is popular with children as a resting and climbing spot, which wouldn't have bothered "Mother Kollwitz" in the slightest.

On the night of October 2, 1990, the "Autonomous Republic of Utopia" was founded here. The area, with increasingly high rents, myriad upscale restaurants and about 100 eateries and cafés of all kinds, has long been a favourite pocket for the former West. New Berliners have taken up residence here as well.

Husemannstrasse, which starts on the northern edge of the square, is the area's model street. The facades of its houses were renovated along the entire block on the occasion of the city's 750th birthday in 1987. Guild signs and wrought-iron lanterns have restored the original look, but this also meant preserving the stove heating and shared toilets. It is a lovely place to sit in the summer and at house number 13, an unconventional Chinese restaurant named **Ostwind** is worth a visit.

Schultheiss Brewery
⋯⟩ Kastanienallee

In the **Knaackstrasse**, on former factory grounds from the 19th century that stretch all the way to Schönhauser Allee, the elegantly renovated **Schultheiss Brewery** has re-opened as the **KulturBrauerei (culture brewery)** where actors, directors, singers, poets and sculptors from all over Europe meet during various events. The Lychener Strasse leads north to Helmholtzplatz, an urban centre surrounded by restaurants.

At the Eberswalder Strasse subway station, in the midst of all the noise, stench and bustle, you'll come across **Konnopke**, a legendary sausage stand. Founded as a family business in 1930, with a tent, table and sausage vat, the name is synonymous today with the best curried sausage in Berlin. The secret is in the family ketchup recipe.

In 1852, **Prater** was founded at Kastanienallee 7-9. Originally just a beer stand, it soon developed into a destination for excursions, public entertainment and as a summer theatre venue and meeting point. Famous German personalities used to sing and speak here regularly. In 1967, the district cultural centre for Prenzlauer Berg set up shop here, and the people started coming for Sunday dances. Now Prater serves as an auxiliary stage for popular theatre, a beer garden and a dance hall.

Popular pubs and shops can be found here in droves under sootblackened facades. Berlin design labels and products from the old East are on offer. The conspicuously well-dressed roaming the streets here have prompted Kastanienallee's new nickname, "Casting Alley".

Young fashion designers have settled along Kastanienallee, and Oderberger Strasse leads to Mauerpark which is reminiscent of Woodstock on warm summer nights. The site at the former Wall location has been converted into a neighbourhood park. Young people play music, talk and drink, or test their fitness on the climbing wall.

Looking left down Schönhauser Allee, you'll see the Gethsemane Church in the Stargarder Strasse, famous as a meeting place for dissidents in 1989.

The painted sign "Orgelfabrik Inh. G. Bacigalupo", Berlin's largest hand organ manufactory from the end of the 19th century, is still visible on a wall in the Schönhauser Allee. It was a virtual Italian colony here. For two or three marks a week, you could rent hurdy-gurdy instruments and play in the streets. When Italians were no longer given permits to play, German hurdy-gurdy men took over until the 1960s. The factory didn't shut down until 1978.

Depending on your mood, the tour ends at the Senefelderplatz underground station, or at Konnopke's sausage stand at the Eberswalder Strasse station.

Parisian flair around Kurfürstendamm and Savignyplatz

Features: The former West, with its well-tended Wilhelminian houses, stately old trees and elegant shops has something Parisian about it, especially in the side streets. **Duration:** 3-4 hours; **Refreshment:** Diekmann (→ p. 19), Soup Kultur (→ p. 21), XII Apostoli (→ p. 20); **U-Bahn:** Wittenbergplatz; **Map:** ⋯⟩ p. 85

If you want to really get into the Parisian flair and the fascination side of West Berlin, you'll have to begin your walk at **Wittenbergplatz**. The **KaDeWe** department store, founded in 1905, dominates the square. The underground station from 1913 has been reconstructed, otherwise most of the buildings here are new.

Continuing to **Breitscheidplatz**, **Tauentzienstrasse** is the main shopping mile for Berliners and tourists alike. Many of the facades, which compete with the new Friedrichstrasse in the old East for appeal, have been given a general overhaul of late, and the KaDeWe, focal point of the "Showcase of the West" during the Cold War, was polished up as well. Its 645,000 square feet make it the second-largest department store in the world. The sculpture "Berlin", on the centre divider of the road, designed by Brigitte and Martin Matschinsky-Denninghoff and presented as part of the project "Sculpture Boulevard" in 1986, has gained new timeliness.

The gurgling fountain at the **Europa-Center** on **Breitscheidplatz** makes for a good spot to rest. The square has become a meeting place for just about everyone. Some dip their feet in the water while others paint passers-by, play music, or take look inside the **Gedächtniskirche**.

The roof rotunda of the famous **Café Kranzler** on the corner of Joachimstaler Strasse looks like a birthday cake with its red and white marquee against the new glass, concrete and steel buildings. In the evening, it transforms into a bar. What was until recently an intersection where you could sit, is now a 16-storey building where the sounds of exotic birds emit from an aviary instead street noises.

Take a left into the Fasanenstrasse to check out the lordly mansions. You'll pass the **Astor Cinema**, where a sensational guest performance by Josephine Baker took place in the "Nelson-Künstlerspiele" revue theatre in 1926. The **Literaturhaus** with its lovely **Café Wintergarten** is an inviting stop, with a **book shop** in the basement. Next door is the **Villa Grisebach**, one of Germany's leading galleries and auction houses, and home to the **Käthe-Kollwitz-Museum** and the renowned **Galerie Pels-Leusden**. If you continue over the bustling Lietzenburger Strasse on to **Fasanenplatz**, things really begin to turn Parisian—and not just because you're walking along **Pariser Strasse** ("Parisian Street"). Head toward **Ludwigkirchplatz**, where the **Zur weissen Maus** bar awaits you with delicious cocktails. The Parisian flair continues as you make your way back down **Bleibtreustrasse**. After the train bridge at the end of Bleibtreustrasse you'll come to **Savignyplatz**, nice by day or by night, with little shops, cafés and restaurants. Particularly pretty is the corridor leading to the S-Bahn railway with an architecture exhibition in the arches.

You can take the train now to Bahnhof Zoo or walk back via Grolmanstrasse and meander around Kurfürstendamm. From **Adenauerplatz** take Bus M29 back to the start.

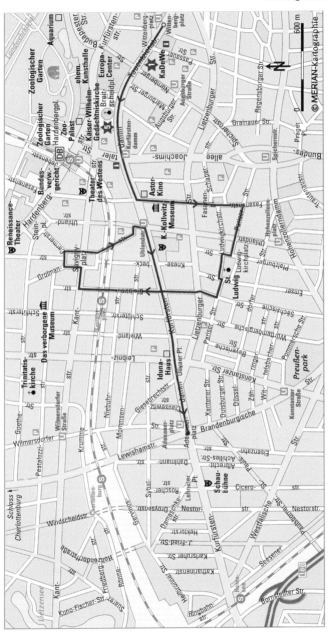

Grunewald: the noble and idyllic east bank of the Havel

Features: This has been one of Berlin's nicest residential neighbourhoods for more than 100 years; **Duration:** 2 hours; **Refreshment:** Schlosshotel, Brahmsstr. 10; **S-Bahn:** Grunewald; **Map:** ⋯⟩ p. 87

The east bank of the Havel is pretty sparsely populated. In 1542, Prince-elector Joachim III purchased the Grunewaldsee lake and laid the cornerstone for his hunting lodge "Zum grünen Wald", built by Caspar Theys. Poachers met with draconian punishment back then, losing both eyes for killing a boar.

Once it became fashionable to spectate at court hunts, the lodge began attracting more and more day trippers on strolls through the countryside. Later, princes parcelled off the land amongst themselves, followed by the few who could afford the "up-scale address". The little colony of villas at Grunewald was planned in the 19th century by the "immigrant" Hamburg merchant Johann Anton Wilhelm von Carstenn. The pit-dwellings on the edge of the colony, where Polish workers who excavated lakes and built the streets lived, became a destination for day excursions. Department store founders Tietz and Wertheim ultimately settled here along with opera singers, distinguished industrialists and chief executives. Author Gerhart Hauptmann manned the fire engine at the volunteer fire department. Berlin's finest residential settlement, developed in the woods in 1890 under the protection of Bismarck, near the city and yet still secluded, is also well suited for cycling tours.

S-Bahnhof ⋯⟩ Villa Koschewski

The walk begins at the **19th-century S-Bahn train station Grunewald**. At the ramp to the train station platform there is a monument honouring the countless Jewish citizens who were transported from here to concentration camps.

Fontanestrasse leads straight on past house number 8, home to movie director Max Reinhardt until he moved to the USA in 1938. Many important figures in Berlin's literary and political history at the time had their homes here. The South African consulate is at **Douglasstrasse** no. 9 in the **Villa Canaris**. Admiral Wilhelm Canaris, who lived here and was responsible for foreign affairs and defence, was sentenced to death for his contacts to the resistance after an assassination attempt on Hitler.

The tennis facilities "Rot-Weiss" are located in the **Gottfried-von-Cramm-Weg**. This bright-yellow rococo palace was a banker's villa known back in the 1920s by the name **Villa Koschewski**. Drawing attention at the corner of **Koenigsallee/Oberhaardter Weg,** is the lordly estate of Walther Rathenau, foreign secretary in 1922 during the Weimar Republic, who was shot down that same year by right-wing radicals.

Koenigsallee ⋯⟩ Tabener Strasse

Artists and intellectuals lived alongside the typically wealthy bankers on the **Koenigsallee**, including Ingeborg Bachmann on the left (no. 53) and Vicki Baum (no. 45), for example. Theatre critic Alfred Kerr lived at **Höhmannstrasse 6** and Leon Jessel might have even composed some of his well-known pieces at his residence at **Regerstrasse 12**. This street used to be called Mahlerstrasse, even back in 1933, when Martha and Lion Feuchtwanger moved away and went into exile.

Taking Hagenstrasse you reach Richard-Strauss-Strasse before turning right into **Brahmsstrasse** with the **Palais von Pannwitz**, former residence of Emperor William II's attorney. The noble Schlosshotel hosted some important guests in the summer of 2006: the German national football team.

Via Leo-Blech-Platz and Wernerstrasse you come to **Bismarckallee**. Delbrückstrasse no. 23, at the corner of **Richard-Strauss-Strasse** was the home of Walter Benjamin. A few houses down, actor Emil Jannings lived at no. 27. Between the Herthasee and Hubertussee lakes, Bismarckallee leads to **Herthastrasse** where Ferdinand Sauerbruch lived in house

no. 11. His bust is located on the lot across the way. House no. 17 was home to Grethe Weiser and the left side of the street belonged to the Mendelssohn family. Thomas Mann and Hermann Hesse were guests in the **corner house at Erdener Strasse no. 8**, residence of publisher Samuel Fischer, and Gerhart Hauptmann was at **Trabener Strasse 54**. Take Trabener Strasse back to the train station. Steps lead up to a half-timbered house, former address of dancer Isadora Duncan, who lived here with Engelbert Humperdinck.

After all the sightseeing, some will need to have a seat at the station and wonder if there is somewhere to get a bite to eat around here.

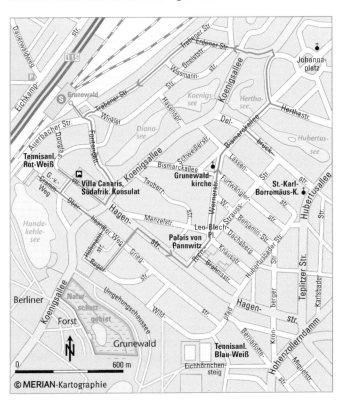

© MERIAN-Kartographie

Excursions in the area

⭐ 9 By steamer from Spandau to Wannsee 👭

Features: If you've never taken a ride on a "Dampfer", or steamer as the Berliners tend to call anything that floats, then you haven't really seen the city yet. Surprisingly, one of the best and most leisurely ways to get a unique look at Berlin is from the many waterways.
Duration: Including Pfaueninsel (Peacock Island), one day.
Food and drink: Food is served on board and Peacock Island has a restaurant and snack stand.
Steamer rides: Reederei Bruno Winkler; tel. 3 49 95 95; Havel Lakes Tour (Unterhavel, Pfaueninsel, Potsdam, Werder).
Stern und Kreisschifffahrt:
Tel. 5 36 36 00, inner-city tours, Havel and Spree tours and charter services. This outfit has plenty of long and short cruises, through the centre, under the bridges, through the new government district and much more. Meanwhile, a number of smaller and larger companies offer tours, and each has a list of its alternating rides at the local tourist information and at their own piers. Exclusive yacht tours are also available.
Reederei Riedel, Tel. 6 93 46 46
U-Bahn: Altstadt Spandau
Map: ⸻⸽ Front jacket

Another great way to get to know Berlin is to travel by boat down the Havel from **Spandau** to **Wannsee**. It is unique for two reasons: one, it is from the water, and two, **Spandau** is unique in and of itself. Its inhabitants still feel more like Spandauer than Berliners, if you ask, and only reluctantly acknowledge that they were incorporated in 1920. When they go to town, they mean the old city centre, as in Spandau city centre. The **Gotisches Haus** (Gothic House), the late medieval home of a great merchant and one of the oldest buildings in Berlin, is now home to a city museum and small tourist office. It is located on the **Breite Strasse** in the pedestrian zone. The **Nikolaikirche** from the 15th century is also worth seeing. Fontane's description of the Margravate of Brandenburg, the former principality in which Berlin is located, has long since lost its validity with industrial estates all around. A painting about the history of the church hangs inside: in 1539, when Prince-elector Joachim, with wife and children, took Holy Communion in the Lutheran manner, the end of Catholicism in Brandenburg was sealed. The tour boats depart from the **Lindenufer**, where the city's fortifications once stood. Close by the Spree flows into the Havel, which then continues southwest toward the Elbe.

The first stretch leads around the back side of the city with Spandau's dockyards area, **Südhafen,** to the left. Behind that lies the former fishing village of **Tiefwerder**, with its wharf, boat houses and some apartment buildings. There are still fishermen here too. After crossing under Heerstrasse, **Pichelsdorf** is on your right.

Although **Pichelswerder** on the left was a lumber transshipment area in the 18th century, it soon became an excursion destination for Berliners. The area is now visibly occupied by watersports clubs, and the traffic here resembles that of the Ku'damm on weekends. If you look back to the right you'll see the **Scharfe Lanke**, the most prestigious bay in Spandau–for those who can afford it.

At the point where the Havel begins to widen, on the hills to the right

Berlin and Surroundings

called the **Weinmeisterhorn,** nuns tended their vineyards back in the Middle Ages. The **Marina Lanke Werft,** at the foot of the slope and at the entrance to the Scharfe Lanke, was Berlin's first marina.

On **Schildhorn,** the headland straight on, Albrecht the Bear triumphed over the Slavic prince Jaczo

in the 12th century. The Schildhorn tavern and its terrace are a favourite summer destination.

To the right is the **Gatow rowing route** (part of the district of Spandau) and the lovely white **Villa Lemm.** The little island **Lindwerder** to the left, which can be reached by ferry from the Havel causeway, has a sailing club and a garden eatery. Berlin's yachtsmen used to favour the docks of the **British Yacht Club** (on the right) because the scotch was cheap outside of the customs zone. The **Grosses Fenster** (Great Window) is the name of the area opposite, an idyllic location for beginner sailors and windsurfers.

A »graceful isle«

The **Schwanenwerder** peninsula, formerly called Sandwerder, was described by French writer Stendhal at the beginning of the 19th century as an isle full of nobility and grace. After 1933, people called it "Bonzenwerder" ("Bigwig Island"). **Joseph Goebbels** lived here, where today the Aspen Institute Berlin advises scientists, entrepreneurs and politicians on contemporary issues, along with Reich architect **Albert Speer**. A bride's school here was meant to breed the proper "Reichsfrau". When the Americans seized the island, **Lucius D. Clay**, "Father of the airlift", lived here until his return to the U.S.

Pack a swimsuit

After that, the expansive **Strandbad Wannsee** beach begins (1,400 yards long, 90 yards wide). The historical landmark buildings designed by municipal builder Martin Wagner, with colonnades, showers and changing cubicles for 30,000 guests, were considered exemplary at the time they were built. It's almost like a seaside holiday location. One idyllic spot that was for some the loveliest spot in all of Berlin has disappeared, however: the **Wannsee-Terrassen** country cottage, which burned down New Year's Eve 2001. The shore took a steep plunge straight down from the tables at the restaurant. The awaited reconstruction has yet to come, but you can still only see Peacock Island and the island Imchen in front of the Kladower strand.

Group 47 got things started here in the adjacent industrialist's villa, where the **Literary Colloquium of Berlin** welcomes authors and theatre people to seminars and conferences. The boat now enters lake Wannsee. Just a short ride away, the vessel docks to allow the visitors to **Peacock Island** to change over to a ferry.

Was it always called "Pfau". as in peacock, or did it used to be "Pau",

If you're tired of walking, you can also comfortably visit Berlin by boat.

as in horse? It is still not completely clear, as both spellings have been found. Either way, the "Pearl of the Havel" was first made famous as a love nest of the Prussian crown prince. Later, between 1685 and 1689, chemist Johann Kunckeel produced highly treasured ruby glass in a foundry on the east side of the island. The land on the island had always been farmed until **Friedrich Wilhelm II** had a fairy-tale castle built by Potsdamer court carpenter Brendel in 1797 for his mistress, Wilhelmine Enke, who later became **Countess Lichtenau**. Friedrich did not get much out of it, however, as he died the year it was completed. His prudish son, Friedrich Wilhelm III, subsequently had his father's mistress arrested and chose to make the castle a summer residence for himself and his wife, Queen Luise. The interior–the castle is only viewable by guided tour–still presents its original furnishings.

Not until the beginning of the 19th century did **Peter Joseph Lenné** transform the majority of the island into a landscaped park. The **Menagerie**, which started in 1822 with exotic animals, became the foundation for the Zoological Gardens. **Kavaliershaus**, in the centre of the island, was designed by **Karl Friedrich Schinkel** in 1824. The aviary to the south is from the same year. The **dairy farm** at the northern end of the island was conceived by Brendel in 1795 as an artificial ruin in Gothic style. The portico to the south was built as a **memorial temple** for Queen Luise (1829). It is a quiet spot with only an occasional screech from one of the roughly 40 peacocks still living wild on the island. The Heilandskirche in Sacrow, a church erected according to plans by Ludwig Persius, lies ship-like on the west bank of the Havel. After the Wall was built, the church was on the wrong side for services, which only took place again after 1989.

Majestic residences in Potsdam, Sanssouci and Babelsberg

Features: The Great Elector had a palace built in Potsdam in the 17th century, and all successive princes ruling from Berlin used it as a second residence. Friedrich the Great's rococo palace, in the meantime, has been incorporated into a Prussian arcadia by landscape artists. Potsdam is unearthing some beautiful historical treasures, and the film studios at Babelsberg beckon with bold stunts.

Duration: 1 day

Food and drink: In Sanssouci, opposite the mill, in Potsdam in the Dutch Quarter, in Babelsberg in the film park.

Route: S-Bahn Zoologischer Garten to Potsdam Stadt, then Tram 98 to Luisenplatz. At the train station, bicycle rentals are available from April to November at City Rad and the signposted tour "Alter Fritz" takes you past the most important sights.

Information: Tourist Information, Brandenburger Str. 3; Tel. 03 31/27 55 80. Information on opening times for palaces and tours: Tel. 03 31/9 69 42 02

Studiotour Babelsberg 👣👣: Enter on the Grossbeerenstrasse; Tel. 03 31/7 21 27 50; www.filmpark.de; Apr–Oct. Daily 10 a.m.–18 p.m., Sep. Mon and Fri closed; adults €17, reduced €15.50, children €12.50, families €55.

Map: ⸱⸱⸱⟩ p. 89, a 3, p. 93

The ruling elite of Berlin never really liked the city much. Potsdam was so close and so splendidly green. **Friedrich II's summer palace** 🔟 there is a favourite among visitor. Fortunately, admission to the park is supposed to remain free of charge (donations are encouraged). After all, this is the largest and, for some, the finest palace complex north of the Alps.

The Great Elector Friedrich Wilhelm, great-grandfather of Friedrich II, was in need of an abode near his beloved hunting grounds, and his advisor, Johann Moritz von Nassau-Siegen, decided to turn a plain little town with a dilapidated hunting lodge on the outskirts of Berlin into a regal paradise. The city palace was finally completed in 1669, but the edifice no longer exists. Only its ruins remain, and they can be inspected later during the tour of town. But first, off to **Sanssouci**.

Carefree in Sanssouci

The park at Sanssouci is aproximately 300 hectares in size, and it does take quite a while to explore all of the expansive grounds with its many sculptures, views and buildings. The **Marlygarten**, a vegetables-only garden commissioned by Friedrich Wilhelm I, is one of Peter Joseph Lenné's most beautiful works of landscape architecture. Friedrich and his wife, Elisabeth of Bavaria, are buried in the **Friedenskirche**.

From the chestnut-lined road you can already see the verdigris copper domes of the palace, a picturesque colour contrast with a blue sky over the vineyard. A flight of stairs with 132 steps leads across the terraces to the top. Friedrich II designed **Schloss Sanssouci** himself in 1744, and Georg Wenzeslaus von Knobelsdorff, the most important northern German architect at the time, was responsible for making it a reality. The chances of actually entering the palace are greater in the morning, since only 1,800 visitors are allowed inside per day. This is meant to protect the castle from damage from the throngs of tourists.

Incidentally, Berliners blame Friedrich's advancing gout on the lack of a cellar, as this could have warded off cold and moisture...

The premises are regarded as the most beautiful in the history of German rococo. The collection in the adjacent **picture gallery** (1762)–with

Peacock Island (→ p. 68), once site of the romantic interludes of Prussian kings, has been a nature reserve since 1924.

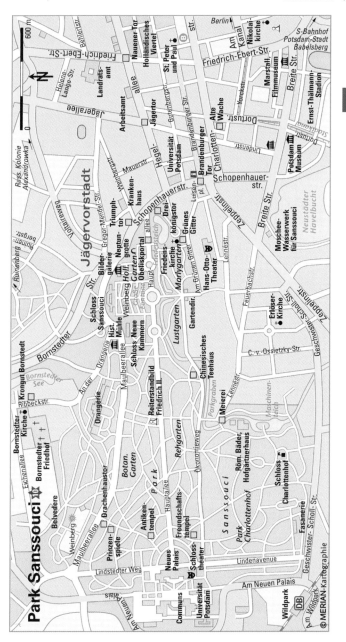

about 90 paintings covering the walls of one 330-foot-long hall–has been open to the public again since 1996 after having been carefully renovated. New marble slabs cover the floors now. The walls are decorated mainly with profane and mythological subjects, including Caravaggio's "Doubting Thomas" and allegedly real works by Raphael. In 1991, on the terrace in front of the palace, Friedrich the Great was given the state funeral he never wanted–for the fifth time!

To reach Friedrich II's summer palace if you're coming from town, you'll go through the wrought-iron **"Grünes Gitter"**, or "Green Gate". The early bon vivant–and later cynic–fulfilled one of his childhood dreams at Sanssouci with an exuberant garden that is more reminiscent of Italy than Brandenburg. There were apricots, grapevines and fig trees, and ancient deities embodying the elements fire, water, air and earth surrounded the basin of the great fountain. The **Chinese Teahouse** glitters gold and is home to a precious porcelain collection. Originally built for Friedrich's collection of ancient stat-

ues, the **Antikentempel** now serves as the tomb of the last Empress of Germany, Augusta Victoria, who died in 1921. The **Belvedere** on the Klausberg (1755-1763) was used for smaller celebrations. Friedrich Carl von Gontard was contracted to build the **Friendship Temple**, with medallion portrayals of classical friendships adorning the Corinthian columns. The **New Chambers** were built in 1747 as an Orangerie and converted later to apartments for guests. The subsequent **Orangerie**, with colonnades and a winter conservatory, shows decidedly Italian influences. The most sumptuously appointed of all is the **New Palace**, which is inlaid with shells and semi-precious stones. The **Roman Baths** were designed by Schinkel and his pupil Ludwig Persius in the style of an Italian manor as an auxiliary building to the Charlottenhof. The **Charlottenhof Palace** served as summer residence to Crown Prince Friedrich Wilhelm IV.

Nostalgic Babelsberg

Emperor Wilhelm I preferred the Tudor style **Babelsberg Palace**, designed by Schinkel and located on the banks of the Havel river, while Prince

The Chinese Teahouse in the park at Schloss Sanssouci is adorned with life-size gold figures.

Karl enjoyed the **Klein-Glienicke,** also a Schinkel creation. The **Cecilienhof Palace,** the last royal construction commissioned by the Hohenzollern family in Prussia, was erected in 1917, albeit to the justified protests of a starving population, for Crown Prince Wilhelm in the **New Garden,** across from Pfingstberg. One of the 176 rooms made history between June and August of 1945 when the heads of government of the Great Powers met here. But this charming manor, which is now a hotel, was not host to the actual conferences and agreements. The meetings were held accross the street, in the **Villa Müller-Grote**.

Europe's film capital of the 1920s is slowly becoming popular again, but it seems to be more for the real estate than for the film business. Television series may be filmed here, but the big productions just aren't coming through.

The city of Potsdam

Passing through the **Brandenburg Gate,** a Roman-style triumphal arch designed by Oswald Mathias Unger and Carl von Gontard in 1770, you arrive in a baroque city. Many of the structures from the time of Friedrich I, however, were destroyed during World War II. The "Soldier King", who unlike his son did not actually conduct any wars, had marshland drained to build quarters for soldiers and craftsmen as part of his expansion of Prussia's military. **Brandenburger Strasse,** where almost all of the houses date from around 1750, could be seen as an early example of estate and row housing. At the time, citizens were required to provide soldiers with lodging on the upper floors, and they were made to show themselves every evening at their windows to make sure they hadn't deserted. There is now a lively pedestrian zone here.

The **Nauener Gate** in **Friedrich-Ebert-Strasse,** painted yellow since the 1920s, now has to make do with a dull grey after years of renovation. This was a decision from the preservation society, abiding by the original colour scheme from 1755. Judging by the Italian flair of the restaurant and café and in front of the eastern gate, however, the guidelines were evidently not adhered to so rigidly.

The **Altes Rathaus** (Old Town Hall, 1753–1755), with its golden Atlas atop the tower, stands gracefully next to Schinkel's mighty **Nikolaikirche** at the **Alter Markt** (Old Market). The Nikolai Church was also destroyed during the war and later reconstructed. Since 2002, the Fortuna Portal from the old Stadtschloss is again on the market square for further expansion. The **Marstall** (Royal Stables), the only edifice standing after the Stadtschloss was destroyed in World War II, now houses the film museum.

The pearl of Brandenburg's capital is without doubt the **Dutch Quarter** (Holländisches Viertel) between Friedrich-Ebert, Mittel and Hebbel streets. When the "Soldier King" summoned Dutch craftsmen, he had hoped they would stay and help enhance the city. From 1733 to 1742 they built as in their homeland but then moved on. Local artists and artisans liked the red houses. **Carl von Ossietzky** printed "Die Weltbühne" ("The World Stage") in the **Gutenbergstrasse**. Later, the area became derelict and was supposed to be demolished. Squatters moved in and after the fall of the Wall, investors smelled the opportunity that existed here. As a result, a redevelopment statute was quickly issued to stop speculators. Still, the rents in the pretty buildings have long exceeded the income of some of the boutiques and galleries.

Potsdam has now begun conjuring images of the former mile-long city canal, as it is depicted running through the historical centre in paintings by Otto Heinrich. The first segment was officially opened in 2001.

Singers as a gift from the Czar

To the north of town is another jewel, the Russian **colony of Alexandrowka**. Czar Alexander I presented Friedrich Wilhelm III with 62 singing soldiers who were given a fully furnished house with a stable and a cow. The houses could be given but not sold. The 13 half-timbered houses with carved gables, built on the example of Russian military villages and set up in a diagonal cross by Lenné, have now been refurbished. There is a museum and a Russian tearoom there.

Rheinsberg Palace: for lovers and Tucholsky fans

Features: The young Friedrich spent four happy years in this palace until, in 1740, his role as king forced him to move to Berlin. Today lovers hire boats here.

Duration: 1 day

Food and drink: The Ratskeller in the town hall opposite the palace.

Route: From the train station Berlin-Charlottenburg take the RE6; with a car, A 24 toward Hamburg, exit Neuruppin, about 50 miles.

Information: Tourist Information Rheinsberg, Am Markt; Tel. 03 39 31/20 59; www.rheinsberg.de

Map: ⤳ p. 89, a 2

Crown Prince Friedrich, later called "the Great", was apparently not the only one who was happier in Rheinsberg than elsewhere. **Theodor Fontane,** not normally prone to praising Brandenburg, even found kind words for Rheinsberg, and Kurt Tucholsky immortalised the place in 1912 with his piece "A Picturebook for Lovers".

Crown Prince receiving again

It is no wonder then that this little town is becoming a favourite among tourists and returning the favour with new hotels, pretty restaurants (albeit with precious few parking spaces), as well as concerts and exhibitions. A statue of Crown Prince Friedrich poses again in front of the entrance to the palace, shining brightly between the houses and trees. Georg Wenzeslaus von Knobelsdorff was the architect who turned this medieval water castle into a cheery little palace with squat towers. The great hall was decked out in marble and mirrors like other palaces of the time.

Pilgrimage site for Tucholsky fans

The castle has been once again brought back to its original state after a long renovation period. Back in the days of the GDR, the entire palace was used as a sanatorium, which meant that some of the demolished walls had to be replaced and bathrooms removed. One of the side wings of the complex contains a pilgrimage site for real fans of Tucholsky. One of his typewriters, a light summer suit, some photographs, letters and books of the Berlin-born author are on display there. Occasionally readings take place.

There was even a scandal in the palace's recent history when an army general demanded the Tucholsky exhibition be closed due to alleged propagandistic misuse of the writer. But things like this don't put anyone off in Rheinsberg. Least of all the lovers who, in search of this location's legendary ambience, drift out on the evening lake.

Rheinsberg has become an important ceramics centre again as well. In a large **sales showroom** in **Rhinstrasse** you can purchase common ceramics or even the blue and white Bürgel ceramics from the Silesian town of Boleslawiec. **Boat tours** are available from the pier at the end of **Seestrasse**. During special cultural events, music festivals, ceramics

Crown Prince Friedrich had a happy childhood in Rheinsberg Palace. The three-winged baroque complex is considered to be one of the most charming palaces in the north of Germany.

fairs or Christmas markets, you can make the trip from Berlin to Rheinsberg with a steam locomotive. From Lichtenberg the trip takes two hours.

Buckow: Pearl of Märkische Schweiz

Features: Bertolt Brecht was able to find a nice spot here. The summer house on the lake, used by himself and his wife, Helene Weigel, is now a museum. After your visit, take a stroll through the sandy woodlands around the lake.

Duration: 1 day

Food and drink: The terrace of the Kurhotel am Scharmützelsee, Ringstr. 5 offers nice seating.

Route: S-Bahn to Strausberg, then by bus or train to Buckow. By car on the B1 toward Frankfurt/Oder, in Müncheberg direction Buckow, about 40 miles.

Information on current opening times: Tel. 03 34 33/4 67

Map: ⸱⸱⸱⸱> p. 89, c 3

In the Märkische Schweiz nature preserve roughly 40 miles east of Berlin is the town of Buckow, fondly referred to as the "Pearl of Märkische Schweiz" by writer **Theodor Fontane**. Bertolt Brecht was also attracted to this spot due to its seclusion. The houses, trees and lake here later permeated the author's works, as one can read in the "Buckower Elegies". He wrote them in 1953 after the uprising of the 17th of June in East Germany.

The **summer house** at **Bertolt-Brecht-Strasse 29** was home to the poet and his wife during the warm months from 1952 until Brecht's death in 1956. In 1977, it was opened with original furnishings as a **museum** with occasional literary events. In the summer months, musical-literary events also take place. It's a pretty museum: a high parlour suffused with light, stained black floorboards in front of the fireplace, a heavy wooden table, chests and benches from the 18th and 19th centuries. The couple's life and works are documented in the boathouse.

EXTRA: Berlin Lexicon

After a view of Potsdamer Platz from the unusual perspective of a cruise down the Landwehrkanal (→ p. 111), the Hiroshima footbridge appears from behind weeping willows, with the ship from the Grand Hotel Esplanade anchored on the bank.

The bear is the symbol of Berlin, but the origins of it are uncertain. Other things are less difficult to explain: for example, where the Wall stood or how Kennedy came to be a "Berliner".

Adlergestell

Berlin's longest street, known by most motorists from traffic reports. It leads 7.4 miles through Treptow.

Adlershof

Europe's most modern technology centre has been planned on 420 hectares in the district of Treptow. Author Anna Seghers ("The Seventh Cross") was born in Adlershof, East German television broadcast its propagandistic "Black Channel" and the popular animated "Sandman" character (long popular in all of Germany and established at the Babelsberg studios) from here, and the Felix Dzerzhinsky Guards Regiment of the GDR was stationed here too.

Allies

Berlin was not formally part of the Federal Republic of Germany after World War II. Instead, it formed a piece of occupied territory of the German Empire under the tutelage of the four allied victorious powers: the Soviet Union, the USA, France and Great Britain. The Allies intervened in the politics and in the rights of the divided city. West Berliners did not have Federal German identification papers but "provisional identification". Their stamps said "German Federal Post Berlin". There was no compulsive military service or any alternative service for West Berliners. Until Reunification in 1990, Berlin's members of parliament were not elected but dispatched from the House of Representatives. The voting powers of Berlin representatives were limited in the capital, Bonn, and they were not allowed to vote for the chancellor or pass legislation. West Berliners experienced the Allies as their "defence" only during the Berlin Airlift. After the reunification they withdrew.

Ampel (traffic light)

At the beginning of the 1920s, Potsdamer Platz threatened to drown in its own traffic chaos. During an informative trip to New York, municipal planners from Berlin's streetcar company discovered a reliable solution: the traffic light. The "traffic tower" was purchased, shipped across the Atlantic to Berlin and installed in 1924 as the first of its kind on the continent. In 1997, the old light was reconstructed in Berlin, a pentagonal tower, 28 feet tall. A clock is built into each side of the replica lamp as well. Police officers once transmitted messages in Morse code via this device. As a space-saving measure, the red-yellow-green lamps are placed horizontally. The old traffic light at the corner of Potsdamer and Stresemannstrasse is not in use.

Avus

Now part of the city motorway at the Funkturm junction, this approximately 6-mile-long motorway and testing track was built between 1913 and 1921 as the first thoroughfare in the world without intersections. A steep north and south curve connected the two straightaways on a 12-mile-long circuit where Grand Prix star Bernd Rosemeyer raced a record 171 miles per hour with his Auto Union car (now Audi). About 7,700 spectators were watching from the grandstands.

Bears

Following Tilo's the bear's death in 2007, Schnute is now Berlin's incumbent city bear, assisted by Maxi, her housemate in the compound at Köllnischer Park behind the Märkisches Museum. Tilo's five offspring, Alex, Bärolina, Atze, Rieke and Peifke have all pursued careers abroad. There has been a city bear in Berlin since 1939. The first to live in the bears' compound were Jule, Lotte, Urs and Vreni, all gifts from the Swiss city of Bern, whose city coat of arms also displays a bear, on the occasion of Berlin's

700th birthday. The difference between the live bears and the one on the coat of arms is that the origins of the live ones are known, whereas we only know that the earliest evidence of the Berlin bear symbol was found on a seal from 1280. It appeared later in letters of the peltmongers' guild in the city seal from 1330 with a margravian eagle. As of 1500, the eagle was perched on the nape of the bear's neck. Under Friedrich I, the bear stood leashed next to the red eagle of Brandenburg and the black eagle of Prussia. Although unleashed by then, the 20th century saw him wearing a crown of five towers. The feathered friends were removed in 1920, two years after the emperor abdicated and the Berlin bear also lost his crown. Now he campaigns for Berlin, sits with stone paws on bridges, adorns beer mugs and snuggles up to tourists in his teddy or plaster versions. The bears regularly congregate by the hundreds, either in plastic or as "buddy bears", to be painted, scolded, loved, auctioned...And when all of Berlin sighs with relief, they meet again by the hundreds, to be painted, scolded, loved...

Berge (mountains)

The sandy soil on which the city was built is not as flat as it may first appear. There are at least 24 natural and just as many man-made mountains, more than a dozen climbing rocks, more than 100 toboggan runs and even an Alpine Association here. The Teufelsberg hosted a world ski championship, albeit with grass runs. It's 377 feet high, but with that in mind, consider that Berlin is already 165 feet above sea level. The alpine sport centre for the city is here and hang gliders (but more likely kites) launch from here while mountain bikers, hikers and joggers use the network of trails. Skiers and sledders of course also use the hill.

Berliner

"Ish bin ein Bear-lee-ner" was the phonetic spelling that interpreter Robert H. Lochner gave to US President John F. Kennedy for rehearsal of his famous quote on the 26th of June 1963. It was essential that everyone could understand him, and that's exactly how he said it. A simple declaration can be, as is plainly evidenced here, the easiest way to become a Berliner. Unlike other cities, origins

Military parade of the victorious Allied powers: France, the USA and Great Britain.

matter very little in Berlin. Here, it's more a matter of staying power, the proof of which can be seen from behind the cemetery walls. Architect Karl Friedrich Schinkel, for example, the man responsible for the neo-classical face of Berlin, may have been born in Neuruppin but he was buried as a Berliner. Marlene Dietrich, baptized in the waters of the Spree, did not just become an American when she went there but was almost "un-Berlined" because of her lack of loyalty. But Berliners are not resentful, at least not for long, and she was ultimately buried in her hometown. A square was even named after her. Hildegard Knef was born in Ulm and the famous cabaret artist Claire Waldoff was born in Gelsenkirchen. Indeed, Berliners can be from anywhere.

Berliner Zimmer

If you stay in a classic guesthouse here, you will probably get to know it as the breakfast room. The Berliner

There are still a few left: the green urinals popularly called "Octagon cafés".

Zimmer (Zimmer = room) is typically characterised by more doors than seem necessary and bad lighting. It is a vestige from better times, when the servants in the side wings served the bourgeoisie in the main house. The connection between the two was this room with a single side window.

Berlinerisch (or Berlinisch)

It's not slang and not at all vulgar. The way Berliners speak is a dialect, a native, regional vernacular that can be heard most often on an excursion into Brandenburg. Its origins: a Low German core melded with Brandenburger Platt German and was enriched by centuries of random phrases from French, Polish, Russian, Yiddish and Latin. Berlinerisch is a very pictorial language, ironic and contrary with a quick-wittedness that is renowned for being slightly, well, not very quick. There are no hard "Gs" in Berlin. Instead, there is a general defiance of High German grammar and pronunciation. Non-Berliners would be ill-advised to attempt the dialect themselves, as the mysteries of this tongue are many–as are the possible blunders.

Berolina

The symbolic figure of Berlin, sculpted in 1895 by Emil Hundrieser–and sometimes called "Bearolina" in the light of her corpulence–was erected on Alexanderplatz at the end of the 19th century before completely disappearing, with full regalia, in 1944. Rumour has it that she took part in the war effort, having been melted down for shells. Berlin art students designed a modern Berolina that was erected on Hausvogteiplatz, but she turned out very slim and not everyone recognises her.

Blockade

In order to force the unification of Berlin to swing in their direction, the

Konnopke's stand is known beyond the borders of Berlin for its curried sausage.

Soviets sealed off access to the city's American, French and British occupied zones in West Berlin in June of 1948. American military governor, Lucius D. Clay, and Berlin mayor, Ernst Reuter, were forced to find a solution. After much deliberation about the plausibility of their plan, they decided on the Berlin Airlift. More than 277,000 flights were eventually made to supply the city with food, coal, chocolate and Father Christmas, who was also transported by military aircraft. The 2.5 million citizens held out for nearly a year until May 12, 1949, when the Soviets lifted their blockade. A monument at Tempelhof Airport, the "Rake of Hunger", memorialises the event. It was a solidarity contribution of sorts, called the "Berlin emergency fund", taken up in the American and British zones that made the entire operation possible.

Brandt, Willy
From 1957 to 1966, Willy Brandt governed as mayor from the Schöneberg Town Hall. As Chancellor he managed to transform West German politics regarding the East–and not just when he famously fell to his knees in Warsaw. He became an honorary citizen of Berlin in 1970.

Café Achteck (Octagon Café)
This is the endearing term for the green, eight-sided public urinals that can still occasionally be seen around town, for example on Chamissoplatz in Kreuzberg.

Capitals
This is the name of the West Berlin ice hockey team that used to push the puck around under the names the Preussen and the Devils. Back then the East Berlin Eisbären skated under the name Dynamo Berlin.

Carillon
Every Sunday afternoon, visitors at the Grosser Tiergarten who are near the government buildings will hear a bell ring from the tower next to the House of World Cultures. This is no typical chime, though. The bell ringer has to climb 187 steps up to a glass cubicle at a height of 140 ft to reach his weighty instrument. The carillon is played on a table, whose wooden rods are connected to the clappers of 68 bells via wires and levers. A lot of strength is necessary to set the rods and pedals in motion. After World War I, Americans brought the instrument, once common in Belgium and Holland, back to Europe.

Cölln

The city on an island (now Fischerin-sel in the Mitte district) in the Spree river was the first documented set-tlement in Berlin: from 1237. It was a colony, probably established by merchants on this spot between the fortifications at Spandau and Köpe-nick. Seven years laters, talk was of Berlin on a mainland ford across the way. In 1307, the two towns united (for the first time) against the robber barons who were stirring up trouble in the area.

Currywurst (curried sausage)

The Currywurst is virtually unknown outside of Germany, and is very typical of Berlin. Indeed, it was in-vented here. It all started when a Berliner was introduced to ribs with ketchup while imprisoned by the Americans. Having liked it, his wife mixed tomatoes and spices until the postwar inmate gourmet was satis-fied. Hertha Heuwer then had the combination of boiled wieners and her special sauce patented (trade-mark no. 721 319) and began selling it in 1949 at her sausage stand on Stuttgarter Platz. Since then, hun-dreds have copied her and made the "Currywurst" a real Berliner.

Eiserner Gustav (Iron Gustav)

In 1928, legendary coachman Gustav Hartmann achieved notoriety by driving his carriage all the way from Berlin to Paris. In addition to that feat, he also created a foundation for the destitute families of dead taxi drivers that still exists. In June 2000, a stat-ue in his memory was fashioned by sculptor Gerhard Rommel weighing more than 1,000 lbs. and made of iron. It sits upon a granite boulder that weighs more than five tons on the corner of Potsdamer Strasse and Schöneberger Ufer.

Erfinder (inventors)

In 1903, Berlin chemist and druggist Hans Schwarzkopf succeeded in cre-ating a product that would revolu-tionise personal hygiene: shampoo. Using his powder, washing your hair became a quick and easy task. The days of curd soap were over. In 1927, the company developed a hair wash-ing liquid that would replace "Berlin-

Der Palast der Republik (aka "Erich's Lamp Shop" in GDR times) is but a memory now. The Stadtschloss is supposed to be rebuilt in its place as the Humboldt Forum.

er powder". Demand was high, and new production plants were built in Tempelhof. In 1947 the cold wave was invented in Germany and in 1955 the first hairspray.

Berlin was also where chemist Andreas Marggraf discovered beet sugar in 1747. The first beet sugar was produced in 1798 in present-day Kaulsdorf by Franz Carl Achard, who continued building the first sugar beet factories in the world until 1805 in Silesia. Of course, even more was invented in Berlin, but not everything was comparably revolutionary.

Erich's Lamp Shop
The popular name for the Palast der Republik in GDR times is a reference to its many lamps and the leader of East Germany. Other names included Palazzo Prozzo, and Ballast of the Republic since it was slated for demolition.

Euro
The eagle on German Euro coins comes from Prenzlauer Berg. Artist Sneschana Russewa-Hoyer, Bulgarian by birth, designed it and her husband, sculptor and medallist Heinz Hoyer, made the prototype. It is now stored in the safe at the Ministry of Finance. Both were working with the Treasury at the time of the GDR. They created the Marabu in 1984, a commemorative coin for Alfred Brehm, and in 1985 another with the first actress to be commemorated on a coin, Caroline Friederike Neuber, who revolutionised the Deutsches Theater in the 18th century.

Exclave
West Berlin terrain surrounded by East German territory and hence only accessible with a special permit. Until the fall of the Wall, several of these existed, such as Steinstücken, 13 hectares of Zehlendorf belonging to the sector but surrounded by the GDR. Russian soldiers and GDR customs controlled a barrier blocking the way from 1951 until the Four Power Agreement in 1972. Inhabitants had to pass through two control stations. For a long time visitors were not allowed on the "Western island in the eastern sea". This led to one man's trick of registering his apartment as a second residence for all the guests of his silver anniversary party. In 1972 a 65-ft-wide access road was built with walls on each side. Curious visitors could now enter via Bernhard-Beyer-Strasse and Steinstücken became an attraction. The exclaves were often garden plots, like the Fichtewiese in Spandau. Hobby gardeners had to arrive at specified times with their papers to be granted access. As recently as 1988, a 100-yd-wide strip was allotted to West Berlin.

Fassbrause
A matter of taste, but Berliners seem to like it. According to the original recipe, it is a sour apple drink, but it is also available in the flavours orange, raspberry or woodruff. The name suggests that it comes from the barrel, but it is actually in a bottle.

Films
Like "The Lives of Others" with Ulrich Mühe (2006), Bernd Böhlich's film "Du bist nicht allein" (2007) plays in Berlin. Andreas Dresen's "Summer in Berlin" (2006) takes place here. "Run Lola Run" (1998) races through the city and "Good Bye Lenin" (2002) bids adieu to the GDR from the capital. Berlin is becoming more and more popular as a film set. Location scouts are on a continual search for undiscovered sites, and the film consultant at the police department can procure props like uniforms or helicopters. The city was a wonderful set in "Life is all you get" (1997), the title in German meaning "Life is a construction site". Historic events are also the subject of many films, and the city does play the leading role in "Berlin Baby-

lon" (2001), a thriller amidst the maze of urban reconstruction.

Fliegeberg

The name of a rise in Berlin-Lichtefelde made by the Lilienthal brothers in 1894 for their flight experiments. In 1868, Otto Lilienthal made the first wing stroke apparatus, and in 1891 he successfully completed the first human flight with a winged leap of 15 meters. He died in 1896 of complications from injuries received during a test flight on Gollenberg near Stölln.

Freiheitsglocke (Liberty Bell)

In 1950, General Clay, "Father of the Airlift" (blockade, p. 102), gave Berlin it largest bell: a 10.2 ton replica of the Liberty Bell in Philadelphia. It now hangs as a symbol of freedom in the clock tower over the main entrance of Schöneberg Town Hall, from 1948 to 1990 seat of Berlin's House of Representatives.

Garderobe

Berliners supposedly imagine a nail in the wall for unnecessary items when they hear this word. Even Theodor Fontane remarked in 1898 that, "As soon as you enter Berlin you can forget chic and elegant." Designers clear their throats cautiously before typically answering questions about fashion in the capital with "interesting". A well-dressed senator incited a wave of indignation with his public denouncement of many Berliners' uncivilised manner of dress, usually a track suit. But high-end labels have long since made their way beyond Kurfürstendamm to Friedrichstrasse, and not just for the tourists. The number of Berlin labels grows from year to year. During the annual Walk of Fashion, Berlin designs can be purchased directly, and the regular fashion trade shows now receive international acclaim. Berlin brands usually offer functional clothes, and it's more than evident that there is no dress code in Berlin. Whether for the Philharmonic or the cabaret, bar or gourmet restaurant, you wear what you want. Venues with a specified mode of dress are accessible by invitation only anyway.

Geisterbahnhöfe (ghost stations)

The name given to subway and other train stations through which West

The Lilienthal brothers used the Lilienberg for their first flight experiments.

trains drove but which were closed to East Germans at the time of the GDR: Stadion der Weltjugend, Oranienburger Tor and Französische Strasse, for example. The trains did not stop and you could only get off when you were back on the West side.

Germania
This was meant to be the name for the National Socialist seat of power after their victory in World War II. Albert Speer drew up the plans, which envisioned a 950-ft-tall Great Hall, next to which the Reichstag would have looked like a matchbox with its 245-ft dome. The gigantomania inspired the architect's father to comment, "You have all gone mad."

Geschichtsmeile (Historical Mile)
Wilhelmstrasse was once compared with the Quai d'Orsay in Paris and London's Downing Street. Being the centre of power, its neoclassical buildings were unfortunately the target of bombings in World War II, which led to much destruction. Today it stretches as one long prefabricated building, with few exceptions, from Pariser Platz to Anhalter Strasse. This inspired the foundation Topography of Terror to put up informative texts and picture plates as an aid to those seeking traces of the Reich Chancellery, the Reich Main Security Office (Prinz-Albrecht-Palais, Centre of Terror), the Reich Presidential Palace, Prussian Ministry of Justice, etc.

Grüner Pfeil (green arrow)
"It wasn't all bad in the GDR," is a famous quote from former citizens of the GDR, and an example of what they mean is the "green arrow", which "West Germans" are only slowly learning to use: a right-turn green arrow when the main light is still red. The test implementation in the West led on the one hand to enthusiasm and on the other to it being totally ignored.

Berlin couturiers present their creations during the Walk of Fashion.

Hertha
"Hertha" was the name of the dual-propeller steamship with blue and white smokestack built in Stettin in 1886 and used by Berlin's football team for a relaxing excursion in 1892. The ship's name inspired the players, who were looking to form a club and needed a name. Hertha BSC was born. In June 1930, the club won the German championship for the first time. In 1964 the club spent 15,000 Marks to Munich 1860 player Alfons Stemmer to improve their chances of joining the newly formed league. The scam was uncovered but went unpunished. Games were bought and manipulated. Hertha rose and fell. Their home is the Olympia Stadium, built in 1936, damaged in the war, modernised in 1974 and renovated in 2006 for the World Cup. And the old steamship, "Hertha"? It cruised the Spree, Havel, Wannsee and Müggelsee lakes as an excursion boat in GDR times under the name "Seid bereit" ("Be Ready"). In 1964, the White Fleet retired it and it was left to rot on the Spree until a man from Kyritz re-

The artistically designed Sophie Gips Courts in Mitte.

furbished it in 1971 and set it back into the water under the name "See-bär" ("Sea Bear"). When Hertha BSC celebrated its 100th birthday in 1992, fans cruised the Kyritz lake district on the Seebär.

Hinterhöfe (back courtyards)

From Kreuzberg to Prenzlauer Berg, if you look behind the pretty façades of the houses you'll often find one, two or three courtyards with side wings and a rear house or garden house. Gardens, however, were fairly rare in the tenements of this former working-class neighbourhood. Many of the courtyards have been gutted in the meantime, making space for trees, flowers and sand boxes. When the courtyards have been maintained (as in the Hasenheide in Kreuzberg), you'll often even find businesses, shops and, more recently, trendy lofts. Old Berlin police ordinances required that every adult have 3 square meters of floor space and 10 cubic meters of air. Children could do with one-third of this. Thus, the size of the courtyards was standard-ised with 17 square feet, enough for a fire engine to turn around.

Hunde (dogs)

There are officially 107,804 registered dogs in Berlin. Add to this about the same number of unregistered dogs, and you have 27 tons of excrement in the streets, parks, fields and woods daily, for which a mere €120 per first dog in pet taxes go towards removal. In 1830, when the dog tax was introduced, there were 6,000 registered animals. For the dogs in the West, spaces with beaches have been made available from Grunewald to Jungfernheide, where they can play free of the leash laws of the city centre. The dogs in the East, however, only have one nice areal and can only enjoy leash-free play in unobserved spaces. But since some inhabitants of the capital cannot seem to survive the struggle of existence without their fighting dogs, these animals are forced to wear a leash and a muzzle to protect other less snappy four-legged Berlin residents.

Interbau

Abbreviation for the Internationale Bauausstellung 1957 (International Building Exhibition), during which noted architects reconstructed the southern part of the Hansaviertel at Tiergarten, which had been heavily damaged during the war. Walter Gropius, Max Taut, Alvar Aalto and Oscar Niemeyer, along with ten land-scape architects, planned a lovely green metropolis. This was the West's answer to the first socialist street in the East, Stalinallee.

Jewish Community

Until 1933, 173,000 Jews lived in Berlin. Of the 8,000 that could still be counted in 1945, many were sim-ply awaiting their emigration permits for America or the Holy Land. The National Socialists had transported and murdered over 55,000 Berlin Jews and forced most others to flee the city and the country. With more than 12,000 members, the Jewish community in Berlin is now the largest in Germany and the third largest in Europe. Since 1990, it has accommodated thousands of immi-grants from Eastern Europe. In 1999, the Central Consistory of Jews re-sumed its works where the Nazis had closed down the Higher Institute of Jewish Studies in 1942. About 50 Jew-ish facilities are protected day and night by security forces in the capital, including six synagogues, the Jewish secondary school and the Jewish kindergarten.

Kakerlaken (cockroaches)

But surely not in Berlin! Oh yes. A man who looks like Rasputin fires the starting gun and off they go, Olga, Pamir, Sergei or Ivan the Terrible, cheered on by the bettors, most of whom cannot see the race. But being there is everything. Cockroach races have been an event in Berlin since 2001. Rasputin in this case is the Russian painter Nikolai Makarow, and he seems to have made a name for himself in Berlin more quickly with his roaches than with his paintings. Insiders knew him for the wild parties in his studio on January 13th, the Orthodox New Year, and in the sum-mertime. Those were where the first races took place. The crowds then began growing and the number of spectators rose to the hundreds. Television crews came. A bank invit-ed him to one of their parties, ac-companied by Ivan the Terrible. It was supposed to be a treat. The roaches have now arrived in the West, in Paris Bar. There are no set dates, it's al-ways a surprise.

Kiez

The term comes was originally Slavic and described outskirt settlements on the banks of the Elbe in medieval times. Later Kiez was used as a name for suburbs and fisher colonies. In the former fishing colony of Köpenick, there is a street with this name. Oth-erwise the term Berliner Kiez is used as a synonym for the home district; that part of the town where you find your local baker, your local pub, take your dog for a walk, greet the neigh-bours and meet for a chat on the cor-ner. To change your "Kiez" is to move to a different city.

KPM

The Königliche Porzellan Manufaktur (Royal Porcelain Manufactory) is the full name and reveals the problem in full as well: there are no more kings (Könige) in Germany. Although Bill Gates allegedly ordered one thou-sand pieces with monogram, there are too few people who want a KPM cup next to their laptop. And who needs a 150-piece set? In 2004, KPM was 241 years old and had to leave its premises to make room for a business that not only had nothing to do with porcelain, but even uses styrofoam instead. The factory nearly met its end in 1763, back before it had been given its advantageous name, but Friedrich the Great saved the day by giving them the title and the blue sceptre as a symbol. A particularly famous set was produced over and over, one of which was created by the Bauhaus designer Trudi Petri. Recently, Milanese designer Enzo Mari, at the head of his master class, created the service "Berlin". After that the KPM belonged to the Investment Bank of Berlin, who have yet to turn a profit from its sales.

Kremser

This was the name of the court councillor who was granted a concession in 1822 for a carrying company that used multi-seated vehicles for passenger transport outside the city walls. Such vehicles, resembling a covered wagon, are still called Kremsers to this day, and not just in Berlin.

Kreuzer

Since the mid-1990s, people have been paying in Kreuzers in Kreuzberg. The Kreuzer is a virtual currency, only honoured in this exchange scheme, now with over 300 Kreuzberger members. An hour of work is worth 20 Kreuzers, and since its inception, there has been a turnover of over one million Kreuzers. It's an exchange of abilities. Someone feeds your cat while you're on holiday, another lets the aspiring hair dresser practise on his head and is perhaps repaid with a bit of help typing his dissertation.

Landwehrkanal

Loaded with fruits, vegetables or construction material for the booming city, ships had to wait up to six days at Berlin's lock awaiting entry. In response, work began in 1845 on the Landwehr canal based on plans by Peter Joseph Lenné. The canal was opened on September 2, 1850. About 6.4 miles in length and 73.5 ft wide, this national waterway flows through Kreuzberg, Tiergarten and Charlottenburg. It is spanned by 37, mostly very low, pedestrian and car bridges. Rosa Luxemburg's body was thrown into the water by Freikorps soldiers in 1919 at the Lichtenstein bridge. A memorial plaque can be found here.

Lenné Triangle

This was the name of the piece of land between the Sony Center, Lenné and Ebertstrasse that became nationally famous in 1988 after a bizarre mass exodus from the West to the East. Positioned west of the Wall, it belonged to the Mitte district and was cut off during the building of the Wall in 1961 and left, fenced in, as wasteland. The senate, however, wanted to exchange it for a West Berlin property near the border, but hundreds of young people had occupied the land in protest against the senate's plans to build a highway through the Lenné triangle. West Berlin could not access the land until the territory was legally exchanged on July 1, 1988. The protestors fled over the wall to avoid arrest and were helped by border patrols, who gave them tea, bread and cigarettes and sent them back to the West by train via Friedrichstrasse.

Litfasssäule (advertising column)

The authorities decided that the posters placed with abandon on house walls and fences was one of the causes of the Revolution of 1848. Uncontrolled bill posting was forbidden and a contract was then drawn up with the printing press owner Ernst Litfass to allow the placement of 150 columns that would be used for censored advertisements. Despite their efforts, any stroll through Berlin may lead you to believe another revolution is not far away...

Die Mauer (The Wall)

⤑ p. 112/113

The Wall was built on August 13, 1961, along a border that ultimately encircled the Western sectors (map, p. 112/113) and ran through the entire city. In the beginning, GDR border patrols sealed off the West with barbed-wire fences and road-blocks. Not two days after this official border was put up, a photograph by Peter Leibing became world-famous: on August 15, 1961, border guard Conrad Schumann jumped the barbed wire at Bernauer Strasse and became the first refugee of the GDR. On August 26 all border crossings were closed, sealing off the Western section of the city from the East as well as from the surrounding territories. The makeshift division was ultimately replaced by nearly 100 miles of concrete wall. Approximately 30 miles of it separated the urban areas. The individual wall sections were 11. 8 feet high and 3.9 feet wide. About 45,000 modules, at a total cost of 38.5 million Marks were placed as "an anti-fascist barrier" to prevent the people who were needed to build the socialist state from fleeing. A 32-mile chain-link fence, 293 watch towers, a 110-ft-wide strip with dog runs, a patrol path and a 330-ft-wide prohibited area completed the "border protection facilities". A piece of it is still standing, artificially preserved, on Bernauer Strasse. You can view the "no-man's land" through slits in the wall.

The wall tore families and friends apart and brought death to 239 people during their attempts to escape. And when it fell in 1989 after a long 28 years, it was cleared and sold off so quickly that hardly anyone can remember exactly where it once stood. You can still make out parts of the border from the tar paths in the tall grass around town, some of it has been built over, and in the city itself there are some sections of wasteland and occasional pieces of the wall that are usually displaced by a construction project. For the sake of history and orientation, a start has been made to trace the city border with a double-row of cobblestones bearing the inscription "Berliner Mauer 1961-1989". A wall bike path in 14 legs leads down the former border strip and commemorates the division and reunification of the city.

Mitte

Is Berlin Mitte in the middle of Berlin, as the name would imply? Clearly not. The geographic centre of the city is in Alexandrinenstrasse in Kreuzberg, 52°30'10 north and 13°24'15 east. That said, Mitte has been an official district since 1920, and the area was synonymous with Berlin for centuries.

Music

Berlin is the capital of music too, according to Universal Deutschland, the country's largest music label, which has now moved to the banks of the Spree. And Berlin has indeed become a centre for music, with more than a thousand rock and pop bands and over 250 musical venues of all sizes. But the city is mainly a talent and trend pool. Few singers or groups are known outside of Berlin and even fewer outside of Germany. Blixa Bargeld's "Einstürzende Neubauten" have been a name for over 20 years and one-time German new-wave star Inga Humpe made it with the band "2-Raum-Wohnung". Sven Regener, singer of Element of Crime, achieved more notoriety as author of "Berlin Blues" than as a musician. The musically hip will know Die Ärzte, Rosenstolz and Wir sind Helden. But it was the scandalous rockers from the East, Rammstein, who were the first German language band to receive a gold record in the States. And then

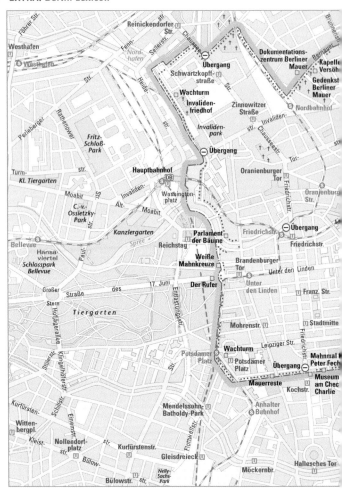

there was Peaches, the first international pop star from the Mitte district! Karl Lagerfeld photographed her, Iggy Pop recorded a song with her, and Madonna paid her the highest compliments for her work. The *Observer* named her, with her mix of hip-hop, techno and punk, the "most exciting pop artist this fall". The stars of 2007 were "Wir sind Helden".

Olympia

In the summer of 1936, the Olympic games were held in Berlin, and the city made a fine impression for a couple of weeks. In January 1933, President Hindenburg appointed Hitler Chancellor, one month later parliament burned in a fire "set by communists" and unexplained to this day, and then an unparalleled wave of

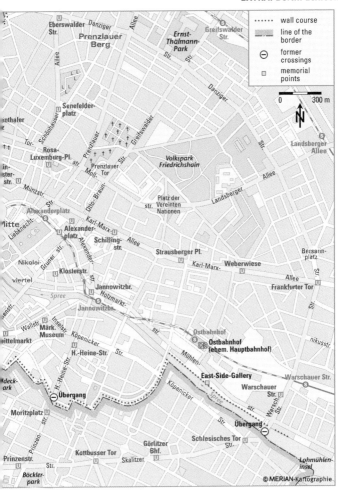

The former path of the Berlin Wall.

terror culminated in World War II. Still, the most successful athlete of these Olympics was not a blond Teuton but black American Jesse Owens, who won four gold medals.

Ostprodukte (products from the former East)

Every year, a trade fair for products from the former East is held in Berlin. It is well-attended, ever more so, perhaps, as the fall of the Wall drifts further into the past. Spreewald gherkins and paté from Rügen, mustard from Bautzen and chocolates from Halle. But now most of these things are available (again) in shops in East and sometimes West Berlin. Whereas people from the West are at a loss when it comes to most of these products, the eyes of people from the former East light up when they hear the names. The quality of some of the products has been improved upon, but with many it makes little difference whether they are now produced in the East or West. Some of the items on offer are undoubtedly from old stock, such as the "brandy-infused" Goldbrand, also called Goldi, or Kahla tableware from Thuringia, or Tempo-Linsen–lentils ready to eat in 10 minutes. The rare shops that exclusively sell commodities from the East also offer forbidden goods that were sold "under the counter" before the Wall fell: from books by censored authors to bottles of Gotano, Vermouth from Gotha, these were all goods that had to be stashed out of sight of the authorities.

Prussian Cultural Heritage

Prussia, of course, no longer exists. Dating from February 26, 1947, the Allied Control Council's law no. 46 dissolved the state. Its art treasures belonged from then on to the victorious nations of World War II. The Soviet Union ceded a large part of its spoils to the GDR. In the West, the Prussian Cultural Heritage Foundation was established in 1959. As part of the Unification Treaty, the organisational and physical consolidation of all collections and museums was resolved under the auspices of the Berlin State Museums – Prussian Cultural Heritage. The movement of the art works began then and has not stopped since.

S-Bahn-Bögen (railway arches)

The Berlin S-Bahn, whose services began in 1882 as the first European elevated railway, was built on a series of numbered brick vaults from Ostbahnhof (no. 1) to Savignyplatz (no. 731). These arches were rented as commercial spaces and then turned into market halls, stables, warehouses and workshops. Many of the busi-

nesses in the arches were closed when the state railway (administered by the GDR), following the currency reform of 1948, demanded that the tenants of the spaces in the West also base their sales on the East German Mark. After East German money (referred to as "alu chips") was abolished, the renaissance of the arches began, which is most picturesquely seen in the spaces under the S-Bahn station Hackescher Markt.

Salons

Berliners would only associate this term with a haircut if a renowned stylist in the capital requested their presence at an intellectual gathering in a private apartment. Mostly, however, as was the case 200 years ago, it's clever young women who use the term at poetry readings with select audiences seated on sofas and armchairs and enjoying snacks and a glass of wine. There are public salons, to which one may be invited, but the chances of getting the attention of a publisher in this city–where they have all but disappeared–is minimal. Sometimes one has to make do with a muse. The Academy of Art estimates more than 400 authors live in Berlin. That would be one-third of German book authors who could handle the city's moderate price levels. Opportunities to read for an unknown audience are plentiful. Every day there are a dozen readings, on lectern stages, in bars and observatories, and of course in department stores, book stores, agencies and cafés. Hundreds of book circles surely meet privately and exclusively on a regular basis.

Scheunenviertel

This term is used liberally in reports, and sometimes in travel guides, in reference to the former suburb of Spandau. The evident disrepair of the area around Oranienburger and Rosenthaler Strasse may have been the reason at the time of reunification for romantic claims that the neighbourhood was formerly a slum for eastern European Jews. But this is not the case. For a long time, it was the preferred residential area of bankers and philosophers, and the rear buildings housed workshops. It did not decay until after the war. The GDR government actually wanted to demolish much of it and rebuild. The real Scheunenviertel (shack district), outside the city walls in the 17th century, where poor immigrants actually did live, was somewhere between the Volksbühne theatre and Rosenthaler Platz.

Schwul (gay)
After Mayor Klaus Wowereit began his term with the now famous words "I am gay and that's okay", the tourism managers in town realised that so much candour could be good promotion and potentially appeal to a new audience of tourists. Even the hotel directory announces with rainbow colours which inn actively welcomes same-sex couples. Berlin has a Gay Museum, dealing with the history and persecution of homosexuals, and since 1987 a bronze teddy bear has been awarded to gay-lesbian productions as the gay brother of the Berlinale film festival bear. A large and open gay and lesbian scene exists in Schöneberg, where lots of bars and cafés and even rainbow-adorned snack stands can be found on Fuggerstrasse, Eisenacher Strasse and Motzstrasse. The scene is also present in Prenzlauer Berg on Gleimstrasse and Greifenhagener Strasse, and in Kreuzberg in Oranienstrasse and at Mehringdamm.

Sperrstunde (closing time)
The West Allies are responsible for the lack of a closing time law in Berlin. In 1949, they yielded to pressure from the head of the hotel and restaurant guild, Heinz Zellermayer. After

years of curfew, Berlin was able to reconnect with its prewar nightlife culture. Today you can still find bars that are open 24 hours a day in even the remotest of areas. But a warning to thirsty visitors: establishments can close at 1 a.m. if they want to, and many want just that.

Städtchen (little city)
It's called Majakowskiring on the map and was partially Kronprinzen and Viktoriastrasse until 1950, but most locals refer to it simply as "Städtchen". Ringstrasse in the Pankow neighbourhood of Niederschönhausen is definitely an historical site in Germany. After World War II, it was sectioned off as a residential area for representatives of the Soviet occupation forces and for those privileged with the task of building the new socialist society. Barriers prevented access and kept unwanted visitors at a distance. The first President of the GDR, Wilhelm Pieck, lived here. His successor, Walter Ulbricht, did too. Party General Secretary of the SED, later First Secretary of the Central Committee, and then Chairman of the State Council of the GDR, Prime Minister Otto Grotewohl, and the writer Johannes Robert Becher called it home. It was the heart of the GDR until 1972, when state leadership moved to Wandlitz.

Stalinallee
Until 1961, this was the name of Karl-Marx-Allee , a 300-foot-wide traffic artery with gigantic apartment blocks 300 to 1,000 feet long. After the war, housewives, pensioners and students had cleared the debris from the area which would later become the first socialist boulevard in Berlin, built between 1952 and 1953. The architects were committed to a Soviet-style neoclassicism with elements borrowed from Schinkel. Nowadays you would call it gingerbread style. In order to live here, one had to have

worked 1,000 hours. Compensation was low rent, a rooftop terrace, a rubbish chute, an intercom and a laundry drying space. Dedication to your building community was a given, and the young pioneers (a GDR youth organisation) sang Happy Birthday to residents. Stalin's death changed the architecture. The second phase of building, from 1961 to 1963, was one of the first projects with concrete slabs. On the eve of June 17, 1953, on the north block at the Weberwiese underground station, the first workers' strike against the standard ten percent increase in productivity took place. The next day saw the solidarity of workers from other factories and other parts of the populace. This incited the Soviet commander to declare a state of emergency in the city and had tanks roll forth to quash the uprising.

Steckschlüssel (Berlin key)

The name of this key in German means "push-through key" and pretty much describes the mechanism of the device that still drives some visitors mad if their host fails to explain how it functions before a late night out. The Berlin key, invented in 1912 in Kreuzberg, has two toothed ends. You open the door from the outside with a three-quarter turn, push the key through and lock the door again from the inside, thus freeing the key from the lock. In most houses, the Berlin key locks have been replaced with security locks and doorbells. Mostly found in older West apartments. The East gave up on it after the war.

Strassenbahn (streetcar)

In 1881, the world's first streetcar rolled into operation in Lichterfelde, in the southwest of Berlin: a two-axle carriage with 26 seats and not unlike today's tram. Inventor and businessman, Werner Siemens, had actually intended to build an elevated electric railway between Wedding and what is now Mehringplatz, but was not given authorisation because officials feared that cart grease would drip on passers-by. Most people would not have been able to travel with the new contraption anyway: a ride cost 20 Pfennigs, more than the average hourly wage. But the invention prevailed, replacing the horse-drawn and steam railcars. By 1929, the 394-mile network was transporting 929.1 million passengers. The rails in West Berlin were closed in 1967 to make room for automobiles, but new tracks are now being laid.

Telespargel (Tele-sparagus)

This nickname is only found in travel guides. The TV tower at Alexanderplatz is actually nicknamed St. Walter because a silver cross appears on the orb when the sun shines on it. Despite Walter Ulbricht's (leader in the GDR) indignation, the defect could not be changed.

Tuschkastensiedlung (paint-box estates)

This is the popular name for the first co-operative residential estate on Falkenberg in Altglienicke, built by future Bauhaus architect Bruno Taut from 1912 to 1915. The colourful façades were not well received by Berliners initially: people declared that the architect should be locked up, and even the papers took part in defaming him as a "Deformer of the general aesthetic".

The synthesis of pragmatic living, aesthetic architecture and social cohabitation soon gained some advocates, however. In the early 1920s, 135 families lived here between Akazienhof and Gartenstadtweg, having fled to the suburb from the tenements of the city.

At the beginning of the 1990s, the Berliner Bau- und Wohnungsgenossenschaft, founded in 1892, regained their former property. After

The "paint-box houses" were built by Bauhaus architect Bruno Taut as Berlin's first co-operative housing project.

renovations, the houses–again to the dismay of some of the occupants–were painted in their original colours: black, blue, lemon-yellow, pastel green, ochre, orange and rust-brown.

Übersicht (overview)

The nicest view of Berlin can be enjoyed via the fastest elevator in Europe. In less than 20 seconds visitors speed to the 24th floor of the beautiful wedge-shaped high-rise at Potsdamer Platz 1 (it's the 331-foot-high, dark-red brick building) to an observation deck at an impressive height of 295 feet. No funny feeling in your stomach, though, and no abrupt braking. Head and stomach arrive simultaneously. And then you look over the city through golden crenellations.

If you decide to climb the 285 steps inside of the Siegessäule, you'll be standing under the skirt of Victoria, or Gold-Else to locals, and looking out over the streets of Tiergarten from a height of 157 feet. The band

U2 filmed one of their videos here. From the café up in the TV tower on Alexanderplatz, a half-hour break will provide you with a full 360° view at 679 feet.

Volxgolf

It was a sensation and the talk of the town: children, functionaries and the unemployed were playing golf between sand, withered grass and weeds where the Olympiahalle was to be built – and where the World Youth Stadium had stood for the Youth of the World 2000 competition. It turned out differently though: Sydney, Australia, got the games and the German secret service decided to take up residence here. But you can still play golf in the middle of the city opposite Potsdamer Platz, south of the Spree at the track junction, even if the course is only vaguely reminiscent of the Volxgolf course. Most of the players are obviously practising for their course license.

Interesting facts about Berlin

Berlin has an expansive public transportation network. You can even reach the lovely outlying areas on the fast and easy S-Bahn.

From bicycle rentals and Turkish baths, to special tours, sightseeing flights and racetracks. Everything you need to know is briefly described for you here.

A historical time line of Berlin

1237
First documentation of Cölln, which eventually merged with Berlin.

1244
Berlin first mentioned in documents.

1307
Cölln and Berlin join to become one city.

1442
Friedrich II builds himself a palace in Berlin.

1539
Elector Joachim II converts to Protestantism.

1640-1688
Friedrich Wilhelm, known as the Great Elector after 1675, founds the Prussian state and expands Berlin as the capital.

1685
The Edict of Potsdam offers protection to persecuted French Huguenots.

1688-1713
Friedrich III crowns himself King Friedrich I of Prussia in 1701 in Königsberg.

1713-1740
Friedrich Wilhelm I, the Soldier King, redesigns the city. The pleasure gardens become military parade grounds. Victims of religious persecution from Bohemia settle in Neu-kölln. An excise tax wall is built around the city to secure the collection of taxes and prevent soldiers from deserting.

1740-1786
Under Friedrich the Great, Berlin becomes a true European capital and a centre of the Enlightenment. Potsdam is expanded, and Sanssouci Palace is built.

1786-1797
Reign of Friedrich Wilhelm II. Peacock Island is laid out in the style of early Romanticism.

1797-1840
Reign of Friedrich Wilhelm III: period of Restoration.

1806-1808
Napoleonic Wars: Berlin is occupied by French troops.

1838
The railway line Berlin–Potsdam is opened. Increase in industry and population.

1840-1861
Friedrich Wilhelm IV leads Berlin to an economic boom.

1848
March Revolution and demands for more democracy.

1861-1888
Wilhelm I appoints Otto von Bismarck as Prussian prime minister.

1866
Berlin is named capital of the North German Confederation.

1871
King Wilhelm I is proclaimed Emperor in Versailles, and Berlin becomes capital of the German Empire. The first economic upwinds are felt.

1888
Emperor Friedrich III dies after just 99 days of rule; his son becomes Emperor Wilhelm II.

1918
The Emperor abdicates and representative Phillipp Scheidemann proclaims the Weimar Republic from the balcony of the Reichstag.

1919
Socialists Karl Liebknecht and Rosa Luxemburg are murdered.

1920
Eight cities, 59 rural communities and 27 rural districts are incorporated into Berlin, increasing its population to 4 million.

1929
The Great Depression and 600,000 unemployed.

1933
Hitler becomes chancellor of the Reich, on February 27th the Reichstag mysteriously burns, on April 1 the boycotting of Jewish businesses begins, and on May 10th books are burned at Opernplatz.

1939
World War II officially begins with the invasion of Poland.

1942
The "Final Solution to the Jewish question" is reached at the Wannsee Conference.

1945
On April 30, Hitler and Eva Braun commit suicide in a bunker below Berlin, on May 2nd the Red Army invades, on May 8th German armed forces capitulate in Karlshorst.

1946
The city is divided into four sectors by the occupation forces.

1948
Currency reform in the West sectors of Berlin, the blockade begins, the Air Lift saves the city.

1949
Founding of the GDR with East Berlin as its capital.

1953
Uprising of June 17th in East Berlin.

August 13, 1961
Construction on the Berlin Wall begins with barbed wire and barricades.

1971
Four Power Agreement: transit routes to West Berlin through East Germany are guaranteed.

1989
The fall of the Wall.

1990
October 3rd: the two Germanies are reunited.

1991
On June 20th Berlin once again becomes Germany's capital.

1993
The president of the Federal Republic changes official residence from Bonn to Berlin.

1994
The Allied powers pull out of Berlin.

1999
The federal government moves to Berlin.

2001
After district reorganisation and consolidation, Berlin is composed of 12 greater boroughs rather than 23 smaller ones.

2006
Berlin is declared UNESCO City of Design.

2008
Tempelhof, the "Mother of all airports", closes down.

Never again speechless

Important words and phrases

yes	*ja*
no	*nein*
my pleasure, you're welcome	*bitte*
thank you	*danke*
Pardon?	*Wie bitte?*
I (don't) understand	*Ich verstehe (nicht)*
I beg your pardon / excuse me / sorry	*Entschuldigung*
Good morning	*Guten Morgen*
Hello	*Guten Tag*
Good evening	*Guten Abend*
My name is ...	*Ich heisse ...*
I come from ...	*Ich komme aus ...*
How are you?	*Wie geht's?*
Thanks, fine	*Danke, gut*
who, what, which	*wer, was, welcher*
how much (how many)	*wie viel(e)*
Where is ...	*Wo ist ...*
when	*wann*
how long	*wie lange*
Do you speak German?	*Sprechen Sie Deutsch?*
Good-bye	*Auf Wiedersehen*
See you soon	*Bis bald*
today	*heute*
tomorrow	*morgen*

Numbers

zero	*null*
one	*eins*
two	*zwei*
three	*drei*
four	*vier*
five	*fünf*
six	*sechs*
seven	*sieben*
eight	*acht*
nine	*neun*
ten	*zehn*
twenty	*zwanzig*
fifty	*fünfzig*
one hundred	*einhundert*
one thousand	*eintausend*

Days of the week

Monday	*Montag*
Tuesday	*Dienstag*
Wednesday	*Mittwoch*
Thursday	*Donnerstag*
Friday	*Freitag*
Saturday	*Samstag*
Sunday	*Sonntag*

With and without a car

How far is it to ...?	*Wie weit ist es nach ...?*
How do I get to ...?	*Wie kommt man nach ...?*
Where is ...?	*Wo ist ...?*
– the next garage	*– die nächste Werkstatt*
– the station/ bus terminal	*– der Bahnhof/ Busbahnhof*
– the nearest/ subway station/ bus stop	*– die nächste U-Bahn-/ Bus-Station/*
– the airport	*– der Flugplatz*
– tourist information	*– die Touristen-information*
– the next bank	*– die nächste Bank*
– the next petrol station	*– die nächste Tankstelle*
Where do I find a doctor/ a pharmacy?/	*Wo finde ich einen Arzt/ eine Apotheke?*
Fill up please	*Bitte voll tanken*
Regular petrol	*Normalbenzin*
Super	*Super*
Diesel	*Diesel*
right	*rechts*
left	*links*
straight ahead	*geradeaus*
around the corner	*um die Ecke*
I would like to rent a car/bike	*Ich möchte ein Auto/ein Fahr-rad mieten*
We had an accident	*Wir hatten einen Unfall*
A ticket to ... please	*Eine Fahrkarte nach ..., bitte*
I would like to change foreign currency	*Ich möchte ... in Euro wechseln*

Hotel

I'm looking for	*Ich suche*
– a hotel	*– ein Hotel*
– a guesthouse	*– eine Pension*
I'm looking for a room for ... people	*Ich suche ein Zimmer für ... Personen*
Do you have any vacancies?	*Haben Sie noch Zimmer frei?*
– for one night	*– für eine Nacht*
– for two days	*– für zwei Tage*
– for one week	*– für eine Woche*
I made a reservation for a room	*Ich habe ein Zimmer reserviert*
Do you offer a special weekend rate?	*Haben Sie zum Wochenende einen Sonderpreis?*
How much is the room?	*Wie viel kostet das Zimmer?*
– including breakfast	*– mit Frühstück*
– half board	*– mit Halbpension*
Can I have a look at the room?	*Kann ich das Zimmer sehen?*
I'd like to have this room	*Ich nehme das Zimmer*
Do you accept credit cards?	*Kann ich mit Kreditkarte zahlen?*

Restaurant

We have booked a table	*Wir haben einen Tisch reserviert*
Could I see the menu please?	*Die Speisekarte bitte*
Could I have the bill please?	*Die Rechnung bitte*
Do you accept credit cards?	*Akzeptieren Sie Kreditkarten?*
I would like to have a cup of coffee	*Ich hätte gern einen Kaffee*
cheers	*Auf Ihr Wohl*
Where are the washrooms (ladies/gents)?	*Wo finde ich die Toiletten (Damen/Herren)?*
waiter	*Kellner*
breakfast	*Frühstück*
lunch	*Mittagessen*
dinner	*Abendessen*

Shopping

Where do I find ...?	*Wo gibt es ...?*
Do you have ...?	*Haben Sie ...?*
What is that/ what do you call this?	*Was ist das/ wie heisst das?*
How much is this?	*Wie viel kostet das?*
I like it (I don't like it)	*Das gefällt mir (nicht)*
That's too expensive	*Das ist zu teuer*
I'll take it	*Ich nehme es*
I'd like to have 100 grams/ one pound/ one kilo	*Geben Sie mir bitte 100 Gramm/ ein Pfund/ ein Kilo*
Thank you, that's it	*Danke, das ist alles*
open/ closed	*geöffnet/ geschlossen*
bakery	*Bäckerei*
shopping centre	*Einkaufszentrum*
department store	*Kaufhaus*
market	*Markt*
butcher's	*Metzgerei*
household goods	*Haushaltswaren*
grocery	*Lebensmittelgeschäft*
stamps for a letter/ postcard	*Briefmarken für einen Brief/ eine Postkarte*
to England	*nach England*
to Australia	*nach Australien*
to Ireland	*nach Irland*

Government offices, banks, customs

Do you have anything to declare?	*Haben Sie etwas zu verzollen?*
I have lost my passport/ my wallet	*Ich habe meinen Pass/meine Brieftasche verloren*
I am looking for a bank machine	*Ich suche einen Geldautomaten*
I would like to place a call to England	*Ich möchte nach England telefonieren*

Useful addresses and travel service

Area: 344.28 square miles.
City boundary: 145 miles; east-west axis 28 miles; north-south axis 24 miles. Berlin is traversed by the Havel and Spree rivers, the Spree joining the Havel in Spandau.
Population: With 3.4 million inhabitants, Berlin is Germany's largest city. About 447,000 Berliners are not natives of Germany, coming from 183 different nations.
Administrative unit: Berlin is the capital of the Federal Republic of Germany as well as a federal state. The city is divided into 12 districs, each with approx. 300,000 inhabitants.
Languages: Berlinerisch, Swabian, Hessian, Turkish, Arabic, English, French, Russian, Polish... and German are spoken in Berlin.
Economy: Almost one-third of the labour force is employed in the service sector. The largest employers are the railways and banks. 94% of all businesses have fewer than 200 employees. About 134,000 people from around the world study at three universities, and roughly 30,000 more at the 13 polytechnics. After Paris and London, Berlin is the third-largest office market in Europe. 3,500 correspondents provide the world with news from the capital round the clock. The unemployment rate was 15.6 percent in August of 2007.

Purchasing tickets in advance is often advisable, but there can be surcharges of for the service, typically ten percent.

Abida   ⇢ p. 141, south F 16
Tickets forwarded worldwide. Credit cards accepted.

Detmolder Str. 65, 10715 Berlin;
Tel. 8 53 20 44

Berliner Festspiele
(Berlin Festival)   ⇢ p. 142, B 17
Budapester Str. 50, Charlottenburg,
10787 Berlin; Tel. 25 48 90

Berlin Ticket in KaDeWe
                               ⇢ p. 142, B 18
Tauentzienstr. 21–24, Schöneberg,
10789 Berlin; Tel. 2 17 77 54

Heckticket
Same-day tickets, often at a discount.
From 4 p.m.
– Ticket kiosk,   ⇢ p. 138, C 11
  Alexanderplatz, opposite McDonalds,
  Mitte; Tel. 24 31 24 31
– Hardenbergstr. 29 d ⇢ p.141, F 13
  (in the Deutsche Bank);
  Tel. 2 30 99 30

ACE Tel. 0 18 02/34 35 36

ADAC Tel. 0 18 02/22 22 22

ADFC
Help for cyclists; Tel. 4 48 47 24

American Express   ⇢ p. 138, A 12
Friedrichstr. 173, Mitte; Tel. 2017400;
Mon–Fri 9 a.m.–6 p.m., Sat
10 a.m.–13 p.m

Berliner Bank in Tegel Airport
                               ⇢ p. 89, b 3
Daily 8 a.m.–10 p.m; Tel. 4 17 85 40

Don't be intimidated by the traffic. Berlin and its surroundings are wonderful by bicycle. Plenty of signs indicate paths, sights and distances.
    Some hotels have bicycles available for their guests. Rentals can also

The two towers facing the Spree rise like the pillars of a modern castle. The futuristic construction has been the official seat of Germany's Ministry of the Interior since 1999.

be made at the train stations Zoologischer Garten (Tel. 29 74 93 19) and Lichtenberg (Tel. 29 71 29 49) and Alexanderplatz (Tel. 24 04 79 91).

Bicycle rental station
– Bergmannstr. 9, ⤳ p. 144, A 23
Kreuzberg; Tel. 2 15 15 66;
U-Bahn: Gneisenaustrasse
– Train Station Friedrichstrasse, Mitte;
Tel. 20 45 45 00; S-Bahn: Friedrichstrasse ⤳ p. 138, A 11
– Rosenthaler Str. 40/41, Hackesche Höfe, Mitte; Tel. 28 38 48 48;
S-Bahn: Hackescher Markt
⤳ p. 138, B 11
– Auguststrasse, Mitte;
⤳ p. 138, B 10
Tel. 28 59 96 61; U-Bahn: Rosenthaler Platz

There are 1,700 Call-a-bikes from DB in Berlin. Call the number on the bike to rent them. You'll need a credit card to make the payment.

BOAT TOURS
Reederei Riedel GmbH
⤳ p.144, C 23
Daily narrated tours, evening cruises and special events. Primary landings:

Hansabrücke, Haus der Kulturen der Welt, Märkisches Ufer/Jannowitzbrücke, Alte Börse, Potsdamer Brücke;
Tel. 6 93 46 46; www.reederei-riedel.de

Haveltour
→ p.88

Reederei Bruno Winkler
⤳ p. 134, C 3
City tours through historical and modern Berlin.
Tel. 3 49 95 95; www.reedereiwinkler.de; daily 11.10 a.m. and 3.10 p.m.; departs Schlossbrücke Charlottenburger Ufer (beside Charlottenburg Palace);
Duration: 3 hrs.

Stern und Kreisschifffahrt GmbH
This operation has 25 lines in and around Berlin. Primary landings: Schlossbrücke, Charlottenburg; Friedrichstrasse, Bahnhof, Mitte; Nikolaiviertel, Mitte; Schlesisches Tor, Kreuzberg; Hafen Treptow; Tel. 53 63 60-0

CAMPING
Campingplatz Am Krossinsee
⤳ p. 139, east E 12
Open all year, the largest and nicest campsite in Berlin. Separate area for

young people, waterskiing, bicycle and boat rental, rooms available.
Wernsdorfer Str. 38, Köpenick;
Tel. 6 75 86 87

CITY TOURS
Most of the theme-oriented tours start at Kurfürstendamm between Zoo (Rankestrasse) and Uhland-strasse. Some begin in the Nikolai district at Alexanderplatz (Forum Hotel). Prices range between €15 and €25 and last 2 to 3 hours. Tip: Most of the important sights in Berlin can be seen from bus lines 100 and 200 leaving Bahnhof Zoo towards Alexanderplatz.

Berlin's TV tower (→ p. 54), pictured here with the Neptune Fountain, offers a lovely panorama of the city.

GETTING THERE AND TRAVEL TIPS
By car
There are direct autobahn connections from Hamburg and Rostock, from Cologne/Bonn via Hanover, from Frankfurt/Main via Braun-schweig and from Munich via Leipzig, from Dresden and Szczecin (German: Stettin)/Poland. All autobahns lead to the Berliner Ring, the beltway around the city.

For those intending to drive to Berlin, a glance at the city's motor-way network is advisable. Each area of town is easily reachable from the correct exit. Brandenburg's rural roads will also take you—if slowly—to the capital.

By bus
BerlinLinienBus is proving a real competitor for rail and air carrier, at least as far as the prices are concerned. More than 350 towns in Germany and Europe, from Hamburg to Munich, Amsterdam, Paris or Vienna, are all connected to Berlin by long-distance bus. The connections to Poland and the Baltic are being expanded.
Busbahnhof (Bus station)
⋯→ p. 140, A 13
Masurenallee 4–6, Charlottenburg;
Domestic travel tel. 8 61 93 31;
European travel tel. 3 01 03 80;
www.berlinlinienbus.de;
U-Bahn: Kaiserdamm,
S-Bahn: Messe Nord/ICC
Bus: 104, X49

By train
Connecting with to its former status as Central Europe's rail hub, Berlin boasts the continent's largest and most modern train station. This has led to the central train stations in the West (Zoologischer Garten) and the East (Ostbahnhof) losing their significance.

The most important railway stations are Hauptbahnhof (central station) in Mitte, Bahnhof Gesundbrunnen to the north and the former Papestrasse Bahnhof, now Südkreuz, to the south. The latter two are also S-Bahn stops on the rail beltway around the inner city. Long-distance trains no longer leave from Ostbahnhof to northern and southern Germany, but still go to Frankfurt/Main and Hanover. Only night trains to Munich and Zurich stop at Bahnhof Zoologischer Garten now. The new stations for regional transport are Jungfernheide, Gesundbrunnen, Potsdamer Platz, Südkreuz and Lichterfelde Ost.

It's not only the Deutsche Bahn going to and from Berlin. The Vogtlandbahn connects the capital with Hof (www.vogtlandbahn.de), Connex travels to Stralsund as well as Gera (www.interconnex.com) and the Harz (www.hex-connex.de).

Deutsche Bahn
Information and Reservations
Tel. 1 18 61, free schedule information
08 00/1 50 70 90; www.bahn.de

By air
Low fares to Berlin are offered from many departure points. The best information is on the internet.

Tegel Airport (TXL)
"Otto Lilienthal" ⤏ p.89, b 3
Infoline tel. 01 80/5 00 01 86; public transport connections: express bus X9 to Bahnhof Zoo (about 30 min.), airport bus TXL runs every ten minutes until 9 p.m. and stops at the new central station; Bus 109 to Jakob-Kaiser-Platz and Zoo; 5 miles to the centre.

Schönefeld Airport (SXF)
⤏ p.89, b 3
Infoline tel. 0180/5000186; RB 14 (train) every 30 Min. from Bahnhof Zoo; S45 via Tempelhof to Messegelände, S9; Express bus X7 from U-Bahnhof Rudow; 12 miles to centre (about 50 min.)

Tempelhof Airport (THF)
⤏ p.89, b 3
Flight information tel. 0180/5000186 (daily 5 a.m.– 11 p.m.); public transport connections: U6 via Stadtmitte and Friedrichstrasse; Bus 119 via Kreuzberg to Kurfürstendamm; 3 miles to centre (closed from Oct. 2008)

Information and reservations
Austrian Airlines
Tegel Airport, Lufthansa counter
Tel. 0 18 03/00 05 20; www.aua.com

Lufthansa
Tegel Airport, main hall;
Tel. 88 75 61 28-9
Schönefeld Airport, Terminal A;
Tel. 88 75 57 15-17
Travel & Touristik GmbH, Friedrichstr. 185–190; Tel. 20 39 19 12-18,
0 18 03/80 38 03; www.lufthansa.com

INFORMATION
Berlin Tourismus
Marketing GmbH ⤏ p. 143, E 18
Am Karlsbad 11, 10785 Berlin;
Tel. 0 30/25 00 25, Fax 25 00 24 24;
www.btm.de

Tourist information
– Brandenburger Tor ⤏ p. 137, F 8
 Pariser Platz, Mitte; south wing;
 Apr–Oct. daily 9.30 a.m.–6 p.m.,
 Nov.–Mar daily 10 a.m.–6 p.m.
– Neues Kranzler Eck
  ⤏ p. 142, A 17
Kurfürstendamm 21/Passage;
Mon–Sat 9.30 a.m.–8 p.m., Sun 9.30 a.m.–6 p.m.
– Bundestagspavillon ⤏ p. 137, E 7
 Pavilion at parliament builiding
– Hauptbahnhof ⤏ p. 137, E 7
Europaplatz entrance; daily
8 a.m.–10 p.m.

Info points
– Tegel Airport ⤏ p. 89, b 3
Lufthansa City Center, Innenring, opposite gate 9; daily 7.30 a.m.–7 p.m.
– Schönefeld Airport
  ⤏ p. 89, b 3

Terminal B, ground floor centre;
Mon–Fri 9 a.m.–7 p.m., Sat, Sun
10 a.m.–6 p.m.
– Services for the disabled
⋯⋯⟩ p. 138, A 12

Berliner Behinderten Verband
Jägerstr. 63 d, Mitte; Tel. 2 04 38 47
– Ground transport for the disabled
Tel. 4 10 21 11 (5 a.m–1 a.m.)

INTERNET
www.btm.de
Berlin tourist information web site:
hotels, public transport, tickets, exhibitions, special offers and more.
www.berlin.de
Berlin's official web site: city administration and offices, events, sports,
city map, businesses and tourist information.
www.berlinonline.de
Database with practical information
about events, cinema, theatre,
restaurants as well as pharmacies,
cultural sites and bank machines.

www.berlin-airport.de
Web site for Berlin's airports Schönefeld, Tegel and Tempelhof, with
arrival and departure times.
www.art-in-berlin.de
Online magazine with current information on art, architecture, literature
and exhibitions in Berlin.

LOST AND FOUND (FUNDBÜRO)
Zentrales Fundbüro (main office)
⋯⋯⟩ p. 143, F 20
Platz der Luftbrücke 6; Tempelhof;
Allgemeine Fundsachen Tel. 75 60 31 01;
U-Bahn: Platz der Luftbrücke

BVG (Berliner Verkehrsbetriebe)-
Fundbüro ⋯⋯⟩ p. 143, D 19
Lost and Found of Berlin's public
transport (BVG)
Potsdamer Str. 180/182;
Tel. 1 94 49; U-Bahn: Kleistpark

Deutsche Bahn (also S-Bahn)
Fundbüro

*During a tour of Museum Island (→ p. 56) one of the attractions is the glass
spindle by architect Ieoh Ming Pei. It is the new symbol of the German Historical
Museum (→ p. 73).*

German railway (including suburban rail lines) lost and found
Tel. 01 80/5 99 05 99

There are nine daily newspapers in Berlin. For a current overview of weekly cultural events you can take a look at the *Tagesspiegel* and the *Berliner Zeitung* on Thursday, for example. In alternating two-week intervals, *Zitty* and *Tip* offer a complete calendar of events with leisure and restaurant tips, theatre, film, festival and event critiques. Once a month the city guide "Prinz" appears with current leisure, lifestyle and eating tips. Furthermore, there is the MERIAN-Magazin Berlin, with exclusive tips, detailed maps and comprehensive travel services.

MEDICAL ASSISTANCE
Medical emergencies
Tel. 31 00 31

Dental emergencies
Tel. 89 00 43 33

Private patient emergency services
Tel. 08 00/7 11 21 12

Poison control centre
Tel. 1 92 40

Emergency pharmacy services
Tel. 1 18 80

POST OFFICE
Offices with longer opening hours:

Friedrichstrasse   ⋯⟩ p.138, A 11
Next to the train station;
Mo–So until 10 p.m.

Flughafen Tegel   ⋯⟩ p. 89, b 3
Tgl. 6.30–21 Uhr

SIGHTSEEING FLIGHTS
Air Service Berlin
View the capital from a bi-plane

(AN-2, €105), DC-3 (used during the Airlift, €150) or helicopter (€105) with departures from Tempelhof, or take a sea plane from Treptow.
Registration 14 days beforehand at Tempelhof airport (after closure, Schönefeld airport): Tel. 53 21 53 21

SPORT
Golf   ⋯⟩ p. 143, E 18
Opposite Potsdamer Platz is a driving range suitable for everyone, from beginner to expert.
Schöneberger Ufer 7; Tiergarten;
Tel. 22 69 78 44,
www.globalgolf-berlin.net; U-Bahnhof:
Gleisdreieck; daily 9 a.m.–10 p.m.

Inline skating
⋯⟩ p. 143, southwest A 16
Almost 2.5 miles of the Kronprinzessinweg in Zehlendorf free of vehicle traffic.
S-Bahn: Nikolassee

Climbing
Magic Mountain Climbing Center
⋯⟩ p. 137, north F 5
"Europe's largest climbing arena" offers 200 routes of varying difficulty and 60 top ropes and magic mountains. The base camp has a spa with sauna and steam bath. Extras: Internet, shop and a fitness studio.
Böttgerstr. 20–26; S-Bahn: Gesundbrunnen

Horse racing
Galopprennbahn Hoppegarten
⋯⟩ p. 139, east F 10
One of the nicest horseracing tracks in Germany. Operating since 1868. Also hosts open-air concerts.
Regular race days from Jun–Oct.;
S-Bahn: Hoppegarten; by car: B1/B5
direction Biesdorf/Kaulsdorf, exit
Dahlwitz-Hoppegarten, 800 m left

Swimming
Badeschiff   ⋯⟩ p. 145 east F 22
Public pool built into the Spree river with a man-made beach on land in

summer; becomes a sauna in winter with a small outdoor terrace.

Eichenstr. 4 (Arena grounds), Treptow; U-Bahn: Schlesisches Tor; daily 10 a.m.–midnight

Turkish baths
Hammam ⸺⟩ p. 145, D 22

Women-only zone with a cosy oriental atmosphere. Massage, baths and rose tea.

Mariannenstr. 6, Kreuzberg; U-Bahn: Kottbusser Tor; Mon 3 p.m.–10 p.m., Tue–Sun noon–10 p.m.

Hot springs at the Europa-Center
⸺⟩ p. 142, B 17

Thermal baths above the rooftops of Berlin. Three steam baths, massage parlour and solarium.

Nürnberger Str. 7, Wilmersdorf; U-/S-Bahn: Zoologischer Garten; Mon–Sat 10a.m.–midnight, Sun 10 a.m.–9 p.m.

Hi-Flyer ⸺⟩ p.143, F 17

Float above Berlin in a hot-air balloon, weather permitting of course.

Wilhelm-/Ecke Zimmerstrasse; Tel. 2 26 67 88 11; daily from 10 a.m

SUGGESTED READING

First published in 1939, "Goodbye to Berlin" by Christopher Isherwood tells the story of a bunch of misfits who made the capital their home before World War II. The film "Cabaret" was based on this novel (Vintage, 1989).

Brian Ladd's elegantly written and well-illustrated "The Ghosts of Berlin: Confronting German History in the Urban Landscape" amounts to a brief history as well as a guide to the city (The University of Chicago Press, 1998).

"Berlin Blues" by Sven Regener is an entertaining look at life and modern-day decadence in the capital. The novel also served as the basis for the successful German film (Vintage, 2006).

TOURS
ADFC ⸺⟩ p. 138, A 10

Be it cycling maps or bike repair, online tour planning or guided tours through Berlin or Brandenburg, this is a full service for cyclists.

Brunnenstr. 28, Mitte; Tel. 4 48 47 24; www.adfc-berlin.de; Mo–Fr 12–20, Sa 10–16 Uhr

Hear We Go audio tours

Currently available in English for the Berlin Wall. Bring your headphones and either a CD, MP3 or mobile phone music player and follow the voice wherever it leads you. This recorded guide will give you a unique look at the once divided city.

MegaeinsVerlag; www.hearwego.de

Babelsberg Studio Tour

Foray into the world of film, present and past. Real sets, props, scenery and shows.

Berliner Autoren Führungen
(Berlin author tours)
⸺⟩ p. 138, B 10

Year-round themed walks: back courtyards, literature, film, city and architectural history.

Grosse Hamburger Str. 29, Mitte; Tel. 2 82 58 77; www.berliner-autoren-fuehrungen.de

Berliner Geschichtswerkstatt
(Berlin history workshop)
⸺⟩ p. 142, C 19

City tours by boat, women's history, literature, emigrant stories and adventures.

Goltzstr. 49, Schöneberg; Tel. 2 15 44 50; www.berlinergeschichtswerkstatt.de

Berlin Walks

For English language tours of the city.

Harbigstr. 26; Tel. 3 01 91 94; www.berlinwalks.com

Fahrrad Kultour

Sightseeing by bicycle, in Brandenburg too.

Tel. 61 70 96 52;
www.fahrrad-kultouren.de

Frauentouren ⟶ p. 139, east F 11
Female figures in the city's sculpture,
history, literature and salons.
Sophienstr. 32; Tel. 2 81 03 08

Kulturbüro ⟶ p. 138, north C 9
Themed tours including, theatre, architecture and art. Bicycle tours too.
Greifenhagener Str. 62; Tel. 4 44 09 36;
www.stadtverfuehrung.de

StattReisen
⟶ p. 136/137, north C/D 5
History, literature, film, theatre, Jewish Berlin, Wall walks, Pankow, Tempelhof, Potsdam.
Malplaquetstr. 5; Tel. 4 55 30 28;
www.stattreisen.berlin.de

Unterwelten ⟶ p. 138, north A 9
"Underworlds" offers tours of the
dark side of the capital city. The
Unterwelt Museum features exhibits
and information on Berlin's "subterranean" history.
Bahnhof Gesundbrunnen;

Tel. 49 91 05 17;
www.berliner-unterwelten.de

ZeitReisen ⟶ p.138, A 12
Tours, excursions and a video bus
ride through history.
Unter den Linden 40, Mitte;
Tel. 44 02 44 50; www.zeit-reisen.de

TRANSPORT
Car
Stretching nearly 32 miles from west
to east and 24 miles from north to
south makes Berlin tempting for a
car ride–until you find yourself stuck
in a traffic jam. Since January 1, 2008,
an emission sticker is required for
cars in the inner city (within the
S-Bahn loop).

If you want to park your car near
Ku'damm or Unter den Linden
or near the shopping areas of other
districts, you will need to purchase a
ticket and expect frequent checks.
The spaces are metered from Mon–Fri
from 9 a.m.–8 p.m. and Sat 9 a.m.–
2 p.m. (or 7 p.m.), around the Hackescher Markt until midnight. The
parking fee for 30 min. is €0.50 to

Hoppegarten: traditional horse racing track.

€2, in the parking garages near Zoo up to €3.50 per hour. Parking without checking the information in detail can very easily end up in your car getting towed at costs of €149 from 7 a.m. to 6 p.m. and €188 at night, on weekends and holidays.

Car rentals are available at Tegel airport and in the Europa-Center.

Public Transport

Berlin has a dense network of subways (U-Bahn) and suburban railways (S-Bahn), complemented by bus lines and night buses starting at 12:30 a.m. All of the subway lines (except the U4) run every 15 minutes on weekend nights and nights before holidays. There are three different fare zones. Prices as of April 1, 2008: a single ticket for two zones (A,B), valid for two hours (not for return journey) costs €2.10 (children and large dogs are €1.40), for all zones €2.80 (reduced €2.00), for short trips (three stations with U-Bahn or S-Bahn or regional train, or six stations with the bus or tram) €1.30 (reduced €1.00). A day pass costs €6.10 (reduced €4.40) for two zones, €6.50 (reduced €4.80) for three zones, a small-group ticket for one day (two zones) is €15.40, for three zones €15.60. Visitors should also think about getting a WelcomeCard, a transferable 7-day pass for two zones that costs €25.40 or, for three zones it costs €31.30.

BVG-Call-Center: Tel. 1 94 49; www.bvg.de; information for your mobile telephone: wap.bvg.de

WelcomeCard

The WelcomeCard is available at all BVG-associated ticket counters, in tourist information centres and in hotels, is valid for either two or three days in Berlin and Potsdam and costs €16.50 for one adult and up to three children under 14 years for two days or €21.00 for three days. In addition to unlimited travel on public transport, this ticket also offers many discounts for excursions, tours and boat rides in both cities for example.

Taxis

The short-trip fare for up to 2 kilometres or five minutes (from hailing) costs €3.50, otherwise €1.58 (7 Km) up to €1.20/Km; Tel. 21 01 01, 44 33 22, 96 20 52, 6 90 22. ; All of the major taxi dispatchers are available under one telephone number: 08 00/8 00 11 44.

Velo-Taxis

They're not the bone-shaking velocipedes, painted with nostalgic images of a better world, that some may know from the so-called Third World. Yellow, orange or green, they're all called velo-taxis, as a symbol of a new awareness of the environment, and are basically the high-tech rickshaws that you'll find in bus lanes, on bicycle paths and in parks pedalling passengers through the capital. In 1997, 150 drivers were the first in the country to cycle into a new occupation. A trial phase became a trial in another sense, as drivers and passengers suffered a barrage of abuse from the sidelines. Finally everything was ready, with three routes run from noon to 6 p.m. until October (1km costs €1). You just have to hail one.

Route 1: Wittenbergplatz to Adenauerplatz; Route 2: Zoo to Brandenburger Tor; Route 3: Brandenburger Platz to Alexanderplatz.

Velo-taxi stands: Wittenbergplatz, Adenauerplatz, Zoo, Brandenburger Tor, Alexanderplatz.

Travel weather

Though the frozen lakes and rivers can be beautiful in the cold winters, Berlin is really a summer city.

Starting in May, with the first rays of sun, the gruff winter Berliners suddenly become noticeably friendlier, as the restaurants and cafés spread out onto the sidewalks.

Maps

Orientation made easy, with grid squares and all
of the important sights and attractions.

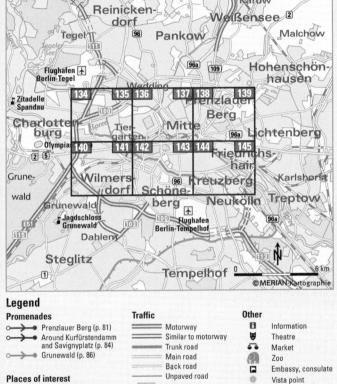

© MERIAN-Kartographie

Legend

Promenades

○━➤ Prenzlauer Berg (p. 81)
○━➤ Around Kurfürstendamm
and Savignyplatz (p. 84)
○━➤ Grunewald (p. 86)

Places of interest

🔟 MERIAN-TopTen
🔟 MERIAN-Tip
▢ Place or building
of interest
✳ Cultural landmark
⛪ Church; monastery
♜ Castle, fortification
☽ Mosque
✡ Synagogue
🏛 Museum
🗿 Monument, memorial
⌒ Caves

Traffic

═══ Motorway
═══ Similar to motorway
─── Trunk road
─── Main road
─── Back road
┈┈┈ Unpaved road
▦ Pedestrian zone
P Parking
B H Bus station;
Bus stop
U Underground
S S-Bahn
DB Train station
✈ ✈ Airport;
airfield

Other

ℹ Information
♟ Theatre
♣ Market
🐒 Zoo
▣ Embassy, consulate
☀ Vista point
✝✝✝ Cemetery
Ψ Ψ Muslim Cemetery
L L L Jewish Cemetery
▭ National park,
nature preserve
✻ National park

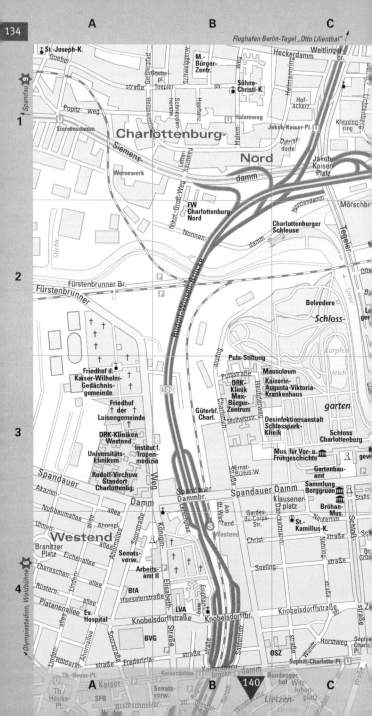

A **B** **C**

Flughafen Berlin-Tegel „Otto Lilienthal"

St.-Joseph-K.
Goebel-
M.-Bürger-Zentr.
Weltlinger br.
Heckerdamm

Popitz- weg
Sühne-Christi-K.
Hofackerz.

Siemensdamm
Halemweg
Jakob-Kaiser-Pl.
Klausing-ring

Charlottenburg-
Dahrendorfel

Wernewerk
Siemens-
damm
Jakob-Kaiser-Platz

Nord

FW Charlottenburg Nord
Mörschbr.

Nonnendamm
Charlottenburger Schleuse

Fürstenbrunner Br.
Belvedere

Fürstenbrunner
Schloss-

Karpfen teich

Friedhof d. Kaiser-Wilhelm-Gedächnis-gemeinde
Puls-Stiftung
Mausoleum
Kaiserin-Augusta-Viktoria-Krankenhaus
garten

Friedhof der Luisengemeinde
DRK-Klinik Max-Bürger-Zentrum
Putzstraße

Güterbf. Charl.
Desinfektionsanstalt
Schlosspark-Klinik

DRK-Kliniken Westend
Mollwitzstr.
Schloss Charlottenburg

Universitäts-klinikum
Institut f. Tropenmedizin
Mus. für Vor- u. Frühgeschichte
gew

Spandauer
Rudolf-Virchow Standort Charlottenbg.
Gartenbau-amt

Akazien-
Damm
Dammbr.
Spandauer Damm
Sammlung Berggruen
Stalls.

Nußbaumallee
allee
Ernst-Bumm-W.
Klausenerplatz
Bröhan-Mus.

Ulmen-
Ahornpl.
Westend
Gardes-du-Corps-Str.
St.-Kamillus-K.
Sch

Westend
Christ-

Branitzer Platz
Eichehallee
Senatsverw.
Seeling-
straße

Eberaschen-
allee
Arbeits-amt II

Rüstern-
BfA
Haeselerstraße
Ev. Hospital
LVA
Knobelsdorffstr.
straße

Platanenallee
allee

Linden-
Knobelsdorffstraße
Knobelsdorffbr.

BVG
Horstweg

Hölderlin-
straße
Fredericia-
OSZ
Sophie-Charlotte-Pl.

Th.-Heuss-Pl.
A Kaiser
Senatsverw.
B 140
Bundesbof
Witzlebenplatz
C

Th.-Heuss-Pl.
SFB
Bredtschneider-
Lietzen-

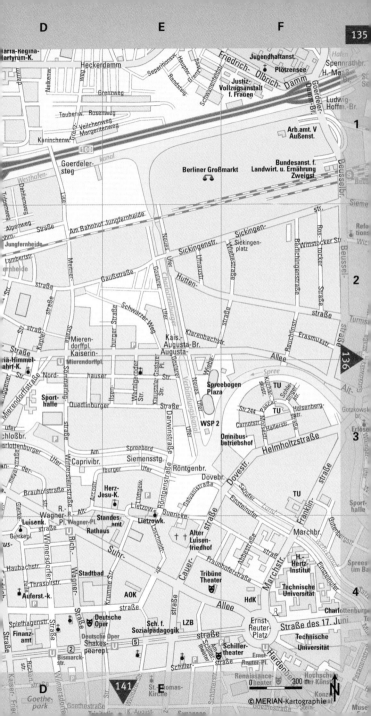

A B C

Spennrathbr.
H.-Maaß-Br.
Südl.
Seestraßenbr.
Ludwig-
Hoffm.-Br.

Hafen

Becken III

Berlin-Spandauer

Nordufer

Fohrer Str.
Buchstraße

Pekinger Pl.

R.-
Koch-
Inst.
Fohrer
Str.

Torfstraßensteg

Schiffahrts-

Westhafen

Westhafen-
str.

Schifferk.

Friedrich-

Krause-

stral

Reusselbr.

Becken II

Behala

Becken I

Westhafen

S Westhafen

5

Beusselstr.

Güterbf.
Moabit

Quitzow-

str.
Unionpl.

Sport-
halle

Putlitzbrücke

Stephan-
pl.

Salt-
wafeter
str.
Putlitz-

Stephan-

Havelberger

Rathenower Str.

straße

Perleberger

Feldzeug-
meisterstraße

Siemens-

Unionstraße

Birken-

straße

Birkenstr.

U

straße

Stadt-
bücherei

Rathenower Str.

Hannoversche

Krupp-

str.

Reforma-
tionskirche

Wiclef-

Straße

Straße

havener

straße

HL.-
Geist-K.

Perle-

Birken-

Witznacker

Kinder-
zentrum

6

Waldenser

St.-
Paulus-
Kirche

Straße

Emdener

Oldenburg

Markt-
halle

Bremer

Bugenhagenstr.

Wilhelmstr.

Bredow

Perle

Lübecker

Krankenhaus
Moabit

Moabit

Bandel-

Dreysestraße

S

Turmstraße

Stadt-
bibliothek

Rathaus

Otto-
platz

Moabit

U Turmstr.

St.-
Laurentius-K.

Ges-
amt

str.

Turmstraße

† †

St.-

Kriminalger.

Amtsgericht

135

Zwingli-

straße

Hansa-
theater

Heimatmuseum

Kl.
Tiergarten

U-haft-
anstalt

Alt-

Gotzkowsky-
br.

Feuerwehr
Moabit

Erlöserk.

Landes-
bildst.

Agricola-

Levetzow-

str.

Zinzen-
dorfstr.

Essener

Str.

Dortmunder

Str.

Holsteiner

Berl.
Kammer-
spiele

Lessingbr.

Spree

Johannis-Kirche

BM des
Innern

Oberwv.-
Gericht

Moabiter
Br.

Gericke-
steg

Kirchstraße

Thomasiusstraße

Alt-

Carl-
von-
Ossietz-
Park

Melanchthonstr.

7

Wullenweber-
steg

Landes-
bildst.

Tile-
Wardenberg-Str.

Hansabr.

Flensburger

Straße

Bundes-
präsidial-
amt

Spener-

Sport-
halle

Wullen-

weberstr.

Grips
Theater

Hanseat-

Hansa-

Akad. d.
Künste

Bellevueufer

Bellevue

St.-
Ansgar-K.

U Hansapl.

Altonaer

Teehaus

Bellevue

Schloss
Bellevue

Spreeweg

Spreestadt
(im Bau)

TU

Schleswiger Uter

Bach-

str.

Handelallee

Engl. Garten

Viertel

Straße

Bismarck

Roon

Moltke

Ernst-
Reuter-
Haus

Klopstockstraße

Händelallee

Kaiser-
Friedrich-
Gedächtnis-Kirche

Großer

Siegessäule

8

Charlottenburger
Tor

des 17. Juni

Straße

Charlottenbg. Br.

Schleuseninsel

Tier-

Berlin-Pavillon

2 5

17. Juni

Bremer

Weg

Weg

Stern

Büffel-
jagd

Eber-
jagd

Flora

Rud.-Drawe-
Inst.

Müller-Breslau-Straße

Tiergarten

Weg

Fuchs-
jagd

Fasanerieallee

Hofjägerallee

A B C

Zoolog.
Garten

Museum für

Zoologischer

Lichtenstein-
br.

Neuer
See

Wisent

Großer Weg

Rousch-

Volks-
lied

142

D E F

Schutzendorfer Str.
Reinickendorfer Str.
Fenn-straße
Fennbr.
Mettannpl.
Am Nordhn.
E.-Hess-Eisstadion
Chausseestr.
Neue Hochstr.
Liesenstr.
Gartenstr.
Ackerstraße
Friedh. d. St.-Hedw.-G., Franz. Domgem.
St.-Sebastians-K.
5
Handels-hochsch.
Wöhlertstr.
Gartenplatz
Heide-ke
Heide-berger
Fennbr.
Kieler Br.
Nordhn-brücke
Nordhafen
Scharnhorststr.
Schwartz-kopffstr.
Schwartz-kopffstr.
Pflugstr.
Stettiner Tunnel
Lazarus-Kranken-haus

Hamburger u. Lehrter Bf. Containerbf.
96
Bundeswehr-krankenhaus

Invaliden-Friedhof
Habersaathstr.
Museum für Naturkunde u. Zool. Mus.
Univ.
Zinnowitzer Str.
Chausseestr.
Honigmond Garden Hotel
Invalide
N
1
Amts-gericht rafanstalt stadion
96
BM für Wirtschaft u. Technologie
Inva-lidenpark
Invalidenstr.
Univ.
Brechthaus/Archiv
Dorotheenstädt. und Friedrichsw. Friedhof
6
Sporthalle
Döberitzer Str.
Mina-Cauer-Str.
Museum für Gegenwart
Pl. v. d. Neuen Tor
Hannoversche
Rob.-Koch-Str.
Humboldt-
Oranien-Tor
Oranien-Tor
138

Komb. tallen-u. Freibad
Friedhof
Leiter Str.
Akademie d. Künste
Sand-krugbr.
Ladestr.
Europa-pl.
Humboldt-hafen
Universitäts-klinikum
Luisenstraße
Philippstr.
Straße
Universität
Charité
Kammer-spiele
Deutsches Theater

Städt. Altenheim Tiergarten
Invalidenstraße
Alt-Moabit
J.-Tschirsche-Str.
Hauptbahnhof
DB S U
Washington-pl.
Alexanderufer
Kapelleufer
Charité
Schumannstr.
Albrecht
Bertolt-Brecht-Pl.
Berliner Ensemble
7
Moabit
B. Benz-Str.
R.-Hirsch-Str.
Heinemann-Br.
Spreebogen-park
Uferstr.
Reinhardtstr.
Karl-pl.
Marienstraße
Admirals-palast
Die Distel

Ingeborg-Drewitz-Allee
Moltke-br.
W.-Brandt-Str.
Otto-v.-Bismarck-Str.
Paul-Löbe-Haus
Künstler-heim Luise
Lüders Haus
2
Schiffbauer
Friedrichstr.
S
Georg

Haus der Kulturen der Welt/Kongresshalle
Paul-Löbe
H.-v.-Gagern-Str.
Scheidemannstraße
Reichstags-gebäude
Deutscher Bundes-tag
Reichstagufer
Marschallbr.
Reichstagufer
Dorotheen
Bundes-presseamt
Dorotheenstr.

Tiergarten
Foster-Dulles-Allee
Platz der Republik
Spreeweg
Sowjetisches Ehrenmal
Platz des 18. März
Brandenburger Tor
Pariser Pl.
Brandenburger Tor
S
Unter den Linden
Unter
Komische Oper

Kleiner Stern
Straße des 17. Juni
Naturschutz-u. Grünfl.amt
Bremer Weg
Amazone
Löwen-denkmal
Ahornsteig
Goethe
Akademie d. Künste
Behrenstr.
Stasi-Die Ausst.
Holocaust-Mahnmal
Hochsch. f. Musik
Bocca di Bacco
8

Tiergarten
Herkules mit der Lyra
Musiker-denkmal
Ebertstraße
Hannah-Arendt-Str.
A. d. Kolonnade
Bundes-ministerien
Jäger-
Tauben-

Mitte
umkmal
Großer-Weg
Königin Luise
Friedrich Wilhelm III.
Musikinstrumentenmus.
Ahornstraße
Lessing
96
Kemper-pl.
Bellevuestraße
Lennéstraße
Ebertstraße
In den Ministergärten
Gertrud-Kolmar-Str.
Voß-
Mohrenstr.
Mohrenstr.
Kronen-
Sta

Wagner
Prinz Wilhelm Kunstgewerbe-museum
Kultur-forum
143
Filmmus.
Sony Center
Potsd. Pl.
Potsdamer Pl.
Bethlehem-kirchpl.
Mus.
Bundes-

0   300 m
Leipziger Str.
© MERIAN-Kartographie
N

imholtzplatz

D **E** **F**

Danziger Str.

Stadt-bibliothek

Städt. Krankenhaus

Kiga

Ernst-Thälmann-Park

Greifswalder Str.

Storkower Str.

Volks-

park

Anton

Saefkow

straße

Kollwitzstr.

Allee

Chodowiecki-

Straße

Jablonski-

Christburger

straße

John-Schehr-Str.

Eugen-Schönhaar-Str.

R.-Schwarz-Str.

Straße

Kollwitz-

platz

agoge

Prenzlauer

Marienburger

straße

Straße

D.-Bonhoerer-Straße

Danziger

Schehr-

Straße

Wasserturm

Immanuel-kirche

Immanuelkirchstraße

Raabestr.

twins

Heim-Roller-Str.

VHS

Pasteur-

Hufeland

str.

Arnswalder Pl.

Otto

str.

Straße

Niederkirchner-

K.-

Str.

Hans-

straße

Knigrode-

Advents-kirche

St.-Marien-Nikolaigem.

St.-Georgen-Gem.

St. Gertrud

Greifswalder Str.

Bötzow-

straße

Friedrichshain

Virchow-

Fitness-center

Prenzlauer Berg

Pl. am Königs-tor

Am

Königs-tor

St.-Bartholomäus-Kirche

Volkspark

St.-Nikolai-Gem.

Georgenkirchst.

Friedenstr.

Mendels

sohnstr.

Friedrichshain

Krankenhaus im Friedrichshain

Moll-

Str.

Barnimstraße

Weinstraße

Freilicht-bühne

Friedrichshain

Stat. Bundes-u. Landesamt

straße

Berolina

Mollst.

Pl. d. Vereinten Nationen

Strausbg.-Str.

Frieden-

Landsberger

Allee

Friedhof der St.-Georgen-Gem.

Haus der Gesundheit

Berolinastraße

Weidenweger str.

Straße

Palisaden-

Friedrichstraße

Auferste-hungs-kirche

Pufendorf-str.

Diestelmeyerstr.

Friedhof d. Parochial-u.-St.-Petri-Gem.

Schillingstr.

des ers ress-

Karl-

Jacobystraße

Kino International

Bezirksamt Mitte

meyerstraße

Neue

Weberstr.

Schönau

St.-Pius-Kirche

straße

Koppen

Gesundheits-amt

Weidenweg

LPVA

Poli-klinik

Magazinstr.

Neue

Blumenstr.

Strausberger Platz

Strausberger Pl.

Blumenstr.

Marx-

Allee

Weberwiese

Singer-

straße

Lichtenberger

Blumenstr.

Str.

straße

Rüdersdorfer

Str. d. Pariser Komm.

Marchlewskistr.

Jannowitzbr.

Holzmarktstr.

Kraut-

Andreas-pl.

Singerstraße

Franz-Mehring-Pl.

St.-Antonius-Kirche

tzbr.

Jannowitzbr.

str.

Spree

A.d. Mich. br.

Michael-br.

Holzmarktstr.

Andreas

Koppen-

Lange Straße

Erich-Steinfurtstr.

Radial-145

Ostbahnhof

Am Ostbahnhof

DB

Schillingbr.

Stralauer Pl.

© MERIAN-Kartographie

0   300 m

Berlinmap

BSR-Verwaltung

9

10

11

12

N

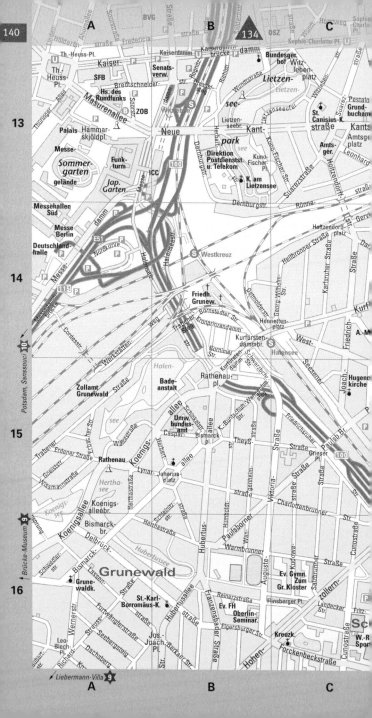

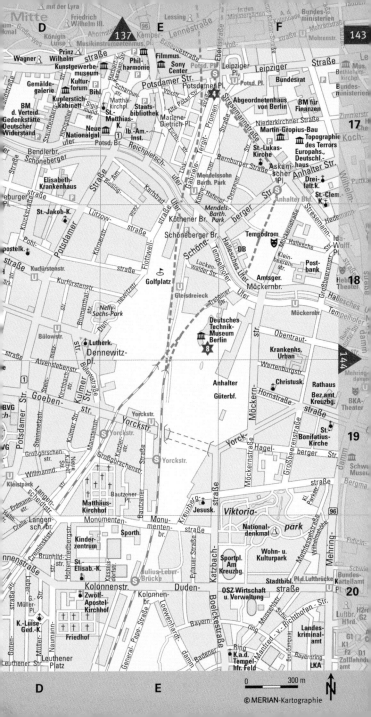

A

A.-Döblin-Pl. 144, C21
A.-Paulus-Str. 142, B20
A.-Schweizer-Pl. 145, E24
Abbestr. 135, F4
Ackerstr. 137, F5
Adalbertstr. 145, D21
Adenauerpl. 141, D14
Admiralbr. 144, C23
Admiralstr. 145, D23
Agricolastr. 136, A7
Ahornallee 134, A4
Ahornpl. 134, A4
Ahornsteig 137, D8
Ahornstr. 142, C18
Akazienallee 134, A3
Akazienstr. 142, C19
Albertstr. 142, C20
Albrecht-Achilles-Str. 141, D14
Albrechtstr. 137, F7
Alexanderpl. 138, C11
Alexanderstr. 138, C11
Alexanderufer 137, E7
Alexandrinenstr. 144, B22
Alice-Berend-Str. 136, C7
Alpenweg 135, D2
Alt-Lietzow 135, D4
Alt-Moabit 136, A7
Alte Jakobstr. 144, B21
Alte Potsdamer Str. 143, E17
Alte Schönhauser Str. 138, C11
Altonaer Str. 136, B8
Alvenslebenstr. 143, D19
Am Berliner-Mus. 144, B22
Am Bf. Westend 134, B3
Am Friedrichshain 139, E10
Am Karlsbad 143, E17
Am Kupfergraben 138, A11
Am Lustgarten 138, B11
Am Nordbahnhof 137, F6
Am Nordhafen 137, D5
Am Ostbahnhof 145, E21

Am Rathaus 142, B20
Am Schillertheater 135, E4
Am Spreebord 135, D3
Am Volkspark 141, F16
Am Weidendamm 138, A11
Am Zeughaus 138, B11
Am Zirkus 137, F7
Amtsgerichtsplatz 140, C13
An der Apostelkirche 143, D18
An der Kolonnade 137, F8
An der Schillingbr. 145, E21
An der Spandauer Br. 138, B11
An der Urania 142, B18
Andreaspl. 139, E12
Andreasstr. 145, E21
Anhalter Str. 143, F17
Anklamer Str. 138, A9
Annenstr. 144, C21
Ansbacher Str. 142, B18
Anton-Saefkow-Str. 139, F9
Arcostr. 135, D3
Arkonaplatz 138, B9
Arndtstr. 144, A24
Arnswalder Pl. 139, F10
Aschaffenburger Str. 142, A19
Askanischer Pl. 143, F17
Auerstr. 139, F12
Augsburger Str. 142, A18
Auguste-Viktoria-Str. 140, B16
Auguststr. 138, A11
Axel-Springer-Str. 144, B21

B

B.-Lichtenberg-Str. 139, E9
B.-v.-Arnim-Ufer 137, D8
Babelsberger Str. 142, A20
Bachstr. 136, A8
Badener Ring 143, E20

Badensche Str. 141, F16
Baerwaldbr. 144, B22
Baerwaldstr. 144, B23
Bamberger Str. 142, A18
Bandelstr. 136, C6
Barbarossaplatz 142, B19
Barbarossastr. 142, B19
Barbrücke 141, E16
Barnimstr. 139, D11
Barstr. 141, E16
Bartningallee 136, B8
Baruther Str. 144, A23
Bautzener Pl. 143, E19
Bautzener Str. 143, E20
Bayerische Str. 141, E15
Bayerischer Pl. 142, A19
Bayernring 143, E20
Bayreuther Str. 142, B18
Behrenstr. 137, F8
Belforter Str. 138, C9
Bellevuestr. 137, E8
Bellevueufer 136, C7
Belziger Str. 142, B20
Bendlerbr. 143, D17
Berchtesgadener Str. 142, B19
Bergfriedstr. 144, C22
Bergmannstr. 144, A23
Bergstr. 138, A10
Berkaer Str. 140, B16
Berlichingenstr. 135, F2
Berliner Str. 141, D16
Bernauer Str. 138, A9
Bernburger Str. 143, E17
Bernh.-Lichtenberg-Str. 134, C1
Berolinastr. 139, D11
Bertolt-Brecht-Pl. 137, F7
Besselstr. 144, A21
Bethaniendamm 145, D21
Bethlehemkirchpl. 143, F17
Beusselbr. 135, F1
Beusselstr. 136, A6
Birger-Forell-Pl. 141, F16

Birkenstr. 136, B6
Bismarckallee 140, A16
Bismarckbr. 140, A16
Bismarckpl. 140, B15
Bismarckstr. 134, C4
Bissingzeile 143, E17
Bleibtreustr. 141, F14
Blücherpl. 144, A22
Blücherstr. 144, A23
Blumenstr. 139, E12
Blumenthalstr. 143, D18
Bodestr. 138, B11
Böckhstr. 144, C23
Böcklerstr. 144, C22
Boelckestr. 143, E20
Bötzowstr. 139, E10
Bonhoefferufer 134, C3
Boppstr. 145, D23
Bornimer Str. 140, B14
Bornstedter Str. 140, B14
Borsigstr. 138, A10
Bouchéstr. 145, F24
Boyenstr. 137, E5
Bozener Str. 142, A20
Brachvogelstr. 144, A22
Brahestr. 134, C2
Brandenburgische Str. 141, D14
Brandesstr. 144, A22
Branitzer Platz 134, A4
Brauhofstr. 135, D3
Bredowstr. 136, B6
Bredtschneiderstr. 140, A13
Breite Str. 138, B12
Breitscheidplatz 142, A17
Bremer Str. 136, A6
Bremer Weg 136, B8
Brommystr. 145, F21
Brückenstr. 139, D12
Brunhildstr. 143, D20
Brunnenstr. 138, B10
Buchstr. 136, B5
Budapester Str. 142, A17
Bülowstr. 142, C18
Bürknerstr. 145, D23
Büschingstr. 139, E11
Bugenhagenstr. 136, B6

Bundesallee 142, A18
Bundesratufer 136, A7
Burggrafenstr. 142, B17
Burgstr. 138, B11

C

Calvinstr. 136, C7
Caprivibr. 135, D3
Carl-Herz-Ufer 144, B22
Carmerstr. 141, F13
Carnotstr. 135, F3
Caspar-Theyss-Str. 140, B15
Cauerstr. 135, E4
Charitéstr. 137, F7
Charlottenbrunner Str. 140, C15
Charlottenburger Br. 136, A8
Charlottenburger Ufer 135, D3
Charlottenstr. 144, A21
Chausseestr. 137, E5
Chodowieckistr. 139, D9
Choriner Str. 138, B10
Christburger Str. 139, D9
Christinenstr. 138, C10
Christstr. 134, B4
Cicerostr. 141, D14
Claudiusstr. 136, B7
Columbiadamm 144, A24
Cordesstr. 140, A14
Courbièrestr. 142, C18
Crellestr. 143, D20
Cunostr. 140, C16
Cuvrystr. 145, F22
Czeminskistr. 143, D20
D.-Bonhoeffer-Str. 139, E9

D

Dachsberg 140, A16
Dahlienweg 135, D1
Dahlmannstr. 141, D14
Damaschkestr. 140, C14
Danckelmannstr. 134, C3
Danziger Str. 139, D9
Darwinstr. 135, E3

Delbrückstr. 140, A16
Dennewitzpl. 143, D19
Dennewitzstr. 143, D18
Derfflingerstr. 142, C18
Dernburgstr. 140, B13
Dessauer Str. 143, F18
Dieffenbachstr. 144, C23
Diestelmeyerstr. 139, F11
Diesterwegstr. 139, E9
Dircksenstr. 138, C11
Döberitzer Str. 137, D6
Dominicusstr. 142, B20
Donaustr. 145, E24
Dorotheenstr. 137, F8
Dortmunder Str. 136, A7
Dovebr. 135, E3
Dovestr. 135, F3
Drakestr. 142, B17
Dresdener Str. 144, C21
Dresselstag 140, B13
Dreysestr. 136, C6
Droysenstr. 141, D14
Dudenstr. 143, E20
Düsseldorfer Str. 141, D14

E

E.-Lasker-Schüler-Str. 142, C18
E.-T.-A.-Hoffmann-Promenade 144, A22
Ebereschenallee 134, A4
Ebersstr. 142, C20
Eberswalder Str. 138, B9
Ebertstr. 137, F8
Edw.-Redslob-Str. 137, F8
Ehrwalder Str. 142, A20
Eichenallee 134, A4
Eichendorffstr. 138, A10
Eichhorststr. 143, E17
Einemstr. 142, C17
Einsteinufer 135, F3
Eisenacher Str. 142, C20
Eisenbahnstr. 145, E22

Eisenzahnstr. 141, D14
Eislebener Str. 142, A18
Elberfelder Str. 136, A7
Elbestr. 145, F24
Elgersburger Str. 140, B16
Elisabetkirchstr. 138, A10
Ella-Kay-Str. 139, E9
Elssholzstr. 142, C19
Emdener Str. 136, A6
Emser Platz 141, E15
Emser Str. 141, F15
Enckestr. 144, A21
Engeldamm 145, D21
Englische Str. 136, A8
Entlastungsstr. 137, E8
Eosanderstr. 135, D3
Epiphaniaweg 134, B4
Erasmusstr. 135, F2
Erbacher Str. 140, A15
Erdener Str. 140, A15
Erdmannstr. 143, D19
Erich-Steinfurth-Str. 139, E12
Erkelenzdamm 144, C22
Erkstr. 145, F24
Ermslebener Weg 141, E16
Ernst-Bumm-W. 134, B3
Ernst-Reuter-Platz 135, F4
Essener Str. 136, A7
Ettaler Str. 142, B18
Eugen-Schönhaar-Str. 139, F9
Eylauer Str. 143, E20
F.-Elsas-Str. 142, B20

F

Falckensteinstr. 145, F22
Fasanenplatz 141, F14
Fasanenstr. 142, A17
Fechnerstr. 141, F15
Fehrbelliner Pl. 141, E15
Feilnerstr. 144, B21
Feldstr. 137, F5
Feldzeugmeisterstr. 136, C6
Fennbr. 137, D5
Fennstr. 137, D5

Feurigstr. 142, C20
Fichtestr. 144, C23
Fidicinstr. 144, A24
Finowstr. 145, F24
Fischerinsel 138, C12
Flemingstr. 136, C7
Flensburger Str. 136, B7
Flinsberger Pl. 140, B16
Flotowstr. 136, A8
Flottwellstr. 143, E18
Flughafenstr. 145, E24
Föhrer Br. 136, B5
Föhrer Str. 136, B5
Fontanepromenade 144, C23
Forckenbeckstr. 140, C16
Forster Str. 145, E23
Fr.-Künstler-Str. 144, B22
Fr.-Stampfer-Str. 144, A22
Fraenkelufer 144, C23
Framstr. 145, E23
Frankenstr. 142, C19
Franklinstr. 135, F4
Franz-Klühs-Str. 144, A22
Franz-Mehring-Pl. 139, F12
Franzensbader Str. 140, B16
Französische Str. 138, A12
Fraunhoferstr. 135, E4
Fredericiastr. 134, A4
Fredersdorfer Str. 139, F12
Freiherr-vom-Stein-Str. 142, A20
Freiligrathstr. 144, C23
Freisinger Str. 142, B19
Friedelstr. 145, E24
Friedenstr. 139, E10
Friedrich-Ebert-Pl. 137, F7
Friedrich-Krause-Ufer 136, B5
Friedrich-List-Ufer 137, E7
Friedrich-Olbrich-Damm 135, E1
Friedrichbr. 138, B11

Friedrichsberger Str. 139, E11
Friedrichsgraben 138, B12
Friedrichsruher Str. 140, C15
Friedrichstr. 138, A11
Friesenstr. 144, A24
Fritschestr. 134, C4
Fritz-Wildung-Str. 140, C16
Frobenstr. 143, D18
Fürbringerstr. 144, A23
Fürstenbrunner Br. 134, A2
Fürstenbrunner Weg 134, A2
Fürther Str. 142, A18
Fuggerstr. 142, B18
Fuldastr. 145, E24
Furtwänglerstr. 140, A16

G
G.-Grosz-Pl. 141, E14
G.-Müller-Pl. 143, D20
G.-Wilhelm-Str. 140, C14
Gabriele-Tergit-Promenade 143, E17
Galvanistr. 135, E3
Gardes-du-Corps-Str. 134, B4
Gartenplatz 137, F5
Gartenstr. 137, F5
Gasteiner Str. 141, F16
Gaussstr. 135, D2
Geibelstr. 144, C23
Geisbergstr. 142, A18
Geisslerpfad 134, A1
General-Pape-Str. 143, E20
Genthiner Str. 143, D18
Georgenkirchstr. 139, D10
Georgenstr. 137, F7
Gerhardtstr. 137, D7
Gerickesteg 136, C7
Gertraudenstr. 138, B12
Gervinus 140, C14
Gierkepl. 135, D4
Gierkezeile 135, D3
Giesebrechtstr. 141, D14

Gieselerstr. 141, E15
Gipsstr. 138, B10
Gitschiner Str. 144, B22
Gleditschstr. 142, C19
Glinkastr. 137, F8
Glogauer Str. 145, F23
Gneisenaustr. 144, A23
Gneiststr. 140, A15
Goebelpl. 134, B1
Goebelstr. 134, A1
Goebenstr. 143, D19
Goerdeler-Damm-Br. 135, F1
Goerdelersteg 135, D1
Görlitzer Str. 145, E22
Görlitzer Ufer 145, F23
Goethestr. 141, D13
Golssener Str. 144, B24
Goltzstr. 142, C19
Gontardstr. 138, C11
Gormannstr. 138, B10
Goslarer Pl. 135, E3
Goslarer Ufer 135, E2
Gossowstr. 142, B18
Gotenstr. 143, D20
Gothaer Str. 142, B19
Gotzkowskybr. 136, A7
Gotzkowskystr. 136, A7
Gr. Hamburger Str. 138, B10
Gr. Querallee 137, E8
Grabowstr. 145, F23
Graefestr. 144, C23
Grainauer Str. 142, A18
Granseer Str. 138, B9
Greifswalder Str. 139, D10
Grenzstr. 137, E5
Grenzweg 135, D1
Griebenowstr. 138, B9
Grieser Pl. 140, C15
Grimmstr. 144, C23
Gröbenufer 145, F22
Grolmanstr. 141, F13
Grossbeerenstr. 143, F19
Grosse Präsidenten-str. 138, B11
Grosse Sternallee 136, C8
Grosser Stern 136, C8
Grosser Weg 136, A8

Grossgörschenstr. 143, D19
Grunerstr. 138, C12
Güntzelstr. 141, F15
Guerickestr. 135, E4

H
H.-Heine-Platz 145, D21
H.-Maass-Br. 135, F1
H.-v.-Fallersleben Pl. 141, D16
H.-v.-Gagern-Str. 137, E8
Habermannpl. 141, F16
Habersaathstr. 137, E6
Habsburgerstr. 142, C19
Hackescher Markt 138, B11
Haeftenzeile 134, B1
Händelallee 136, B8
Haeselerstr. 134, A4
Hafenpl. 143, E17
Hagelberger Str. 143, F19
Hagenauer Str. 139, D9
Halemweg 134, B1
Halenseestr. 140, A14
Hallerstr. 135, F3
Hallesche Str. 143, F18
Hallesches Tor Br. 144, A22
Hallesches Ufer 143, F18
Hammarskjöldpl. 140, A13
Hannah-Arendt-Str. 137, F8
Hannoversche Str. 137, F6
Hans-Otto-Str. 139, E10
Hansabr. 136, A7
Hanseatenweg 136, B7
Hardenbergplatz 142, A17
Hardenbergstr. 135, F4
Harzer Str. 145, F23
Hasenheide 144, C23
Haubachstr. 135, D4
Hauptstr. 143, D20
Hauptw. 135, E1
Hausvogteipl. 138, B12

Havelberger Str. 136, B5
Hebbelstr. 134, C4
Heckerdamm 134, C1
Hedemannstr. 143, F18
Heidelberger Str. 145, F23
Heidestr. 137, D5
Heilbronner Str. 140, C14
Heilmannring 134, A1
Heimstr. 144, B24
Heinr.-Roller-Str. 139, D10
Heinrich-Heine-Str. 144, C21
Heinrichpl. 145, D22
Heisenbergstr. 135, F3
Helgoländer Ufer 136, C7
Helmholtzstr. 135, F3
Helmstedter Str. 142, A19
Helmstr. 143, D20
Henriettenplatz 140, B14
Herbartstr. 140, B13
Herbert-v.-Karajan-Str. 143, E17
Herbertstr. 140, B15
Herkulesufer 142, C17
Hermannpl. 145, D24
Hermannstr. 145, D24
Herschelstr. 134, C2
Herthastr. 140, A16
Hertzallee 142, A17
Hessische Str. 137, F6
Heubnerweg 134, B3
Hildebrandstr. 143, D17
Hildegardstr. 141, F16
Hiroshimastr. 143, D17
Hitzigallee 143, D17
Hobrechtbr. 145, E23
Hobrechtstr. 145, E23
Hochmeisterpl. 141, D15
Höchste Str. 139, E10
Hölderlinstr. 134, A4
Hofackerzeile 134, C1
Hofjägerallee 136, C8
Hohenfriedbergstr. 143, D20
Hohenstaufenpl. 145, D23

Hohenstaufenstr. 142, A19
Hohenzollerndamm 140, B16
Hoher Bogen 141, D16
Hollmannstr. 144, A22
Holsteiner Ufer 136, B7
Holtzendorffplatz 140, C14
Holtzendorffstr. 140, C13
Holzmarktstr. 139, D12
Hornstr. 143, F19
Horstweg 134, C4
Hubertusallee 140, B16
Hufelandstr. 139, E10
Humboldtstr. 140, B16
Husemannstr. 139, D9
Hussitenstr. 138, A9
Huttenstr. 135, E2

I
Iburger 135, D3
Ida-Wolff-Pl. 143, F18
Ilsenburger Str. 135, E3
Immanuelkirchstr. 139, D10
In den Ministergärten 137, F8
Ingeborg-Drewitz-Allee 137, D7
Innsbrucker Str. 142, B20
Inselbrücke 138, C12
Inselstr. 138, C12
Invalidenstr. 137, D7

J
J.-Morgenroth-Pl. 141, E15
Jablonskistr. 139, D9
Jacobikirchstr. 144, B22
Jacobystr. 139, D11
Jägerstr. 137, F8
Jagowstr. 136, A7
Jahnstr. 145, D24
Jakob-Kaiser-Platz 134, C1
Jannowitzbr. 139, D12
Jansastr. 145, E24
Jasmunder Str. 138, A9
Jebensstr. 142, A17
Jenaer Str. 142, A19

Jerusalemer Str. 138, A12
Joachim-Friedrich-Str. 140, C15
Joachim-Karnatz-Allee 137, D7
Joachimstaler Str. 142, A18
Joachimstr. 138, B10
Johannaplatz 140, B15
Johannisstr. 138, A11
Johanniterstr. 144, B22
John-F.-Kennedy-Pl. 142, B20
John-Foster-Dulles-Allee 136, C8
John-Schehr-Str. 139, F9
Josef-Joachim-Pl. 140, A16
Jüterboger Str. 144, A24
Jungfernbr. 138, B12
Jungfernheide 135, D2
K.-August-Platz 141, E13
K.-Buntschuh-Str. 140, B15

K
K.-Niederkirchner-Str. 139, E10
Kaiser-Friedrich-Str. 135, D3
Kaiser-Wilh.-Platz 142, C20
Kaiserdamm 140, A13
Kaiserdammbrücke 140, B13
Kaiserin-Augusta-Allee 135, D3
Kaiserin-Augusta-Br. 135, E2
Kalckreuthstr. 142, C18
Kalischer Str. 141, D16
Kamminer Str. 135, D3
Kaninchenweg 135, D1
Kantstr. 142, A17
Kapelleufer 137, E7
Karl-Liebknecht-Str. 138, B12
Karl-Marx-Allee 139, D11
Karl-Marx-Str. 145, D24

Karl-Schrader-Str. 142, C19
Karlpl. 137, F7
Karlsgartenstr. 145, D24
Karlsruher Str. 140, C14
Kastanienallee 138, B10
Kath.-Heinroth-Ufer 142, B17
Katzbachstr. 143, E20
Katzlerstr. 143, E19
Kaubstr. 141, D15
Keibelstr. 138, C11
Keithstr. 142, B17
Kemperpl. 137, E8
Keplerstr. 135, D2
Kesselsdorfstr. 143, E20
Kiehlufer 145, F24
Kieler Br. 137, D5
Kieler Str. 137, D5
Kielganstr. 142, C18
Kirchbachstr. 143, D19
Kirchstr. 136, C7
Kl. Hambgurger Str. 138, A10
Kl. Parkstr. 143, F19
Klarenbachstr. 135, E2
Klausenerplatz 134, B3
Klausingring 134, C1
Klaustaler Str. 135, E3
Kleinbeerenstr. 143, F18
Kleiner Stern 137, D8
Kleiststr. 142, B18
Klingelhöferstr. 142, C17
Klixstr. 142, C19
Klopstockstr. 136, B8
Klosterstr. 138, C12
Kluckstr. 143, D18
Knaackstr. 138, C9
Knesebeckstr. 141, F14
Kniprodestr. 139, F10
Knobelsdorffbr. 134, B4
Knobelsdorffstr. 134, A4
Koburger Str. 142, B20
Kochstr. 144, A21
Köbisstr. 142, C17
Königin-Elisabeth-Str. 134, B4
Koenigsallee 140, A15

Koenigsalleebr. 140, A15
Köpenicker Str. 138, C12
Körnerstr. 143, D18
Körtestr. 144, C23
Köthener Br. 143, E18
Köthener Str. 143, E18
Kohlfurter Str. 144, C22
Kollwitzplatz 139, D9
Kollwitzstr. 138, C10
Kolmarer Str. 139, D10
Kolonnenbr. 143, E20
Kolonnenstr. 143, D20
Kommandantenstr. 144, B21
Konstanzer Str. 141, D15
Koppenpl. 138, B10
Koppenstr. 139, E12
Kottbusser Damm 145, D23
Kottbusser Str. 145, D22
Krausenstr. 144, A21
Krausnickstr. 138, A11
Krautstr. 139, E12
Krefelder Str. 136, B7
Kremmener Str. 138, B9
Kreuzbergstr. 143, E20
Kronenstr. 138, A12
Kronprinzendamm 140, B14
Krumme Str. 135, E4
Kruppstr. 136, C6
Kucharskistr. 135, F3
Kudowastr. 140, C16
Kufsteiner Str. 142, A20
Kulmbacher Str. 142, A18
Kulmer Str. 143, D19
Kuno-Fischer-Pl. 140, B13
Kuno-Fischer-Str. 140, B13
Kurfürstendamm 140, B15
Kurfürstendammbr. 140, B14
Kurfürstenstr. 142, B17
Kurmärkische Str. 143, D18
Kurstr. 138, B12

Kyffhäuserstr. 142, C19

L

Ladestr. 137, E6
Lambertstr. 135, D2
Landecker Str. 140, C16
Landgrafenstr. 142, C17
Landhausstr. 142, A19
Landsberger Allee 139, F11
Landshuter Str. 142, B19
Lange Str. 139, E12
Langenbeckstr. 139, F10
Langenscheidbr. 143, D20
Langenscheidtstr. 143, D19
Lassenstr. 140, A16
Laubestr. 145, F24
Lausitzer Platz 145, E22
Lausitzer Str. 145, E23
Leberstr. 143, D20
Lebuser Str. 139, E11
Lehniner Pl. 141, D14
Lehrter Str. 137, D5
Leibnizstr. 141, E13
Leipziger Pl. 143, F17
Leipziger Str. 143, F17
Lenaustr. 145, D23
Lennéstr. 137, E8
Leo-Blech-Pl. 140, A16
Leon-Jessel-Pl. 141, 15
Leonhardtstr. 140, C13
Lerschpfad 134, B3
Lesser-Ury-Weg 137, D6
Lessingbr. 136, B7
Lessingstr. 136, B7
Letterhausweg 134, B1
Leuschnerdamm 145, D22
Leuthener Platz 143, D20
Leuthener Str. 143, D20
Levetzowstr. 136, A7
Lewishamstr. 141, D13
Lexisstr. 145, F23
Liberdastr. 145, E23
Lichtenberger Str. 139, E12

Lichtensteinallee 142, B17
Lichtensteinbr. 142, B17
Liebknechtbr. 138, B12
Liegnitzer Str. 145, E23
Liesenstr. 137, E5
Lietzenburger Str. 141, E14
Lietzenseebr. 140, B13
Lietzenseeufer 140, B13
Lilienthalstr. 144, C24
Lilli-Henoch-Str. 139, F9
Lindauer Str. 142, C19
Lindenallee 134, A4
Lindenstr. 144, A22
Linienstr. 138, A10
Linkstr. 143, E17
Lise-Meitner-Str. 135, D1
Littenstr. 138, C11
Lobeckstr. 144, B22
Loewenhardtdamm 143, E20
Lohmeyerstr. 135, D3
Lohmühlenbr. 145, F23
Lohmühlenpl. 145, F23
Lohmühlenstr. 145, F23
Los-Angeles-Pl. 142, A18
Loschmidtstr. 135, E4
Lottumstr. 138, C10
Luckenwalder Str. 143, E18
Ludwig-Erhard-Ufer 137, E7
Ludwig-Hoffm.-Br. 135, F1
Ludwig-Kirchpl. 141, F14
Lübbener Str. 145, F22
Lübecker Str. 136, B6
Lüdtgeweg 135, E3
Lützowpl. 142, C17
Lützowstr. 142, C17
Lützowufer 142, C17
Luisenplatz 135, D3
Luisenstr. 137, F6
Luitpoldstr. 142, B19
Lutherbr. 136, C8
Lynarstr. 140, A15

M

Maassenstr. 142, C18
Märkischer Pl. 138, C12
Märkisches Ufer 138, C12
Magazinstr. 139, D12
Magdeburger Pl. 143, D17
Maienstr. 142, C18
Mainzer Str. 145, E24
Manfred-v.-Richthofen-Str. 143, F20
Manitiusstr. 145, E23
Mannheimer Str. 141, E16
Mansfelder Str. 141, D15
Mansteinstr. 143, D19
Manteuffelstr. 145, D22
Marburger Str. 142, A18
Marchbr. 135, F4
Marchlewskistr. 139, F12
Marchstr. 135, F4
Margeritenweg 135, D1
Marheinekepl. 144, A23
Mariannenpl. 145, D21
Mariannenstr. 145, D22
Marienburger Str. 139, D9
Marienstr. 137, F7
Markgrafenstr. 144, A21
Marlene-Dietrich-Pl. 143, E17
Marschallbr. 137, F7
Martin-Luther-Str. 142, B18
Masurenallee 140, A13
Matthäikirchpl. 143, E17
Matthiasstr. 139, F11
Mauerstr. 137, F8
Max-Dohrn-Str. 134, C2
Max-Urich-Str. 137, F5
Maybachufer 145, D23
Mecklenburgische Str. 141, E16
Mehringbr. 144, A22

Mehringdamm 143, F20
Mehringplatz 144, A22
Meierottostr. 141, F14
Meinekestr. 142, A18
Meininger Str. 142, B20
Melanchthonstr. 136, C7
Melchiorstr. 145, D21
Memhardstr. 138, C11
Mendelssohnstr. 139, D10
Meraner Str. 142, B20
Merseburger Str. 142, C20
Messedamm 140, A13
Messedammbrücke 140, A14
Methfesselstr. 143, F20
Mettmannpl. 137, D5
Metzer Str. 138, C10
Michaelbr. 139, D12
Michaelkirchpl. 145, D21
Michaelkirchstr. 145, D21
Mierendorffpl. 135, D2
Mierendorffstr. 135, D3
Mindener Str. 134, C3
Mittelstr. 137, F8
Mittenwalder Str. 144, A23
Moabiter Br. 136, B7
Möckernbr. 143, F18
Möckernstr. 143, F18
Mörschbr. 134, C2
Mohrenstr. 137, F8
Molkenmarkt 138, C12
Mollstr. 139, D10
Mollwitzstr. 134, B3
Moltkebr. 137, E7
Mommsenstr. 141, D13
Monbijoustr. 138, A11
Monumentenbr. 143, E20
Monumentenstr. 143, D20
Moritzstr. 144, B22
Morsestr. 135, F3
Motzstr. 142, A19
Mühlendamm 138, B12
Mühlendammbr. 138, C12

Mühlenstr. 145, F21
Müllenhoffstr. 144, C23
Müller-Breslau-Str. 136, A8
Münchener Str. 142, B19
Münstersche Str. 141, D15
Münzstr. 138, C11
Mulackstr. 138, B10
Museumstr. 138, B11
Muskauer Str. 145, E22
Mussehlstr. 143, F20

N
Nachodstr. 142, A19
Nansenstr. 145, E24
Nassauische Str. 141, F16
Naumannstr. 143, D20
Nehringstr. 134, C4
Nelkenw. 135, D1
Nestorstr. 141, D14
Neue Blumenstr. 139, D11
Neue Grünstr. 144, B21
Neue Hochstr. 137, E5
Neue Jacobstr. 144, C21
Neue Kantstr. 140, B13
Neue Kulmer Str. 143, D19
Neue Prom. 138, B11
Neue Rossstr. 138, C12
Neue Weberstr. 139, E11
Neuenburger Str. 144, A22
Neues Ufer 135, E2
Neufertstr. 134, C4
Neustädtische Kirch-str. 137, F7
Niebuhrstr. 141, D13
Niederkirchner Str. 143, F17
Niederlagstr. 138, B12
Niederwallstr. 138, B12
Nikol.-Gross-Weg 134, B2
Nikolsburger Pl. 141, F15
Nithackstr. 134, C3
Nollendorfpl. 142, C18

Nollendorfstr. 142, C18
Nonnendamm 134, B2
Nordhauser Str. 135, D3
Nordhfn.brücke 137, D5
Nordkurve 140, A14
Nordsternpl. 142, B20
Nordufer 136, B5
Nostitzstr. 144, A23
Novalisstr. 138, A10
Nürnberger Pl. 142, A18
Nürnberger Str. 142, A18
Nussbaumallee 134, A3
O.-Braun-Str. 139, D11

O
O.-Palme-Pl. 142, B17
Obentrautstr. 143, F18
Oberbaumstr. 145, F22
Oberwallstr. 138, B12
Oberwasserstr. 138, B12
Oderberger Str. 138, B9
Ohlauer Str. 145, E23
Ohmstr. 139, D12
Olbersstr. 134, C2
Oldenburger Str. 136, A6
Olivaer Platz 141, E14
Onckenstr. 145, F24
Oppelner Str. 145, F22
Oranienb. Tor 138, A10
Oranienburger Str. 138, A11
Oranienplatz 144, C22
Uranlenstr. 144, B21
Osnabrücker Str. 134, C2
Ossastr. 145, F24
Otto-Dix-Str. 137, D7
Otto-Grüneberg-Weg 134, C4
Otto-Suhr-Allee 135, D3
Otto-v.-Bismarck-Allee 137, E7
Ottoplatz 136, A7
Ottostr. 136, A7

P
Palisadenstr. 139, E11
Pallasstr. 142, C19
Pannierstr. 145, E24
Pappelpl. 138, A10
Paretzer Str. 141, E16
Pariser Pl. 137, F8
Pariser Str. 141, E14
Parochialstr. 138, C12
Pascalstr. 135, F3
Passage 141, F14
Passauer Str. 142, B18
Pasteurstr. 139, E9
Paul-Lincke-Ufer 145, D23
Paul-Löbe-Allee 137, D7
Paulsberger Br. 140, C15
Paulsborner Str. 140, B16
Pekinger Pl. 136, C5
Penzberger Str. 142, B19
Perleberger Brücke 137, D5
Perleberger Str. 136, B6
Pestalozzistr. 140, C13
Pfalzburger Str. 141, F15
Pflügerstr. 145, E23
Pflugstr. 137, F5
Pfuelstr. 145, F22
Philippstr. 137, F6
Planckstr. 138, A11
Planufer 145, C23
Platanenallee 134, A4
Platz am Königstor 139, D10
Platz d. Republik 137, E7
Platz d. Vereinten Nationen 139, E11
Platz der Luftbr. 143, F20
Platz des 18. März 137, E8
Platz v. d. Neuen Tor 137, F6
Pohlstr. 143, D18
Pommersche Str. 141, E15
Popitzweg 134, A1
Poststr. 138, B12
Potsdamer Br. 143, D17

Potsdamer Pl. 143, E17
Potsdamer Str. 143, D18
Prager Pl. 142, A19
Prager Str. 142, A19
Prenzlauer Allee 139, D10
Prenzlauer Berg 139, D10
Prenzlauer Tor 138, C10
Prinz-Georg-Str. 142, C20
Prinzessinnenstr. 144, C22
Prinzregentenstr. 142, A19
Propststr. 138, C12
Pücklerstr. 145, E22
Pufendorfstr. 139, F11
Pulsstr. 134, B3
Putlitzbrücke 136, B6
Putlitzstr. 136, B6
Puttkamerstr. 144, A21

Q
Quedlinburger Str. 135, D3
Quitzowstr. 136, B5

R
R.-Luxembg.-Pl. 138, C10
R.-Schwarz-Str. 139, F9
R.-Wagner-Pl. 135, D4
Raabestr. 139, D10
Rahel-Varnhagen-Prom. 144, A22
Randsteig 135, E1
Rankepl. 142, A18
Rankestr. 142, A18
Rathausbr. 138, B12
Rathausstr. 138, B12
Rathenaupl. 140, B15
Rathenower Str. 136, C5
Ratiborstr. 145, F23
Rauchstr. 142, B17
Ravensberger Str. 141, D15
Regensburger Str. 142, A19
Reichenberger Str. 145, E23
Reichpietschufer 142, C17
Reichstagufer 137, E7

Reichweindamm 134, C1
Reinerzstr. 140, B16
Reinhardtstr. 137, E7
Reuchlinstr. 135, F2
Reuterpl. 145, E23
Reuterstr. 145, E24
Rheinsberger Str. 138, A9
Rich.-Wagner-Str. 135, D4
Richard-Strauss-Str. 140, A16
Riehlstr. 140, B13
Riemannstr. 144, A23
Ringbahnstr. 140, B14
Ritterstr. 144, B21
Robert-Koch-Pl. 137, F6
Rochstr. 138, C11
Rönnestr. 140, C14
Röntgenbr. 135, E3
Röntgenstr. 135, E3
Rognitzstr. 140, B13
Rolandufer 138, C12
Rosa-Luxemburg-Str. 138, C11
Rosenheimer Str. 142, B19
Rosenstr. 138, B11
Rosenthaler Pl. 138, B10
Rosenthaler Str. 138, B10
Rosenweg 135, D1
Rostocker Str. 135, F2
Rudolf-Wissell-Brücke 134, B2
Rudolstädter Str. 141, D16
Rückertstr. 135, D4
Rüdersdorfer Str. 139, F12
Rüsternallee 134, A4
Rütlistr. 145, E24
Ruhlsdorfer Str. 144, A22
Ruhrstr. 141, E15
Rummelsburger Platz 145, F21
Rungestr. 138, C12
Ruppiner Str. 138, B9
Rykestr. 139, D9
S.-Delitzsch-Platz 138, C12

S
Saarbrücker Str. 138, C10
Sächsische Str. 141, E15
Saldernstr. 134, B4
Salzbrunner Str. 140, C16
Salzburger Str. 142, B20
Salzufer 135, F3
Salzwedeler Str. 136, B5
Sanderstr. 145, D23
Sandkrugbr. 137, E6
Savignyplatz 141, F13
Schadowstr. 137, F8
Schandauer Str. 145, F24
Schaperstr. 141, F14
Scharnhorststr. 137, E5
Scharounstr. 143, E17
Scheidemannstr. 137, E8
Schiffbauerdamm 137, E7
Schillerstr. 141, E13
Schillingbr. 145, E21
Schillingstr. 139, D12
Schillstr. 142, C18
Schinkelstr. 140, B15
Schinkestr. 145, D23
Schleiermacherstr. 144, B23
Schleinitzstr. 140, B16
Schlesingerstr. 135, F3
Schleswiger Ufer 136, A8
Schleusenbrücke 138, B12
Schlossbr. 135, D3
Schlosspl. 138, B12
Schlossstr. 134, C4
Schlüterstr. 141, E13
Schmidstr. 145, D21
Schneppenhorstweg 134, B1
Schöneberger Br. 143, E18
Schöneberger Str. 143, E18
Schöneberger Ufer 143, D17
Schönhauser Allee 138, C9

Schönhauser Tor 138, C10
Schönholzer Str. 138, B9
Schönleinstr. 145, D23
Schröderstr. 138, A10
Schützenstr. 144, A21
Schulenburgring 143, F20
Schulweg 139, F11
Schulzendorfer Str. 137, E5
Schumannstr. 137, F7
Schustehrusstr. 134, C4
Schwäbische Str. 142, B19
Schwanenfeldstr. 135, E1
Schwartzkopffstr. 137, F5
Schwarzbrücke 140, B15
Schwarzer Weg 135, E2
Schwedlerstr. 140, A16
Schwedter Str. 138, B9
Schweiggerweg 134, B1
Schwerinstr. 142, C18
Schwiebusser Str. 144, A24
Sebastianstr. 144, C21
Seelingstr. 134, B4
Seesener Str. 140, C15
Segitzdamm 144, C22
Sellerstr. 137, E5
Separitionsweg 135, E1
Seydelstr. 144, B21
Seydlitzstr. 136, C7
Shakespearepl. 135, D4
Sickingenplatz 135, F2
Sickingenstr. 135, E2
Siemensdamm 134, A1
Siemensstg. 135, E3
Siemensstr. 136, A6
Sigismundstr. 143, D17
Sigmaringer Str. 141, F15
Simsonweg 137, E8
Singerstr. 139, D12
Skalitzer Str. 145, D22

Sömmeringstr. 135, D3
Solmsstr. 144, A23
Sonnenallee 145, E24
Soorstr. 134, A4
Sophie-Charlotte-Pl. 134, C4
Sophie-Charlotten-Str. 134, B2
Sophienstr. 138, B10
Spandauer Damm 134, A3
Spandauer Dammbr. 134, B3
Spandauer Str. 138, B11
Spenerstr. 136, C7
Spennrathbr. 135, F1
Speyerer Str. 142, B19
Spichernstr. 142, A18
Spielhagenstr. 135, D4
Spittelmarkt 138, B12
Spreeufer 138, B12
Spreewaldpl. 145, E22
Spreeweg 136, C8
Sredzkistr. 138, C9
Stallschreiberstr. 144, B21
Stallstr. 134, C3
Stauffenbergstr. 143, D17
Steinacher Str. 142, B20
Steinmetzstr. 143, D19
Steinpl. 141, F13
Stephanpl. 136, B5
Stephanstr. 136, B5
Storkower Str. 139, F9
Str. 244 135, F3
Str. am Schoelerpark 141, F16
Str. d. Pariser Komm. 139, F12
Str. des 17. Juni 135, F4
Stralauer Platz 145, E21
Stralauer Str. 138, C12
Stralsunder Str. 138, A9
Strassburger Str. 138, C10
Strausberger Platz 139, E11
Strausberger Str. 139, E11
Strelitzer Str. 138, A9
Stresemannstr. 143, F17

Stromstr. 136, B7
Stübbenstr. 142, B20
Stülerstr. 142, C17
Stuttgarter Platz 141, D13
Suarezstr. 140, C13
Sybelstr. 141, D14

T
Taubenstr. 138, A12
Taubenw. 135, D1
Tauentzienstr. 142, A17
Tauroggener Str. 135, D3
Tegeler Str. 137, D5
Tegeler Weg 134, C2
Tellstr. 145, E24
Tempelhofer Ufer 143, E18
Teutoburger Pl. 138, C10
Th.-Dehler-Str. 142, B17
Th.-Heuss-Pl. 140, A13
Th.-Heuss-W. 137, F5
Tharandter Str. 142, A19
Thielenbr. 145, E23
Thomasiusstr. 136, C7
Thrasoltstr. 135, D4
Tieckstr. 137, F6
Tiergartenstr. 142, C17
Tiergartenufer 136, A8
Tile-Wardenberg-Str. 136, A7
Toeplerstr. 134, B1
Torfstrassensteg 136, C5
Torstr. 138, A10
Trabener Steg 140, B14
Trabener Str. 140, A15
Trautenaustr. 141, F15
Trebbiner Str. 143, E18
Tucholskystr. 138, A10
Tulpenweg 135, D1
Turmstr. 136, A6

U
Ufnaustr. 135, E2
Uhlandstr. 141, F14
Ulmenallee 134, A4
Unionpl. 136, A5
Unionstr. 136, A5
Universitätsstr. 138, A11

Unter den Linden 137, F8
Unterwasserstr. 138, B12
Urbanstr. 144, B23
Usedomer Str. 138, A9

V
Veilchenweg 135, D1
Veteranenstr. 138, B10
Viktoria-Luise-Pl. 142, B19
Virchowstr. 139, F10
Volksparksteg 142, A20
Vorbergstr. 142, C19
Vossstr. 137, F8
Voxstr. 143, E17
W.-Brandt-Str. 137, E7

W
Wadzeckstr. 138, C11
Waghäuseler Str. 142, A20
Waisenstr. 138, C12
Waldemarstr. 144, C21
Waldenserstr. 136, A6
Waldstr. 136, A6
Wallenbergstr. 141, E16
Wallotstr. 140, A15
Wallstr. 138, B12
Wangeneimersteg 140, B15
Wangenheimstr. 140, B16
Warmbrunner Str. 140, B16
Warneckstr. 141, D16
Wartburgpl. 142, B20
Wartburgstr. 142, B20
Wartenburgstr. 143, F19
Washingtonpl. 137, E7
Wassertorplatz 144, C22
Wassertorstr. 144, B22
Waterloobr. 144, B22
Waterlooufer 144, A22
Wegelystr. 136, A8
Wegenerstr. 141, E15
Weichselplatz 145, F24
Weichselstr. 145, E24
Weidendorfer Br. 138, A11

Weidenweg 139, F12
Weigandufer 145, F24
Weimarer Str. 141, E13
Weinbergsweg 138, B10
Weinmeisterstr. 138, B10
Weinstr. 139, E11
Welserstr. 142, B18
Weltlingerbr. 134, C1
Werftstr. 137, D7
Werkstättenweg 140, A15
Wernerstr. 140, A16
Wernigeroder Str. 135, E3
Weserstr. 145, E24
Westarpstr. 142, B19
Westfälische Str. 140, C14
Westhafenstr. 136, B5
Weydemeyerstr. 139, D11
Weydingerstr. 138, C10
Wichmannstr. 142, B17
Wiclefstr. 136, A6
Wiebestr. 135, F2
Wielandstr. 141, E14
Wiener Br. 145, F23
Wiener Str. 145, E22
Wikingerufer 136, A7
Wildenbruchbrücke 145, F24
Wildenbruchstr. 145, F24
Wilhelmsaue 141, E16
Wilhelmshavener Str. 136, B6
Wilhelmshöhe 143, F20
Wilhelmstr. 137, F8
Willibald-Alexis-Str. 144, A24
Willmannd. 143, D19
Wilmersdorfer Str. 135, D4
Wilmsstr. 144, B23
Wilsnacker Str. 136, C6
Windscheidstr. 140, C13
Winsstr. 139, D10
Winterfeldtpl. 142, C18

Winterfeldtstr. 142, B19
Wintersteinstr. 135, D3
Wissmannstr. 140, A15
Wittenbergpl. 142, B18
Wittstocker Str. 135, F2
Witzlebenplatz 140, C13
Witzlebenstr. 140, C13
Wöhlertstr. 137, F5
Wörther Str. 138, C9
Wolgaster Str. 138, B9
Wolliner Str. 138, B9
Wrangelstr. 145, E21
Württembergische Str. 141, E15
Wullenwebersteg 136, A8
Wullenweberstr. 136, A7
Wundtstr. 134, C4

X
Xantener Str. 141, D14

Y
Yorckstr. 143, E19
Yitzak-Rabin-Str. 137, E8

Z
Zähringerstr. 141, E14
Zehdenicker Str. 138, B10
Zeughofstr. 145, E22
Ziegelstr. 138, A11
Zietenstr. 142, C18
Zillestr. 134, C4
Zimmerstr. 144, A21
Zinnowitzer Str. 137, F6
Zinzendorfstr. 136, A7
Zionskirchplatz 138, B9
Zionskirchstr. 138, B9
Zossener Br. 144, A22
Zossener Str. 144, A22
Züllichauer Str. 144, B24
Zwinglistr. 136, A7

Here you will find a list of all the sights, museums, hotels (H) and restaurants (R) mentioned in this guide.

The index also includes keywords as well as all the MERIAN TopTen and MERIAN Tips from the guide. If a term is frequently used, a bold-type numeral indicates the main entry in the printing, a cursive numeral indicates a photograph.

A

Ackselhaus (H) 14
Adenauerplatz 84
Adlergestell 100
Adlershof 100
Adlon (H) *12*, 13
Advance Ticket Sales 124
Advertising column 110
Airports 125
Albrechtshof (H) 14
Alexanderplatz 53
Allies 100
Alte Bibliothek 61
Alte Nationalgalerie 57, **72**
Altes Museum 56
Altes Zollhaus (R) 25
Ampelmännchen-Galerie (traffic-light men) 30
Ana e Bruno (R) 19
Antiques 30
Aquarium in the Zoologischer Garten 47
Arc (R) 27
Artisans 32
Automobile breakdown 124
Avus 100

B

Babelsberg 91
Babelsberg Palace 94
Back courtyards 109
Bags 35
Bahnhof Zoo 47
Banks 124
Bars 37
Bauhaus-Archiv 72, *74*
Bears 100
Bedroom 35
Beer gardens 25
Bergmann 103 (R) 28
Berlin at a glance 124
Berlin key 116
Berlin Lexicon 98
Berlin Wall Documentation Center 72
Berliner 101
Berliner Bonbonmacherei 47
Berliner Dom 54
Berliner Rathaus 54
Berliner Zimmer 102
Berlinisch 102
Berlinische Galerie 72
Berolina 102
Bicycle Rental 124
Bleibtreu (H) 13
Blockade 102
Blockhaus Nikolskoe (R) 27
Boat Tours 125
Bocca di Bacco (R, MERIAN Tip) 21
Bode Museum 57, **72**
Bogota (H) 15
Borchardt (R) *17*, 22
Botanischer Garten 65
Botanisches Museum 65
Brandenburg Gate 54, *65*
Brandenburg Gate (Potsdam) 95
Brandenburger Hof (H) 13
Brandt, Willy 103
Brecht, Bertolt 97
Brecht-Weigel Memorial 72

Brücke Museum 73
Buckow 97

C

Cabaret 38
Café Adler (R) 28
Café Aedes (R) 27
Café am Neuen See (R) 26
Café am Ufer (R) 26
Café der Schwartz'schen Villa (R) 26
Café Einstein (R) 27
Café Kranzler 84
Café Lebensart (R) 28
Café Milagro (R) 28
Cafés 27
Camping 125
Capitals 103
Capt'n Schillow (R) 26
Carillon 103
Central memorial of the Federal Republic of Germany 61
Chamäleon 38, *40*
Charlottenburg 18, 62
Chinese Teahouse *94*
Churascaria Brasil Brasiliero (R) 19
Cinemas 39
CineStarMAX 47
City tours 126
Closing time 115
Clubs 39
Cockroaches 109
Cölln 104
Concerts 40
Cooking 32
Curried sausage 104

D

Dal Buongustaio (R) 19
Dance Clubs 39
DDR Museum 73
Department Stores 31
Der Spielball 47
Deutsches Guggenheim Berlin 73
Deutsches Technikmuseum Berlin (MERIAN Tip) 49

Die Fabrik (H) 16
Diekmann (R) 19
Diekmann im Weinhaus
  Huth (R) 22
Dogs 108
Dutch Quarter (Pots-
  dam) 95

E
Ellington (R) 14
Engelbecken (R) 19
Entrecôte (R) 22
Erich's Lamp Shop 105
Euro 105
Europa-Center **62**, 84
Events 42
Exclave 105
Excursions 88, 91, 96, 97

F
Fabrics 35
Facts about Berlin 120
Fasanenplatz 84
Fashion 32
Fassbrause 105
Festivals 42
FEZ Wuhlheide 47
Film 106
Film and Television
  Museum 73
Flammende Herzen (R)
  28
Fliegeberg 106
Florian (R) 19
Fontane, Theodor 96
Food and Drink 17
Forsthaus Paulsborn
  (H) 14
Fort Hahneberg 47
Forum Fridericianum
  60
Frauenhotel
  Artemisia (H) 15
Freischwimmer (R) 26
French Cathedral 55
Friedrich the Great,
  statue 62
Friedrichstrasse 54
Funk (H) 16
Funkturm (Radio
  Tower) 62

G
Galeries Lafayette *29*,
  31, 55
Galleries 70
Ganymed Brasserie (R)
  22
Garderobe 106
Gates (H) 15
Gay 115
Gedächtniskirche **62**, 84
Gedenkstätte Berlin-
  Hohenschönhausen 74
Gemäldegalerie in the
  Kulturforum **67**, 74
Gendarmenmarkt 55
German Cathedral 55
German Historical
  Museum 60, **73**
German State Opera 61
Germania 107
Gethsemanekirche 83
Getting there 126
  By air 125
  By bus 124
  By car 124, 131
  By steamer 88
  By train 124
Ghost stations 106
Glienicker Brücke 68
Gothic House 88
Grand Hyatt (H) 13, *15*
Green arrow 107
Grips-Theater 48
Grunewald 86
Grünfisch (R) 21

H
Hackesche Höfe
  (MERIAN TopTen)
  50, 55
Hackescher Markt (H) 14
Hamburg Railway
  Station 74
Hartmanns (R) 21
Hasir (R) 22
Haus am Checkpoint
  Charlie 74
Haus der Kulturen der
  Welt (House of World
  Cultures) 66
Havel 47, 86, **88**

Hecker's Hotel (H) 15
Heinrich-Zille Museum
  74
Hertha 107
Hidden Museum 73
Historical Mile 107
History 120
Holocaust Memorial 56
Honigmond Garden
  (H, MERIAN Tip) 14
Hoppegarten *131*
Horvath (R) 22
Hotels 12
Housewares 31
Hugos (R) 19
Humboldt University 61

I
Information 127
Interbau 109
InterContinental (H) 13
Internet 128
Inventors 105
Iron Gustav 104
Ishin (R) 24

J
Jewellery 34
Jewish cemeteries **68**,
  81, 82
Jewish Community 109
Jewish Museum
  (MERIAN TopTen)
  70, 74
Junior-Museum 49

K
KaDeWe (MERIAN
  TopTen) **31**, *35*, 84
KaDeWe (R) 19
Kadima (R) 23
Kaiser-Wilhelm-Gedächt-
  niskirche (MERIAN
  TopTen) *60*, 62
Kastanie (R) 27
Käthe-Kollwitz Museum
  75, 84
Kellerrestaurant im
  Brecht-Haus (R) 25
Kids 46
Kiez 109

Kinderinsel 48
Klipper (R) 27
Knoblauch-Haus 57
Kollwitzplatz 82
Konnopke (R) **25**, 83, 117
Köpenick 64
Köpenick town hall 64
KPM 109
Kremser 110
Kreuzberg 21, 28
Kreuzer 110
Kronprinzenpalais 61
Ku'damm 18, 27, **62**, 84
Kulturforum 67
Künstlerheim Luise (H, MERIAN Tip) 16
Kurfürstendamm 18, 27, **62**, 84

L
Labyrinth 48
Landwehrkanal *98/99*, 110
Le Cochon Bourgeois (R) 21
Le Piaf (R) 20
Lenné Triangle 110
Liberty Bell 106
Liebermann Villa on Wannsee 75
Lindenufer 88
Literaturhaus 84
Little city 115
Lost and Found 128
Lubitsch (R) 20
Ludwigkirchplatz 84

M
Machmit-Museum 49
Maedchenitaliener (R) 23
Magazines/newspapers 129
Margaux (R) 22
Marjellchen (R) 20
Markets 32
Märkische Schweiz 97
Märkisches Museum 47, **75**
Martin-Gropius-Bau 76
Marx-Engels-Forum 56

Maultäschle (R) 23
Maxim-Gorki-Theater 61
Maxwell (R) 23
Medical Assistance 129
Mitte 22, 28, **53**, 111
Monday Museums (MERIAN Tip) 72
Motel One Berlin-Alexanderplatz (H) 16
Mountains 101
Müggelsee 47, *79*
Museum Berggruen 76
Museum für Fotografie 76
Museum für Gegenwart 74
Museum für Gestaltung 72
Museum für Naturkunde 76
Museuminsel 56
Museums 70
Museumsdorf Düppel *46*, 49
Music 34, 111
Music Venues 39
Musicals 38

N
Nefertiti *56*
Neue Wache (New Watchhouse) 61
Neuer Berliner Kunst-verein 77
Neues Museum 57
Neuköllner Oper (MERIAN Tip) 41
New National Gallery 67
New Synagogue (MERIAN Tip) 76
New Synagogue/Centrum Judaicum (MERIAN Tip) 76
Nightclubs 37
Nightlife 36
Nikolaikirche 57
Nikolaikirche (Potsdam) 95
Nikolaiviertel 57

O
Octagon Café 103
Olympia 112
Olympia Stadium 63
Open-air spots 25
Opera 40
Operncafé (R) 28
Opernpalais 61
Osteria No. 1 (R) 21
Overview 116

P
Palais von Pannwitz 87
Pan Asia (R) 23
Paris Bar (R) 19
Park Klein Glienicke 68
Pergamon Museum (MERIAN TopTen) 57, *73*, **76**
Pfaueninsel (Peacock Island) **68**, 90, *92*
Pichelsdorf 88
Pichelswerder 88
Post Office 129
Potsdam 91
Potsdamer Platz (MERIAN TopTen) *52*, **57**, 80
Prater 83
Prater (R) 27
Prenzlauer Berg 22, 28, **81**
Prices legend (H) 2
Prices legend (R) 2
Products from the former East 113
Prussian Cultural Heritage 114
Public Transport 132
Puppentheater Museum 49

Q
Quartier 206 *10*
Quasimodo 39

R
Readings 39
Reichstagsgebäude (Parliament Building, MERIAN TopTen) *8*, 67

Reinhard's (R) 24
Remise Schloss
  Glienicke (R) 25
Residenz (H) 15
Restaurants 17
Revue 38

S
S-Bahn railway arches
  114
Sale e Tabacchi (R) 21
Salons 114
Salumeria Culinario 24
Samâdhi (R) 24
San Giorgio (R) 20
Sanssouci (MERIAN
  TopTen) 91
Sarah Wieners Speise-
  zimmer (R) 24
Savignyplatz **63**, 84
Savoy (H) 13
Schall & Rauch (R) 28
Scharfe Lanke 88
Schaubühne *36*
Scheunenviertel 114
Schinkel-Klause (R) 24
Schloss Bellevue 67
Schloss Charlottenburg
  63
Schloss Klein-Glienicke
  26, 68
Schloss Rheinsberg
  96
Schlossbrücke 58
Schlossplatz 60
Schultheiss-Brauerei
  83
Schwanenwerder 90
Schwules Museum 76
Sea Life Center 58
Seehof am Lietzensee
  (H) 15
Senefelderplatz 81
Ships (R) 25
shiro i shiro (R) 22
Shoes 34
Shopping 29
Siegessäule 67
Sightseeing flights
  129
Soap 34

Soup Kultur (R) 21
Sowjetisches Ehrenmal
  68
Spandau 66, **88**
Spielbank (casino) 39
Splendid (R) 25
Sport 35, 129
St. Hedwig's Cathedral
  61
St. Matthäus-Kirche 67
Stalinallee 115
Steglitz 24, **65**
Strandbad Wannsee 90
Streetcar 116
Suggested reading 10
Sweets 35
Synagogues 83

T
Tadschikische Teestube
  (R) 28
Taxis 132
Tearooms 27
Telespargel 116
Thai Inside
  (R, MERIAN Tip) 25
The Regent (H) 14
The Ritz-Carlton (H) 14
The Story of Berlin 77
The Wall 111
Theatre 40
Theodor Tucher (R) 24
Tiefwerder 88
Tiergarten 66
Tiergarten-Dreieck 67
Tips for Families 46
Tizian (R) 25
Tours 10
Toys 35
Trade Fairs 42
Traffic light 100
Transport 131
Travel tips 124
Travel weather 132
Treptow 68
Trippen (MERIAN Tip)
  34
TTT (R) 28
Tucholsky, Kurt 96
Türkenmarkt
  (MERIAN Tip) 32

Tuschkastensiedlung
  116
TV tower 54

U
Ufa-Fabrik 47
Unter den Linden 60
Unterwelten-Museum
  128

V
Van Loon (R) 27
VAU (R) 22
Vaudeville 38
Velo-Taxis 132
Villa Canaris 86
Villa Griesebach 84
Villa Koschewski 86
Volxgolf 117

W
Waldbühne (MERIAN
  TopTen) 64, *66*
Walking Tours 80, 81,
  84, 86
Wannsee 47, **88**, 90
Water tower 82
Weigel, Helene 97
Weinmeisterhorn 89
Weissensee 68
WelcomeCard 132
Wintergarten Café im
  Literaturhaus (R) 28
Wittelsbach (H) 16
Wittenbergplatz 84
World Clock 54

X
XII Apostoli (R) 20

Z
Zehlendorf 25, **68**
Zeughaus 60
Zillemarkt (R) 27
Zitadelle Spandau 66
Zollpackhof (R) 27
Zoologischer Garten 64
Zur letzten Instanz (R)
  24

Dear Reader,
We welcome feedback from you regarding our travel guide books. Please write to us if you have changes that need to be made, suggestions on how we can improve our book, or if you just really liked something:

TRAVEL HOUSE MEDIA GmbH, Postfach 86 03 66, 81630 München
E-mail: merian-live@travel-house-media.de, Internet: www.merian.de

THE AUTHOR
This guide book was written by **Gisela Buddée**. After completing a degree in education and Art, she worked as an editor at *Hamburger Rundschau* and Verlag VSA, among other companies. Since 1994 she has lived and worked in Berlin as a freelance journalist. In the MERIAN *live!* series she wrote the "Rügen", "Harz", "Languedoc-Roussillon", "Côte d'Azur" and "Provence" books.

If you are interested in any of the maps from MERIAN Guide Books, please write to us:
iPUBLISH GmbH, geomatics
Berg-am-Laim-Strasse 47
81673 Munich, Germany
email: geomatics@ipublish.de

If you are interested in placing an advertisement:
KV Kommunalverlag GmbH & Co KG
MediaCenterMünchen
Tel. 0 89/92 80 96 - 44
email: kramer@kommunal-verlag.de

PHOTOS
Cover photo: The Brandenburg Gate (mauritius images/imagebroker.net) Bildagentur Waldhäusl/Arco Digital Images/Therin-Weise 98/99; Boening/Zenit/laif 20, 73; Jahreszeitenverlag/GPG/Renner 26; Kirchner/laif 10/11; Maecke/GAFF/laif 36; E. Pansegrau 4/5, 8; H. Sittl 97, 126; Westrich/laif 17; Wohner/Look 125; Grand Hyatt Berlin 15; all other photos: G. Schneider.

© **2008 TRAVEL HOUSE MEDIA GmbH, Munich**
MERIAN is registered trademark of the GANSKE PUBLISHING GROUP.

All rights reserved. Reprinting, even in part, as well as the distribution via film, radio, TV and Internet, photomechanical broadcast, or via sound media and data processing systems of any kind only allowed with written permission from the publisher.

All of the information in this guide book is researched and confirmed to the best of our abilities. However, prices, opening times and other information can change. The publisher assumes no liability for any mistakes.

PROGRAM HEAD
Dr. Stefan Rieß
HEAD OF EDITING
Susanne Kronester
TRANSLATION
Jeffrey Wisdom
EDITOR
Kevin White
DESIGN
wieschendorf.design, Berlin
MAPS
MERIAN-Kartographie
LAYOUT
bookwise, Munich
PRINTER
Appl, Wemding
BINDER
Auer, Donauwörth
PRINTED ON
Eurobulk paper from Papier Union

First Edition

A company of the
GANSKE PUBLISHING GROUP

Berlin

MERIAN Tips

Tips and recommendations for connoisseurs and individuals

1 Honigmond Garden Hotel
A paradise in the big city, with a heavenly garden and very central (→ p. 14).

2 Künstlerheim Luise
Each of the guest rooms here is designed by a different artist, each its own work of art (→ p. 16).

3 Bocca di Bacco
A culinary highlight: fantastic Italian food and wine from almost all Italian producing regions (→ p. 21).

4 Thai Inside
Fresh food, friendly staff, fair prices; central and still almost secluded (→ p. 25).

5 Türkenmarkt
Loud and colourful, this bustling bazaar in the middle of Kreuzberg has food, fabric, porcelain, household goods and clothing (→ p. 32).

6 Trippen
This young but traditional shoe store has integrated its workshop into the shop's layout (→ p. 34).

7 Neuköllner Oper
Berlin's smallest opera house: not a temple to the highbrow, just the high art of intelligent entertainment (→ p. 41).

8 Deutsches Technikmuseum
Old cars, ships and a Science Center: for children and adults alike (→ p. 49).

9 Montags-Museen
More than a dozen museums open on Mondays, a benefit for anyone on a just a short holiday (→ p. 72).

10 New Synagogue / Centrum Judaicum
Once the site of Germany's largest synagogue, now host to exhibitions, concerts and readings (→ p. 76).

←···· MERIAN TopTen
on page 1

S
- S1 Wannsee ↔ Oranienburg
- S2 Blankenfelde ↔ Bernau
- S25 Teltow Stadt ↔ Hennigsdorf
- S3 Erkner ↔ Ostbahnhof
- S3 Erkner ↔ Ostkreuz
- S41 Ring ↻ im Uhrzeigersinn
- S42 Ring ↺ gegen Uhrzeigersinn
- S45 S46
- S46 Königs Wusterhausen ↔ Westend
- S47 Königs Wusterhausen ↔ Südkreuz
- S47 Spindlersfeld ↔ Südkreuz
- Spindlersfeld ↔ Bundesplatz (nur Mo-Fr)
- Spindlersfeld ↔ Schöneweide
- S5 Strausberg Nord ↔ Westkreuz
- Strausberg Nord ↔ Potsdam Hbf
- S7 Ahrensfelde ↔ Potsdam Hbf
- S75 Ahrensfelde ↔ Lichtenberg
- S75 Wartenberg ↔ Spandau
- S8 Grünau (Zeuthen ↔) Grünau ↔ Hohen Neuendorf
- S85 Grünau ↔ Pankow (↔ Hohen Neuendorf)
- (Grünau ↔) Schöneweide ↔ Waidmannslust
- S9 Flughafen Berlin-Schönefeld ↔ Spandau
- S9 Flughafen Berlin-Schönefeld ↔ Warschauer Straße

🌙 S-Bahn-Nachtverkehr
nur Fr/Sa ca. 0.30-5.00 Uhr
Sa/So und vor Feiertagen
ca. 0.30-6.30 Uhr

U
- U1 Warschauer Straße ↔ Uhlandstraße
- U2 Pankow ↔ Ruhleben
- U3 Nollendorfplatz ↔ Krumme Lanke
- U4 Nollendorfplatz ↔ Innsbrucker Platz
- U5 Hönow ↔ Alexanderplatz
- U6 Alt-Tegel ↔ Alt-Mariendorf
- U7 Rathaus Spandau ↔ Rudow
- U8 Wittenau ↔ Hermannstraße
- U9 Osloer Straße ↔ Rathaus Steglitz

U7 U-Bahn-Nachtverkehr
Sa/So oder Feiertagen
ca. 0.30-6.30 Uhr

Kremmen · Wittenberge
Stralsund · Rostock · Templin Stadt

Oranienburg
Lehnitz
Borgsdorf
Birkenwerder

Sachsenhausen (Nord)

Hohen Neuendorf
Frohnau
Hermsdorf

Hennigsdorf
Heiligensee
Schulzendorf

Rathaus Reinickendorf
Karl-Bonhoeffer-Nervenklinik

Alt-Tegel
Borsigwerke
Holzhauser Str.
Otisstr.
Scharnweberstr.
Kurt-Schumacher-Platz

Tegel TXL

Afrikanische Str.
Rehberge

Seestr.
Amrumer Str.

Wedding

Siemensdamm · Rohrdamm · Halemweg
Paulsternstr.
Jakob-Kaiser-Platz

Beusselstr.
Westhafen

Haselhorst
Zitadelle
Altstadt Spandau

Jungfernheide
Birkenstr.

Turmstr.
Mierendorffplatz

Rathaus Spandau
Spandau
Stresow
Pichelsberg
Olympiastadion
Heerstr.

Ruhleben
Olympia-Stadion
Neu-Westend
Th.-Heuss-Pl.
Kaiserdamm
Messe ZOB
ICC

Westend
Sophie-Charlotte-Platz
Deutsche Oper
Bismarckstr.

Richard-Wagner-Platz

Ernst-Reuter-Platz

Tiergarten
Hansaplatz

Messe Nord/
ICC
Wilmersdorfer Str.
Savignyplatz

Messe Süd
Westkreuz
Charlottenburg
Uhlandstr.
Halensee
Adenauerplatz
Kurfürstendamm

Zoologischer Garten
Wittenbergplatz

Nollendorfplatz

Grunewald
Spichernstr.
Hohenzollernplatz
Güntzstr.

Augsburger Str.
Viktoria-Luise-Platz

Hohenzollerndamm
Fehrbelliner Platz
Blissestr.

Konstanzer Platz

Berliner Str.
Bayerischer Platz
Rathaus Schöneberg

Eisenacher Str.

Heidelberger Platz
Rüdesheimer Platz
Breitenbachplatz
Podbielskiallee
Dahlem-Dorf
Thielplatz
Oskar-Helene-Heim
Onkel Toms Hütte
Schlachtensee
Mexikoplatz

Bundesplatz
Friedrich-Wilhelm-Platz
Walther-Schreiber-Platz
Schloßstr.
Feuerbachstr.

Innsbrucker Platz
Friedenau

Rathaus Steglitz
Botanischer Garten
Lichterfelde West

Krumme Lanke
Lankwitz

Nikolassee

Lichterfelde Ost

Zehlendorf
Sundgauer Str.

Wannsee
Griebnitzsee
Babelsberg
Park Charlotten- Sanssouci hof

Brandenburg
Magdeburg

Osdorfer Str.

Potsdam Hbf
Medienstadt Babelsberg
Rehbrücke

Lichterfelde Süd

Wilhelmshorst

Caputh-Geltow
Caputh-Schmerwitz
Ferch-Lienewitz

Seddin
Michendorf
Saarmund
Genshagener Heide

Teltow Stadt

Teltow
Großbeeren
Birkengrund
Ludwigsfelde
Blank

Dessau · Jüterbog

Jüterbog · Lutherstadt Wittenberg/Falkenberg (Elster)